RESPONSIBLE DRIVING

Heathrow, Florida

Glencoe McGraw-Hill

New York, New York   Columbus, Ohio   Woodland Hills, California   Peoria, Illinois

REVIEWERS

James Lewis, President
CALIFORNIA ASSOCIATION OF SAFETY EDUCATORS

Richard Mikulik, Driver Education Instructor
MISSION HIGH SCHOOL
SAN FRANCISCO, CALIFORNIA

Barbara Brody, Past President
AMERICAN DRIVER TRAFFIC SAFETY EDUCATION
ASSOCIATION (ADTSEA)

John Svensson, President
TRAINING AND RESEARCH INSTITUTE FOR
ADVANCED DRIVER DEVELOPMENT, INC. (TRIADD)
GUELPH, ONTARIO, CANADA

Pat Venditte, Driver Education Instructor
CORNHUSKER DRIVING SCHOOL
OMAHA, NEBRASKA

Thomas Cardarella, Driver Education Instructor
M & N DRIVING SCHOOL
ENFIELD, CONNECTICUT

Scott Callahan, Driver Education Instructor
KITTITAS HIGH SCHOOL
KITTITAS, WASHINGTON

Craig Dill, Driver Improvement Coordinator
CALIFORNIA STATE AUTO ASSOCIATION
SAN FRANCISCO, CALIFORNIA

Editorial and Production services by Visual Education Corporation,
Princeton, New Jersey

Glencoe/McGraw-Hill

A Division of The McGraw·Hill Companies

Printed in the United States of America.

Send all inquiries to:
Glencoe/McGraw-Hill
21600 Oxnard Street, Suite 500
Woodland Hills, California 91367

ISBN: 0-02-653382-0 (Student's Edition; casebound)
1 2 3 4 5 6 7 8 9 071 05 04 03 02 01 00 99

ISBN: 0-02 653383-9 (Student's Edition; softbound)
1 2 3 4 5 6 7 8 9 071 05 04 03 02 01 00 99

COORDINATING AUTHOR

Dr. Francis C. Kenel
STAFF DIRECTOR OF TRAFFIC SAFETY (RETIRED)
AMERICAN AUTOMOBILE ASSOCIATION
HEATHROW, FLORIDA

CONSULTING AUTHORS

Dr. James Aaron
DRIVER PERFORMANCE CONSULTANT
PALM HARBOR, FLORIDA

Dr. John W. Palmer
ASSOCIATE PROFESSOR
ST. CLOUD STATE UNIVERSITY
ST. CLOUD, MINNESOTA

Dr. Maurice E. Dennis
COORDINATOR AND PROFESSOR
TEXAS A&M UNIVERSITY
COLLEGE STATION, TEXAS

Richard Russell
ADVANCED DRIVING CONCEPTS
DARTMOUTH, NOVA SCOTIA, CANADA

Charles A. Butler
DIRECTOR, SAFETY SERVICES
AAA TRAFFIC SAFETY DEPARTMENT
HEATHROW, FLORIDA

PREFACE

Well, this is it. You're going to learn to drive, and you're probably in a big hurry to get behind the wheel. However, driving is something that you cannot rush into. There is a great deal of essential driving information that you need to know first. It's important that you understand that risk is always present for the driver but that good drivers learn more effectively to manage risk. Good drivers reduce risk by managing visibility, time, space, and the available traction. We want you to be a good driver.

We've spent many years working on safe driving strategies and attitudes and at the same time working with young people such as you who can't wait to drive. *Responsible Driving* has been written with you in mind. We want you to know the rules and the facts about driving, but we also want you to know why they are important. This book tells you the *What* and *How* about driving, and it always tells you the *Why*.

The American Automobile Association, which you probably know as the AAA or Triple A, is part of the team that helped put *Responsible Driving* together. The AAA is an organization that has the greatest resources in the world on driving. We have used these resources in *Responsible Driving* to help you understand what driving is all about.

As you begin reading *Responsible Driving,* you'll see that the first unit is titled "Starting with You." It begins that way because we care about you, the AAA cares about you, and we want you to care about yourself and those with whom you will share the roadway. You're at the beginning of a very big moment in your life—the day you get your driver's license. We're happy to have the opportunity to help you learn how to use it safely and responsibly.

DR. FRANCIS C. KENEL
DR. JAMES AARON
DR. JOHN W. PALMER
DR. MAURICE E. DENNIS
RICHARD RUSSELL
CHARLES A. BUTLER

CONTENTS

ix

UNIT 4   Planning for Your Future   295

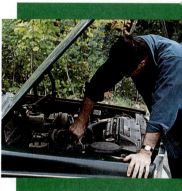

SPECIAL CONTENTS

CULTURAL CROSSROADS

CHAPTER

FOR NEW DRIVERS

CHAPTER

CONNECTIONS

CHAPTER

BUILDING SKILLS: READING MAPS

BUILDING CURRICULUM SKILLS

UNIT 1

Starting with You

Driving begins with you. You must ask how *you* will deal with the risk of driving, how *you* will handle the responsibility of driving, and how *you* will respond to social pressures that may affect your driving. This unit will help you consider these questions, questions that only you can answer.

4

CHAPTER 1

Assessing and Managing Risk

Whenever you walk or ride on our nation's streets and roadways, you become part of the highway transportation system. It is important to learn how to use the system safely and responsibly.

LESSON ONE
The Highway Transportation System and Risk Management

LESSON TWO
Understanding and Applying the SIPDE Process

LESSON THREE
Understanding and Using the Smith System

LESSON FOUR
The Value of Taking a Driver Education Course

OBJECTIVES

1. Name the three parts of the highway transportation system.
2. Explain how and by whom the highway transportation system is regulated.
3. Describe five ways that you can reduce risk when using the highway transportation system.

KEY TERMS

highway transportation system (HTS)
collision
risk
visibility
margin of space

The Highway Transportation System and Risk Management

A vast network of highways, streets, and roads crisscrosses the United States. Each day, millions of drivers travel these roadways.

As you prepare to join the other drivers on our nation's roads, remember that your goal is not just to learn to drive. It is to learn to drive safely and responsibly.

What Is the Highway Transportation System?

Motor vehicles, streets and highways, drivers, cyclists, and pedestrians—these are all part of the **highway transportation system,** or the **HTS.** The main goal of this complex system is to enable people and goods to move from place to place as safely and efficiently as possible.

Highway Concept and Design

Early American roads were built along the routes of existing trails and were constructed with little or no planning. Nowadays an army of engineers is needed just to plan today's more complex highways.

Engineers must plan the route of a highway, the construction of bridges along the route, exit and entrance ramps, where traffic signs are going to be located, and anything else pertaining to the highway. Curves must be planned carefully to make sure they are banked, or tilted, properly.

More than 206 million registered vehicles travel within the HTS, ranging from large vehicles, such as tractor-trailers and buses, to small vehicles, such as motorcycles and mopeds. There are vehicles of every imaginable description, from flashy new luxury cars to battered old pickup trucks.

Motor vehicles in the HTS differ in more than just appearance and age, however. They also vary in how they handle. A heavy truck, for instance, does not accelerate, steer, or brake the same way that a lightweight sports car does. How well an owner cares for his or her vehicle also affects its performance.

Motor vehicles vary, too, in safety features and in their ability to provide protection to drivers and passengers in case of a **collision,** or crash.

For example, drivers of solidly built vehicles equipped with air bags are far less vulnerable to injury than are motorcyclists or the drivers of most subcompact cars.

Roadways

Nearly 4 million miles of roadways link the states, counties, cities, and towns of the United States. These roadways range from multilane superhighways to twisting country roads to vehicle-choked city streets.

Some roadways are smooth and well maintained, while others are peppered with cracks, bumps, and potholes. Driving the great assortment of roads found in the HTS is a challenge, especially at night and in poor weather.

People

The people who use the highway transportation system include more than 180 million licensed drivers, passengers, cyclists, and pedestrians—in other words, just about everyone! Most of these people act responsibly when using the roads, whether driving, riding, or walking.

Some people, however, behave in an unsafe or irresponsible manner. They drive recklessly, cross streets without looking, and weave their bikes through heavy traffic. Such people pose a serious danger to other roadway users. This is just a sample of the behaviors that drivers must anticipate and learn to cope with.

How Is the HTS Regulated?

Federal, state, and local governments work together to regulate the highway transportation system. For example, federal law established a

FYI

During daylight hours, you can see the low beams of an oncoming vehicle from 4,700 feet away, or a little less than a mile. You can see an oncoming vehicle without headlights only from 2,500 feet away, or about half a mile.

CONNECTIONS

Math

The way highways in the highway transportation system are numbered can tell you something about the road on which you're traveling. If you know your numbers, such signs can give additional information.

If the number on a highway sign is odd, it means that the road goes north and south. An even-numbered sign means that the road goes east and west.

Interstate numbers range from 4 to 99. The greater the even number, the farther north you are. The greater the odd number, the farther east you are.

Imagine that you are on Interstate 90. That's an even number and close to 99, so you are traveling either east or west in the northern part of the United States.

maximum speed limit of 55 miles per hour in 1974. This law was changed in 1995 to allow the individual states to set their own highway speed limits. Enforcing speed limits and other traffic laws is the job of state and local police.

Federal and State Requirements

To set uniform standards for various aspects of vehicle and driver safety, the federal government passed two other important laws.

The National Traffic and Motor Vehicle Safety Act requires automakers to build certain safety features, such as safety belts and shatterproof windows, into their motor vehicles. This law also requires manufacturers to correct vehicle defects discovered after vehicle models are sold.

The National Highway Safety Act established specific guidelines for state motor vehicle safety programs. Each state must follow these guidelines. They govern such matters as vehicle registration and inspection, driver licensing, traffic laws and traffic courts, and highway construction and maintenance.

The National Highway Safety Act allows each state to set its own statutes, or laws, that concern highway safety. Many of these statutes are of special interest to teenage drivers. In 12 states, for example, teens under a certain age—usually 17 or 18—are not allowed to drive at night. In other states, teenagers must be enrolled in high school before they can get and keep their driver's licenses.

Cities and towns, too, pass driving regulations that must be obeyed within their limits. For example, in many cities, drivers may turn right at red lights except where expressly prohibited.

◆ *Risk is always present. The chances that you will be in a collision within the year are 1 in 9.*

How Can You Reduce Risk Within the HTS?

Driving involves **risk**—the chance of injury to yourself or others and the chance of damage to vehicles and property. The first important step toward responsible driving is realizing that this risk is *real*—probably much more real than you think.

- In any given year, the likelihood of your being involved in a collision is about 1 in 9. Your chances of suffering an injury that is serious enough to disable you are about 1 in 83.

- About 35 percent of the deaths of 15- to 20-year-olds occur through motor vehicle crash injuries.
- Eighty-five percent of traffic deaths occur in the first collision in which the vehicle's occupants are involved.
- More than 39 percent of vehicle occupant deaths in 1997 involved only one vehicle.

No matter how confident you may feel or how well you've mastered the basics of driving, the risk of being involved in a collision is always present. There are, however, actions you can take to maximize your control over driving situations and to minimize the risk.

◆ *Most drivers overestimate their ability to manage risk and underestimate actual risk.*

Understanding and Reducing Risk

Many factors contribute to the degree of risk when you drive. Some are obvious, such as bad weather or poor roads. Others, such as the condition of your vehicle, may be less obvious, but they are just as important to consider.

Driving responsibly means assessing the risk and doing all you can to reduce or control it. Here are five ways to do that.

Keep your vehicle in top condition. Are your brakes working properly? Are your tires properly inflated and your windows clean? The better the condition of your vehicle, the more control you have when you're driving.

Anticipate the actions of others. Wise drivers drive defensively. They identify cues to behavior that help them predict how other roadway users will act or react. Because drivers and pedestrians often act without thinking or communicating, you must learn to search for clues.

Take steps to protect yourself and others. Wearing safety belts can save you and your passengers from death or serious injury. Turning on your low-beam headlights at all times, even during daylight hours if your vehicle is not equipped with automatic daytime running lights (DRLs), reduces risk by increasing the ability of others to see you.

Drive only when you're in sound physical and mental condition. Are you feeling alert and clearheaded? Are you concentrating on

◆ *Poor weather can be a contributing factor in the degree of risk that drivers face.*

your driving—or thinking about tomorrow night's date? To drive safely, you need to be 100 percent behind the wheel.

Make a conscious effort to develop your driving skills. Working to improve your driving habits and abilities will help protect you and your passengers.

Managing Visibility, Time, and Space

As you learn to drive, you will learn numerous guidelines to help you make sound driving decisions. One basic principle underlies virtually all of these guidelines: the wise management of visibility, time, and space.

Visibility refers to what you can see from behind the wheel and how well you see it and to the ability of others—pedestrians and other drivers—to see you. When you are driving, reduced visibility means increased risk. On the other hand, when you take steps to increase visibility, you decrease risk.

Time and space come into constant play when you are driving. Time can refer to the ability to judge your speed and the speed of other vehicles. It can also refer to how long it will take your vehicle or another vehicle to stop or intersect paths.

Space refers to distance. Wise drivers keep a **margin of space** between their vehicles and other vehicles when they drive. This allows them room to maneuver.

You will read about visibility, time, and space throughout this book, because all three are crucial elements in safe and responsible driving. In fact, managing the various factors related to visibility, time, and space is the key to reducing risk when you drive.

WHAT WOULD YOU DO?

What factors are contributing to risk? What steps can you take to reduce risk?

Lesson 1 Review

1. What are the three parts of the highway transportation system?
2. Who regulates the highway transportation system? Give examples.
3. What are some ways that you can reduce driving risk when using the highway transportation system?

Understanding and Applying the SIPDE Process

OBJECTIVES

1. Define and explain the steps of the SIPDE process, including the approximate time/distance needed to *search, identify, predict, decide,* and *execute.*
2. Describe how the SIPDE process can be applied while you are driving.

KEY TERM
SIPDE process

Driving is challenging because you need to do many tasks at once. You have to control the vehicle, watch the roadway and off-road areas, read signs, and be alert for the sudden actions of other road users.

Although as a young driver you will have good reflexes, you will not have the skills of experienced drivers. You need to develop visual skills, decision-making skills, and vehicle-handling skills to become a safe driver.

Because you have so much to keep track of when you're driving, it is helpful to use an organized system to gather and process information. An organized system will help you make sound decisions and reduce driving risk.

What Is SIPDE?

One easy-to-use system for dealing with the challenge of driving is known as the **SIPDE process**—short for *search, identify, predict, decide,* and *execute.* SIPDE is a five-step process.

1. *Search* the roadway and the off-road areas 20 to 30 seconds ahead for information that can help you plan a path of travel. (Twenty to 30 seconds equals about 1½ to 2 blocks at 25 to 30 mph in the city and about ⅓ to ½ mile at 50 to 65 mph on the highway.)
2. *Identify* objects or conditions within 12 to 15 seconds ahead that could interfere with your planned path of travel.
3. *Predict* what actions or changes in conditions on or near the roadway could increase the level of risk.

◆ **The SIPDE process can help you to manage risk in many different situations.**

◆ *Use your rearview and side mirrors to help you search all around your vehicle.*

4. *Decide* what action or actions to take (such as reduce speed, increase speed, steer, brake, or steer and brake simultaneously) at least 4 to 5 seconds ahead of time to control or reduce risk.

5. *Execute* your decision.

Let's see how you can use the SIPDE process to manage visibility, time, and space.

Search

When you search, you should try to gather as much information as possible about what is happening on or near the roadway.

Use a systematic search pattern to gather information. First, search the road 20 to 30 seconds ahead, then look to the sides. Then glance in your rearview and sideview mirrors to check for traffic behind you. Next, check the sides of the road again. Then again survey the road ahead for ongoing and oncoming traffic.

Identify

To identify information important to you as a driver, you need to do more than simply look. You have to think about what you're looking for. Your aim is to identify as early as possible any objects or conditions that could become a threat to your path of travel.

Much as a detective investigates a crime scene seeking important clues, a driver needs to investigate the roadway and identify possible problems as far in advance as possible—at least 12 to 15 seconds ahead.

Suppose you are driving on a narrow two-way street in a residential neighborhood. Vehicles are parked along the street, vehicles are behind you, vehicles are coming toward you in the other lane, and people are on the sidewalk. Along your side of the street, you identify a young girl on a bicycle. As you get nearer to her, you can see that she is wobbling and having trouble steering the bicycle.

TIPS FOR NEW DRIVERS

Identifying Information

Identify these objects and conditions as you drive:

- vehicles, pedestrians, or objects that are in your path or could enter your path
- vehicles, pedestrians, or objects close to the back or sides of your vehicle
- vehicles, objects, or roadway features that limit your visibility and may conceal objects or conditions
- signs, signals, and roadway markings
- roadway surface conditions

Predict

As you search the roadway and note the position of vehicles, pedestrians, and objects, you try to predict what might happen and prepare for it.

In the situation with the young girl on the bicycle, you might predict the possibility of her veering into your path or falling off her bike in front of your vehicle.

Decide

Once you have identified a potentially threatening object or condition and predicted what might happen, you can decide how best to minimize the risk of a collision.

Keep in mind that most situations allow you a choice of actions. As with any decision, you need to weigh the possibilities. What are the likely consequences of the actions you're considering? Which actions will be most effective in minimizing risk to yourself and others? The purpose of using the SIPDE process is to give yourself as much time as possible to make a wise decision.

What will you decide to do as you get closer to the girl on the bike? Remember that a slight change of speed or position is usually better than a major change in either speed or position.

You could steer closer to oncoming vehicles while passing her. You could tap your horn lightly to warn the girl that you are behind her. You could reduce your speed. You decide to combine all three of these actions in order to minimize risk.

Execute

The final step in the SIPDE process is to execute the decision you have made. In most instances, executing a decision simply means making a routine maneuver. Occasionally, however, you may have to take some kind of emergency action.

Here are the steps you would execute to avoid colliding with the girl on the bicycle. First, slow down and prepare to stop if necessary. Next, wait for a break in the oncoming traffic. Then, lightly tap your horn. Honking loudly might frighten the girl into losing control of her bike.

Energy Tips

Use the SIPDE process to help you judge when to reduce speed or increase following distance and thereby avoid unnecessary stops. Each time you stop and then accelerate again, you burn extra fuel.

◆ *Bicyclists and parked vehicles present potentially threatening conditions to the driver.*

Finally, cautiously pass the bicyclist, allowing her as much space as possible. By waiting for a break in the traffic flow before steering around the girl, you will minimize the risk of colliding with an oncoming vehicle.

Applying the SIPDE Process

The SIPDE process fosters safe driving by enabling you to manage visibility, time, and space. While it is important to understand what the process is, it is far more important to practice applying it.

When you're behind the wheel, simply knowing what the letters SIPDE stand for won't help you drive safely. What *will* help you is making the principles of this process an automatic part of your own thinking—and driving.

For example, you can minimize risk by using the SIPDE process to identify threatening objects or conditions as far in advance as possible. The sooner you realize that you may be faced with a threatening situation, the sooner you can take action to reduce the risk.

Similarly, you can keep threatening objects or conditions apart by using the SIPDE process to help you separate one from another. For instance, suppose you are driving along a two-lane road. Up ahead, you see a bus approaching. At the same time you also see a group of boys walking along your side of the road. Rather than pass both the boys and the bus at the same time, you should adjust your speed so that you pass each one separately. By passing them separately in this way, you have simplified the situation and reduced the risk of a collision.

Lesson 2 Review

1. What are the steps of the SIPDE process?
2. How can the SIPDE process be applied while driving?

WHAT WOULD YOU DO?

Using the SIPDE process, explain how you would manage risk in this situation.

Understanding and Using the Smith System

OBJECTIVES
1. Explain the importance of the Smith System.
2. Describe the guidelines of the Smith System, including Aim high and look ahead, Keep your eyes moving, Get the big picture, Make sure others see you, and Leave yourself a way out.

KEY TERM
Smith System

Like the SIPDE process, the **Smith System** is a series of principles designed to help you drive safely and defensively.

What Is the Smith System?

The Smith System consists of five driving guidelines, which are discussed in the following sections. Understanding and using these guidelines is far more important than memorizing their exact wording.

Aim High and Look Ahead, Not Down

Look well ahead of your vehicle as you drive. Do not look down at the road directly in front of you. As a general rule, try to look about 20 to 30 seconds ahead. Remember that 20 to 30 seconds ahead means about 1½ to 2 blocks at 25 to 30 mph in the city and about ⅓ to ½ mile at 50 to 65 mph on the highway. Note that aiming high and looking ahead is similar to the first step, search, in SIPDE.

◆ *Spot possible dangers early by aiming high and looking well ahead, not down.*

Keep Your Eyes Moving

Roadway and off-road conditions are always changing. Search the scene constantly. Stay alert for changes on or near the roadway or potentially dangerous conditions that might require you to adjust the speed or position of your vehicle.

Get the Big Picture

Search the whole scene, not just a part of it. As you approach an intersection, for example, you need to search for vehicles and pedestrians

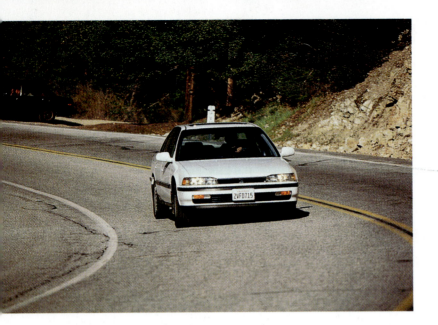

◆ *Driving with your low-beam headlights on insures that others will be able to see you.*

moving in all directions, for traffic-control devices, and for anything that might block your vision or otherwise increase risk.

Make Sure Others See You

Communicate with drivers and pedestrians. If your vehicle is not equipped with automatic daytime running lights, drive with your low-beam headlights on, even during daylight hours. Position your vehicle so that others can see you, signal your intention to turn, and tap the brake pedal so that your brake lights warn following drivers that you're slowing or stopping.

Leave Yourself a Way Out or a Margin of Safety

Always leave yourself a path of escape—a way to avoid a collision. Position your vehicle so that you keep a margin of space around it. In the earlier example of the girl riding the bicycle, for example, leaving yourself a way out meant waiting for a break in the oncoming traffic before steering around her.

Lesson 3 Review

1. What is the importance of the Smith System?
2. What are the guidelines of the Smith System?

WHAT WOULD YOU DO?

RIGHT LANE CLOSED AHEAD

How would you use the Smith System in this situation?

The Value of Taking a Driver Education Course

OBJECTIVES
1. Describe the advantages to be gained from a driver education course regarding knowledge and the ability to manage time, space, and visibility.
2. Name some factors that might affect your ability to drive safely.

The responsibility for operating your vehicle safely is yours. Driver education will help you meet that responsibility.

What Can You Gain from a Driver Education Course?

Driver education helps you become an alert and knowledgeable driver capable of dealing successfully with a wide range of driving situations.

Knowledge

Through driver education, you will gain:
- an understanding of the ways in which your personality, emotions, and maturity affect your driving.
- an understanding of how to maneuver and control your vehicle so as to minimize risk in different driving environments.
- an insight into the ways in which alcohol and other drugs impair driving and a knowledge of the penalties for their use.
- a knowledge of traffic laws, rules of the road, signs and signals, and roadway markings.
- a foundation of consumer information, such as guidelines for buying, insuring, and maintaining a vehicle and tips for trip planning.
- an understanding of how a vehicle works.
- a knowledge of what to do in case of emergency.
- an awareness of limiting factors for yourself and your vehicle.

Ability to Manage Visibility, Time, and Space

Driver education will increase your awareness of the roadway and its surroundings. You will learn how to better manage visibility, time, and space. You'll learn to better maximize your own safety as well as that of your passengers, other drivers, and pedestrians.

◆ *Driver education will help you learn to become a responsible driver.*

Dr. Francis C. Kenel
Staff Director of Safety (Retired), AAA

Risk means the chance of injury, damage, or loss. The purpose of this book is to help you develop the knowledge, skills, and habits that can enable you to manage risk.

The most important skill of good drivers is positioning the vehicle so that their ability to see and the ability of others to see them is maximized. When a vehicle is positioned properly, adjusting speed becomes easier. Equally important is using safety belts and restricting driving if you are not in top physical condition.

Driver education will help you evaluate and respond to the constantly changing driving environment more effectively. You will learn how to better manage and minimize risk by thinking ahead and by preparing for threatening situations that may develop.

Awareness of Limiting Factors

To become a safe and responsible driver, you need more than driving skill. You also need to understand that there are factors that can seriously interfere with your ability to drive, such as:

- the feeling that there is little or no risk involved in driving and that if a collision occurs, it's "the other person's fault."
- the effects of an illness or injury—or the side effects of the medicine you may be taking for it.
- your emotional state.
- the effects of alcohol and other drugs.

The knowledge you gain through driver education and the experience you acquire behind the wheel will develop your driving skills and decision-making abilities. How you use these skills and abilities, however, is up to you. Only you can decide to be a *responsible* driver.

WHAT WOULD YOU DO?

What threatening conditions do you see? How do you think you should handle them?

Lesson 4 Review

1. How can a driver education course be of value to you?
2. What factors might interfere with your ability to drive safely?

Using the Map Scale

People drive to get from one place to another. But they don't always know how to get there or how far they will have to drive. One way to make sure of your destination and the distance you'll need to travel is to use a road map.

Suppose you want to drive from San Jacinto, California, to Indio, California. You'll travel north on highway 79 to Route 10 and then southwest to Indio. Now you know how you're going to drive there, but how can you determine approximately how many miles you'll be traveling?

Look at the map scale to help you figure out the distance. The numbers along the top show the distance in miles. The scale shows you that 1 inch on the map is equal to about 25 miles.

You can use a ruler or a piece of string to estimate your traveling distance. Just find out how many inches long your route on the map is, and then multiply by 25.

Try It Yourself

1. About how far is it from San Jacinto to Indio along highways 79 and 10?
2. If you travel at an average speed of 50 miles an hour, how long will it take to get from San Jacinto to Indio?
3. Driving at the same average speed, how long will it take you to get from Perris to La Jolla?

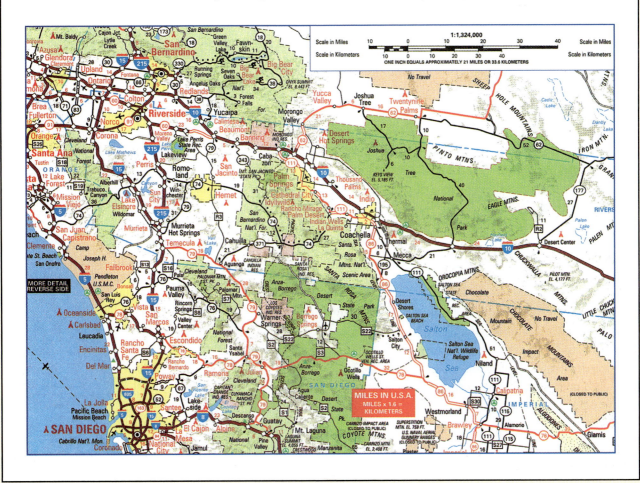

Lesson One

1. Motor vehicles, roadways, and people make up the highway transportation system. The main goal of this system is to enable people and goods to move from place to place as safely and as efficiently as possible.
2. Federal, state, and local governments work together to regulate the highway transportation system.
3. Five ways that you can reduce driving risk are to keep your vehicle in top condition, anticipate the actions of others, take steps to protect yourself and others, drive only when you're in sound physical and mental condition, and make a conscious effort to develop your driving skills.

Lesson Two

1. SIPDE is short for *search, identify, predict, decide,* and *execute.*
2. Using SIPDE, drivers search the roadway and off-road areas 20 to 30 seconds ahead for information that can help them select a planned path of travel, identify objects or conditions 12 to 15 seconds ahead that could interfere with their planned path of travel, predict what actions or changes in conditions on or near the roadway could increase the level of risk, decide at least 4 to 5 seconds ahead what action or actions to take to control or reduce risk, and then execute their decision.

Lesson Three

1. The Smith System is a series of principles designed to help you drive safely and defensively.
2. There are five guidelines to the system. Aim high and look ahead. Keep your eyes moving. Search the whole scene to get the big picture. Make sure others see you. Leave yourself a path of escape in order to avoid a collision.

Lesson Four

1. Through a driver education course you can gain a knowledge of vehicles and driving and develop your ability to manage visibility, time, and space.
2. You can become aware of factors that can seriously interfere with driving ability, such as your emotional state, the effects of an illness or injury, or the effects of alcohol and drugs.

PROJECTS

1. Obtain a copy of your state driver's manual. Read the table of contents, then take some time to skim through the book. What topics are emphasized? What charts and illustrations are included? Are sample test questions included?
2. As a passenger, identify objects on or near the road ahead. What actions might you take to minimize driving risk? Try to predict what other drivers will do. Compare your predictions with what actually happens.

*inter*NET
CONNECTION

Search the Glencoe Web site to find statistics on the number of licensed drivers in your state. Find out how many of them are teens.
www.glencoe.com/sec/driver.ed

CHAPTER TEST

Write the letter of the answer that best completes each sentence.

1. The highway transportation system is made up of
   a. motor vehicles, people, and buildings.
   b. roadways, people, and motor vehicles.
   c. cars, trains, and airplanes.

2. Searching the road 20 to 30 seconds ahead
   a. is equal to looking about ½ mile ahead at 25 to 30 mph in the city.
   b. is equal to looking about ⅓ to ½ mile ahead at 50 to 65 mph on the highway.
   c. is equal to looking about ½ block ahead at 25 to 30 mph in the city.

3. Driving with your headlights on during daylight hours
   a. increases your chances of being seen.
   b. increases engine efficiency.
   c. allows you to pass in a no-passing zone.

4. When you gather information about the roadway and surroundings, you
   a. execute.
   b. predict.
   c. search.

5. Under the National Traffic and Motor Vehicle Safety Act, automakers must
   a. provide for vehicle registration.
   b. build safety features into their vehicles.
   c. offer a choice of models to customers.

6. Risk in driving
   a. does not pertain to good drivers.
   b. depends on the confidence of the driver.
   c. is always present.

7. The Smith System
   a. is a three-step process.
   b. is regulated by the National Motor Vehicle Safety Act.
   c. are principles that help you drive safely.

8. Driver education can provide you with
   a. a knowledge of the rules of the road.
   b. discounts on vehicle purchases.
   c. automobile insurance.

9. The HTS is regulated by
   a. the National Highway Safety Act.
   b. the FBI.
   c. federal, state, and local governments.

10. *Visibility* refers to your ability to
    a. see and be seen.
    b. judge the speed of your vehicle.
    c. drive without wearing eyeglasses.

Write the word or phrase that best completes each sentence.

Smith System	designers	SIPDE
visibility	HTS	

11. The goal of the _____ is to enable people and goods to move safely and efficiently.

12. When you drive, reduced _____ means increased risk.

13. "Make sure others see you" is a basic principle of the _____.

14. _____ is a system designed to help you gather information in an organized way.

DRIVER'S LOG

In this chapter, you have learned about ways to manage risk while driving. Write three paragraphs that give your personal view on the following:
- How would you evaluate the possibility of your being involved in a collision? Explain.
- What kinds of situations do you feel hold the greatest risk for you as a driver?
- What steps will you take to manage the risks that you consider the most serious?

CHAPTER 2

Getting Ready: Your State Driving Test

You will learn a great deal about driving that will help you with your state driving test. It is important that you know how to prepare yourself and your vehicle for the test. Knowing how to prepare will help you succeed.

LESSON ONE
Introducing Graduated Driver Licensing

LESSON TWO
Getting Ready for the Knowledge Test and the In-Vehicle Test

LESSON THREE
Getting the Vehicle Ready for the Test

LESSON FOUR
Taking the Final Test: The In-Vehicle Test

OBJECTIVES

1. Discuss the purpose of graduated driver licensing.
2. Name the three stages of the graduated licensing system.

KEY TERM

graduated driver licensing (GDL)

Introducing Graduated Driver Licensing

No matter how much you have practiced, you cannot go from being a beginner to a fully experienced, safe driver overnight. For this reason, some states are introducing a system called **graduated driver licensing (GDL).** It is based on the idea that a teen with a new driver's license needs time and guidance to gain driving experience and skills in reduced-risk settings.

The Stages of the GDL System

In some states, a person will have full driving privileges as soon as he or she passes the driving tests. In states with a GDL system, newly licensed drivers will graduate from one licensing stage to the next as they achieve the goals at each level. AAA offers guidelines to states setting up a GDL system. Most GDL systems include three stages.

Stage 1: The Learner's Permit

The first stage in the GDL system lasts four to six months. The new driver practices basic driving skills and safe driving practices under totally supervised conditions.

Recommendations for eligibility To qualify for Stage 1, the new driver should:
- be the minimum age required by the state.
- have a parent's written permission.
- have passed the state's vision and written knowledge tests.

Recommended components Stage 1 drivers should be:
- in possession of a learner's permit.
- supervised at all times by a licensed driver who is at least 21 years old.
- required to take a basic driver education course.
- provided with 30 to 50 hours of behind-the-wheel driving certified by a parent, guardian, or licensed instructor.

TIPS **FOR NEW DRIVERS**

Don't Rush Yourself

If your state has not implemented a graduated driver licensing system, you might want to consider creating a plan of your own based on the GDL recommendations in the lesson. For several months after you have received your license, continue to practice driving only with a licensed adult in the vehicle. Then drive unsupervised for another 50 hours, limiting your driving to the hours between 5 A.M. and midnight. Remember that when you are behind the wheel, you have assumed responsibility for yourself and for others. Take that responsibility seriously: Lives depend on it.

- required to remain free of any at-fault crashes or moving violations for at least six months before progressing to the next stage.
- penalized more for traffic violations than are experienced drivers.

Stage 2: Intermediate/Probationary License

During unsupervised, low-risk driving practice, the new driver is exposed to more demanding situations than those in Stage 1.

Recommendations for eligibility To qualify for Stage 2, the driver should:
- be at least the minimum age required by the state.
- have completed a minimum of four to six months of supervised driving.
- have successfully completed Stage 1.
- have passed the road test given by an approved agency.

Recommended components Stage 2 drivers should be:
- required to pass an advanced driver education course.
- required to complete 50 more hours of behind-the-wheel driving.
- restricted from driving between midnight and 5 A.M., unless accompanied by an adult who is at least 21 years old.
- required to remain free of any at-fault crashes or moving violations for at least 12 months or until age 18.
- penalized more for traffic infractions than are experienced drivers.

Stage 3: Full License

This license allows the driver unrestricted driving privileges.

Recommendations for eligibility To qualify for Stage 3, the driver should:
- be at least 18 years of age.
- have successfully completed Stage 2.
- have passed a final road test.

Additional recommendations for the GDL system include the mandatory use of seat belts and a limit on the number of passengers, which in no case should exceed the number of seat belts in the vehicle.

FYI

States with GDL laws have experienced crash and traffic violation reductions of 5 to 16 percent.

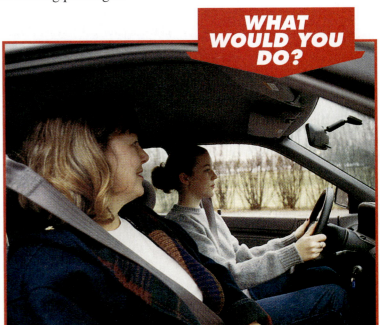

WHAT WOULD YOU DO?

This new driver lives in a state with a GDL system. What rules in Stage 1 is she observing?

Lesson *1* Review

1. What is the purpose of graduated driver licensing?
2. What are the three stages of the GDL licensing system?

OBJECTIVES

1. Name four ways in which you can prepare yourself for the knowledge test, and describe how you would go about implementing each.
2. List three preparations you can make for the in-vehicle test, and explain how to carry out each of the preparations.

Getting Ready for the Knowledge Test and the In-Vehicle Test

In addition to a vision test, you must pass a knowledge or written test and a driving performance test. Application and testing procedures for obtaining a driver's license vary from state to state. To find out what the requirements are where you live, check your state driver's manual or ask your driver education instructor.

In a number of states, your driver education teacher will administer the in-vehicle performance test, or road test, after you have passed a knowledge test. In some states, your teacher will arrange for an examiner to come to your school to give the test. In both of these cases, you will take your in-vehicle performance test in the vehicle you've been using during the driver education course. In other states, you must make your own arrangements with the department of motor vehicles to take all the necessary tests.

How Can You Prepare for the Knowledge Test?

Getting ready to take the knowledge test for your driver's license is not much different from preparing for a test in school. Study the material in advance, be well rested when you take the test, and think carefully before answering the questions.

Study Wisely

Your state driver's manual contains the information that you will need in order to study for the knowledge test. Follow these guidelines for studying the manual.

• Read one section at a time. Use a marker to highlight important information you think may be on the test, or keep a notebook in which you write this information.

TIPS **FOR NEW DRIVERS**

Practicing for the In-Vehicle Test

When practicing your driving, here are some of the skills you may need to demonstrate. You will learn about these skills in Chapters 8, 9, and 10:

- parallel parking
- starting and stopping smoothly
- shifting gears
- backing up safely
- turning

- passing
- following at a safe distance
- signaling
- executing turnabouts

- Reread the section and summarize it for yourself. Write your summary in your notebook.
- Study with someone else who is going to take the test, or ask a friend or family member to quiz you on information from the manual.
- Take the sample test, if there is one in your state's manual. If there is anything in the manual that you don't understand, ask your driver education instructor to explain it to you.
- Review the chapter and unit tests in this book. Look up the answers if you don't remember them.

Budget your study time. Don't wait until the last minute and then try to cram for the test. Figure out how much time you have to study. Then decide how much time you'll devote to studying each day or week, perhaps leaving additional study time just before you take the knowledge test.

Keep in mind that the real purpose of studying the driver's manual is not just to pass the test. Your true goal is to learn driving rules and safe practices so that you can be a responsible driver.

Get Yourself Ready Physically

Get a good night's sleep before the test. No matter how much you have learned, you'll never pass the test if you're too sleepy to think clearly.

Don't skip meals before taking the test. Eating right will keep your energy level high and help you focus your thoughts.

Bring the Necessary Papers

If you have to go to the department of motor vehicles office to take your test, you will have to bring several documents with you. You'll need proof of age and identity. The best proof of both is your birth certificate.

Some states require that you bring proof that you have satisfactorily completed a course in driver education if you are under age 18 or 19. In most cases, a parent or some other adult who has a driver's license will have to accompany you.

FYI

While most states still give road tests in actual traffic, some states do all their testing on closed courses. These tests usually emphasize parallel parking, turns, and turnabouts.

◆ *Before taking your knowledge test, ask a friend or family member to quiz you on the material in the manual.*

Check the driver's manual or call the department of motor vehicles beforehand to find out the specific documents your state requires. People who work for a state's department of motor vehicles usually allow no exceptions to the rules. If the manual says to bring your Social Security card with you, then be sure to do so. Failure to bring necessary documents may result in your not being able to take the test.

Stay Calm

As you prepare for the knowledge test and on the day that you actually take it, stay calm. Read each question carefully, and take time to think before selecting your answer. If you get stuck on a question, skip it and return to it later.

Don't let a tough question throw off your concentration. Just relax and keep going. Generally, there is no time limit on how long you have to complete the test (so long as it is before the department's closing time).

How Can You Prepare for the In-Vehicle Test?

To pass the in-vehicle or road test, you need to show the examiner that you have a working knowledge of the rules of the road and that you have mastered basic driving skills. As with most tests, the key to success is advance preparation.

◆ *Practice the manuevers you find especially difficult, such as backing or three-point turns.*

Know What You Are Doing

Practice, practice, practice—that's the best advice for preparing for the in-vehicle test. The more hours you spend behind the wheel, the more skilled and confident you will become as a driver.

When you practice driving, ask the person you're with to point out any areas in which you might need improvement. Spend extra time perfecting any maneuvers you find difficult.

Be alert for road signs as you practice. Be sure you understand what each sign means and what procedures you should follow at each. Review your driver's manual if you're uncertain about any sign or traffic rule.

Remember, too, that driving is more than just a series of physical movements. Becoming a good driver means exhibiting sound judgment and decision-making skills. In other words, knowing how to make a left turn is important, but knowing when it is safe to make the turn is even more important.

If possible, practice driving in the same vehicle in which you will take your test. Ideally, this should also be the vehicle you'll be driving *after* you get your driver's license. At the very least, your practice vehicle should be similar to the one you'll be using. If, for example, you'll be using a stick shift on the day of the test, be sure to practice driving in a stick-shift vehicle.

Be Alert and Ready

Many of the same suggestions made earlier about preparing yourself for the knowledge test apply for the in-vehicle test. To be at your best, get a solid night's sleep before the day of the test, and don't skip meals before the test.

Bring What You Need

For the in-vehicle test, you will need certain documents. Your state may require you to present your valid driver's permit as well as proof of vehicle registration and adequate insurance for the vehicle you're driving. You may also need proof that the vehicle has been properly inspected and has passed an emissions test. Check your state driver's manual to learn what documents your state requires.

Also bring enough money or a check to pay the licensing fees, and any other items you may need, such as a seat or back cushion and your prescription glasses or sunglasses, if you need to wear them when you drive.

Lesson 2 Review

1. How can you plan to study for the knowledge test?
2. What preparations can you make for the in-vehicle test?

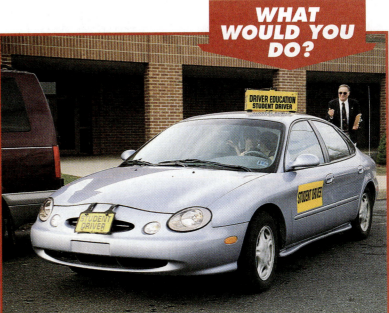

WHAT WOULD YOU DO?

Your in-vehicle test is exactly one week away. What will you do between now and then to prepare for the test?

OBJECTIVES

1. Name two ways in which you can prepare your car for the in-vehicle test.
2. List the actions you should take before and on the day of the test.

Getting the Vehicle Ready for the Test

If you are not going to take your in-vehicle test in the school's driver-training car, you will have to provide the vehicle. Be sure the one you use is as ready for the test as you are.

How Can You Get the Test Vehicle Ready?

The vehicle you drive for your test should be in top condition. It should be clean inside and out. All windows should be in good condition, and the door handles should work properly. In addition, the vehicle should be in good mechanical condition. The last thing you need on the day of your test is a mechanical or other problem.

Choose Your Vehicle Wisely

If you have a choice of what vehicle to use for your test, choose one that is in good all-around condition and that you feel comfortable driving.

Remember that you may have to show proof that the vehicle is registered and insured and that it has been properly inspected and has passed an emissions test. Do *not* bring to the test a vehicle that:

- you have seldom or never driven.
- frequently stalls.
- restricts your ability to see.
- does not have safety belts.
- has muffler problems.
- you have difficulty getting into or out of.

FOR NEW DRIVERS

Choosing a Vehicle for the Test

Suppose you have practiced in and are equally comfortable driving two cars, both of which are in good mechanical condition. Which car should you choose to use for your in-vehicle test? Here are some tips that may make your decision easier.

- Choose a car with an automatic transmission over one with a manual transmission. Nervousness can make you have trouble coordinating the clutch, the gearshift, and the accelerator.
- Choose a smaller car over a larger car. Smaller cars are generally easier to maneuver.
- Choose a conservative, family-type car over a sports car or "souped-up" vehicle. Make a good first impression on the examiner.

Check Out the Vehicle in Advance

Before the day of the test, conduct basic predriving checks of the following items:

- defroster/defogger
- brakes
- clutch and gas pedals
- all lights
- horn
- fluid levels
- tire pressure
- windshield wipers and windshield washer fluid

By checking out the test vehicle in advance, you can make sure that whatever is not in good working order will be fixed in time for the test. Be sure you know where all the controls are and how to operate them.

On the day of the test:

- Clean the interior of the vehicle.
- Clean the windows.
- Adjust and clean the mirrors.
- Clean the lights.
- Verify that you have enough fuel.

Remove any obstructions from inside the car, such as packages or hanging ornaments. Be sure your vehicle's safety belts are working properly.

To review other suggestions for advance preparation of your vehicle, see Chapters 7 and 17.

◆ *Be sure that your mirrors— inside and outside—are clean and that you adjust them properly.*

Lesson 3 Review

1. Why is it important to check out your vehicle in advance of taking the test?
2. What predriving checks should you make on your vehicle before you take the test?

WHAT WOULD YOU DO?

Which car would you choose for your test next week? Explain your choice.

OBJECTIVES

1. Name at least four guidelines to keep in mind when taking the in-vehicle test.
2. Describe in detail what each guideline entails.

Taking the Final Test: The In-Vehicle Test

The big day has finally arrived: You're about to take the in-vehicle test for your driver's license. You've practiced driving for many hours, but you feel nervous just the same. You want to pass the test on your first try.

What Should You Do Once You Are Sitting Behind the Wheel?

The examiner who rides with you during your test will evaluate your skill at handling the vehicle as well as your ability to drive safely and responsibly. In most states, you will fail the test automatically if you violate a traffic law or commit a dangerous act.

Make All Necessary Adjustments First

Before you start the engine, recheck your vehicle to see if any adjustments are needed.

- Make sure your seat is adjusted so that you have a clear view of the road and can reach the accelerator and brake pedals comfortably. If you use a seat or back cushion, put it in place.
- Make sure your head restraint on the back of your seat is correctly adjusted.
- Make sure the rearview and sideview mirrors are positioned for maximum visibility.
- Make certain that no objects inside the vehicle are blocking your view.
- Fasten your safety belt.

Follow these procedures after you've started the engine.

- If necessary, turn on window defrosters and windshield wipers.
- Turn on the low-beam headlights.
- If the radio is on, turn it off.
- Check your mirrors and blind spots before starting to drive.

◆ *Concentrate on your driving and the examiner's instructions during the in-vehicle test.*

Concentrate on What You Are Doing

Follow these guidelines for keeping your mind on your driving during the in-vehicle test.

Listen carefully to any instructions. Follow the examiner's instructions exactly. If you don't understand something the examiner says, ask for clarification.

Don't chat with the examiner. During the test, the examiner may say very little to you. Don't let it bother you if your examiner is the silent type. This may just be his or her personality. On the other hand, if your examiner is talkative and asks a lot of questions, don't let that distract you from concentrating on driving.

Don't worry about what the examiner is writing. During the test, expect the examiner to be writing and making notes on a form. Don't assume the examiner is being critical. Many categories have to be tested and noted. The examiner may be writing favorable comments too.

Don't let a mistake throw you. If you make a mistake, maintain your concentration. Don't let a minor error rattle you so much that you make a worse mistake. If you're going through a complicated maneuver, move the vehicle slowly, paying special attention to the gear you're in, the direction your wheels are turned, and the obstacles and traffic around you.

Stay Calm

Because this is an important test and you care about the results, you are going to be nervous. This is natural. But you can do some things to minimize your nervousness and help you concentrate on your driving.

Be well prepared. If you have practiced a great deal, you should be prepared for the in-vehicle test. Thorough preparation is the best defense against making mistakes during the test.

Admit that you're nervous. It's helpful to admit that you're nervous in a situation that is making you tense. Even though you're prepared, be aware of how you feel, and don't be afraid to tell your examiner. Don't be disappointed, however, if the examiner does not reassure you.

Have a positive attitude. Remember that you are well prepared. Be confident that you are going to do your best.

Bring support. The licensed driver who drives you to the test should be positive, optimistic, supportive, and calm. However, do not expect that person to be allowed to accompany you while you are taking the in-vehicle test.

SAFETY TIPS

If your vehicle has automatic shoulder belts, be sure you also fasten your lap belt for maximum protection.

Don't rev the engine when you are stopped at a stop sign or red light or while you are stopped in traffic. Revving the engine wastes fuel and may annoy the examiner.

Judy L. Alton
Sergeant, Texas Department of Public Safety

When you take the in-vehicle test, try to relax. Imagine that the examiner is your best friend. In Texas we grade on four categories: control, observation, position, and signaling. Controlling the vehicle is knowing how to handle it. Observation is making sure you look at all times—turn your head so the examiner can tell when you are looking. Position has to do with always maintaining the proper lane position. You should signal to make a turn or lane change and also with your horn if you need to give a warning.

Breathe deeply. Pay attention to the way you're breathing. When people are anxious, they tend to hold their breath. Deep breathing will keep the oxygen moving through your system and help you stay calm.

Exercise Good Judgment

Show the examiner that you are a mature, responsible person. Always be courteous, both to the examiner and to the pedestrians and other drivers you may meet on the roadway. Above all, do not smoke while you are taking the in-vehicle test.

Demonstrate the skills you learned in your driver education course. Allow yourself plenty of time to pull out into traffic. Search the path ahead for any object or condition that could raise the level of risk. Follow other vehicles at a proper distance. Be alert for traffic control devices, and remember to signal your intentions.

Lesson 4 Review

1. What adjustments will you need to make to your vehicle before you start your engine?
2. How can you concentrate and stay calm during the in-vehicle test?

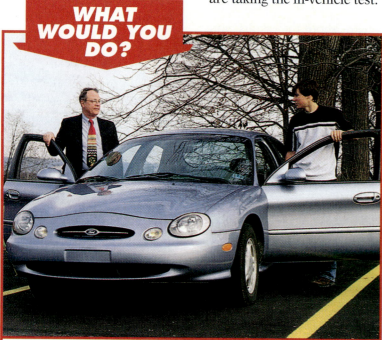

WHAT WOULD YOU DO?

The examiner is ready for you to begin the in-vehicle test. What actions will you take before starting the engine?

The High Cost of Fuel

Oil, the precious resource that is the source of the gasoline that powers our motor vehicles, has been the cause of a confusing mix of benefits and drawbacks to the Inuits of Alaska. In the 1800s, these native people witnessed the exploration of their homeland by navigators searching for a quick Arctic sea route from the New World to the wealth of Asia. This sea route, the Northwest Passage, was finally traveled in 1903 by the Norwegian explorer Roald Amundsen.

Today the Inuits are affected by another exploration—the search for oil in the waters of the Northwest Passage. With the discovery of oil at Prudhoe Bay on Alaska's north coast, human-made oil-drilling islands have been built amidst the 18,000 islands of the 4,000-mile-long Northwest Passage.

The trans-Alaska pipeline carries the oil from Prudhoe Bay to ports in southern Alaska, where it is transferred to huge ice-breaking tankers that carry the oil to refineries outside of Alaska.

For many Inuits, the frozen-over sea is like the land. Driving a ship through it is like driving a bulldozer across a farmer's field. The tankers also pose a danger to the environment, such as that caused when the *Exxon Valdez* struck a reef and poured 10.9 million gallons of crude oil into Prince William Sound. The oil destroyed wildlife that lived in these waters and was absorbed in the gravel beaches along the shoreline.

The threat to the environment and to the Inuit way of life are somewhat balanced by the increased income and other material gains that oil has brought to these Native Americans of Alaska. In the Alaskan Native Claims Settlement Act of 1971, the U.S. government gave Alaskans with at least one Native American grandparent a share in the oil-rich lands.

The Inuits are in the forefront of a movement that while recognizing the need for oil and its economic benefit, also recognizes the need to protect the environment. The threat of pollution has been an important topic in the five Inuit Circumpolar Conferences that have been held since 1977 to discuss the future of Arctic peoples.

What Do You Think Now?

How can the need for oil and the economic advantages it brings be balanced by the need to protect and preserve the environment?

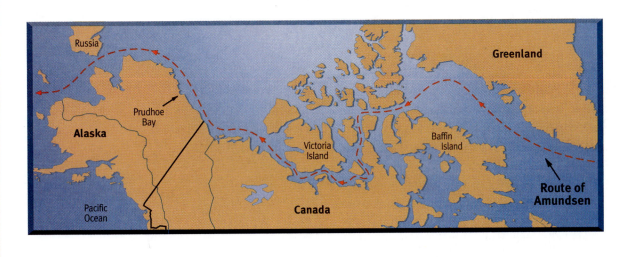

KEY POINTS

Lesson One

1. No matter how much you practice for your driving test, you can't go from being a complete beginner to being an experienced driver overnight. For this reason, some states have implemented a system called graduated driver licensing (GDL).

2. GDL is a three-stage system that gives people time to increase their driving skills gradually in low-risk settings. A GDL system generally includes beginning, intermediate, and full licensing stages.

Lesson Two

1. To prepare for the knowledge test, study your state driver's manual thoroughly. Read one section at a time and summarize it, study with a friend, and take any sample tests. Go for the test well rested, and take with you any documents you may need. When you take the test, stay calm, read each question carefully, and take time to think before selecting your answer.

2. To prepare for the in-vehicle test, practice driving as much as you can, preferably in the same vehicle in which you will take your test.

Be alert and ready by getting a good night's sleep before the day of the test. Bring what you need, including correct documentation, money or a check, and other necessary items, such as sunglasses and a cushion.

Lesson Three

1. Be sure the vehicle you choose for the test is in top condition. Check out your vehicle before you take the test.

2. Conduct predriving checks the day before the in-vehicle test. Check the brakes, fluid levels, pedals, lights, horn, tires, defoggers, and windshield wipers. On the day of the test, make sure that your vehicle's windows, mirrors, lights, and interior are clean.

Lesson Four

1. When taking the in-vehicle test, first make all necessary adjustments before you start to drive: seat, head restraint, mirrors, and safety belt. Stay calm. Be prepared, admit you're nervous, be positive, and breathe deeply.

2. Concentrate on what you are doing while you are driving. Listen carefully to the examiner, don't chat with him or her, and try not to worry.

PROJECTS

1. Write five questions that you think may be on your knowledge test. Exchange questions with a partner in your class. Try to answer your partner's questions. Check all answers in your driver's manual.

2. Interview two people who have acquired their licenses in the past year. What maneuvers were they required to make during the in-vehicle test? What was easiest and hardest about the test. Discuss your findings with your class.

*inter*NET
CONNECTION

Drive through the Web to learn more about graduated driver licensing, including the status of GDL in your state.
www.glencoe.com/sec/driver.ed

CHAPTER TEST

Write the letter of the answer that best completes each sentence.

1. With a graduated driver licensing system, you
   a. must be 21 years old to drive alone.
   b. increase your driving skills and privileges gradually.
   c. are penalized less severely than an experienced driver for traffic violations.

2. Your goal in studying for the knowledge test is to
   a. learn the rules of the road so that you can be a responsible driver.
   b. pass your driving test.
   c. answer all the questions correctly.

3. Three ways to prepare for your knowledge test are to
   a. eat right, sleep well, and study.
   b. study, bring documents, and exercise.
   c. eat right, read, and check the brakes.

4. If you are not going to take your test in the school's driver education car,
   a. the driving instructor will provide a car.
   b. you will have to pay more for your license.
   c. it will be up to you to provide the vehicle.

5. If possible, practice driving in
   a. many different vehicles.
   b. the same vehicle in which you will take your test.
   c. a rental car.

6. One way to stay calm during the in-vehicle test is to
   a. rev the engine.
   b. breathe deeply.
   c. take the sample test.

7. When taking your in-vehicle test, it is
   a. okay to tell the examiner that you are nervous.
   b. a good idea to chat with the examiner.
   c. helpful to play audiocassettes.

8. You should check your car's fluid levels
   a. the day before your in-vehicle test.
   b. in the presence of the examiner.
   c. during the knowledge test.

9. If you violate a traffic law while taking your in-vehicle test, you
   a. will automatically fail the test in most states.
   b. can usually still pass the test.
   c. will be banned from driving for one year.

10. Your best proof of age is your
    a. parent's sworn testimony.
    b. birth certificate.
    c. driver's permit.

Write the word or phrase that best completes each sentence.

clarification	documents	license
emissions inspection	responsible	

11. Being a(n) _____ driver means exhibiting sound judgment and decision-making skills.

12. You may need proof that the vehicle you bring for the test has passed a(n) _____.

13. If you do not understand something the examiner says, ask for _____.

14. Take with you to the test all the _____ that you will need.

DRIVER'S LOG

In this chapter, you have learned how to prepare yourself and your vehicle for the state driving test. Do you think you will have more difficulty with the in-vehicle test or the knowledge test? Write two paragraphs in which you analyze the reasons for the difficulty and explain what you will do to remedy the situation.

CHAPTER 3

Knowing Yourself

Whenever you get behind the wheel of a vehicle, you must be certain that you are both physically and emotionally fit to drive. It is important to recognize and control physical and emotional factors that might impair the driving task.

OBJECTIVES

1. Describe three effects your emotions can have on your driving.
2. Describe at least six ways to control the effects your emotions may have on your driving.

KEY TERM

peer pressure

Emotions Affect Your Driving Ability

Responsibility. Maturity. Self-control. No doubt you've heard these words spoken many times by parents, teachers, and other adults.

As a new driver, those same words will again take on important meaning for you. When you're driving, it's not just skill that matters. It's your ability to think clearly and make sound, responsible driving decisions.

How Do Emotions Affect Your Driving?

Everyone experiences strong feelings, both positive and negative: joy, sadness, anger, fear. Such feelings are part of what it means to be alive.

When you experience a strong negative emotion, you may feel the need to do something forceful. If you're driving, you may have an impulse to act out your emotion by driving aggressively—a very dangerous and irresponsible attitude to take. Aggressive driving incidents have increased so much that there is even a term—*road rage*—to describe the violence sometimes associated with these incidents.

◆ *Strong emotions can have an effect on your driving. They can interfere with your ability to manage risk.*

Inattention

Strong feelings may focus your attention on one thing. If you've just won a tough game, maybe you review the big play over in your mind. Maybe you're thinking about your boyfriend or girlfriend.

Emotions can interfere with your driving by taking your attention away from the road. You may be so preoccupied that you speed or take other risks, without even realizing what you are doing.

Lack of Concentration

Sometimes you can't seem to concentrate on anything. You may feel anxious about a date or excited about getting an A on a test. Let someone else drive or wait until you're better able to focus on the driving task.

Ability to Process Information

Safe driving is a full-time job for your mind as well as for your body. You have to see and hear the signs and signals of the roadway. You also have to use good judgment based on the information you gather.

If you are having a strong emotion, your ability to process roadway information may be diminished. This decreases your ability to manage risk.

How Can You Control Emotions?

Though sometimes it may not seem possible, you *can* learn to control your emotions when you have to. You can also take steps to avoid or minimize problems relating to your emotional state.

Maintain a Responsible Attitude

You exhibit a responsible attitude when you show respect for order and safety and take responsibility for your actions. You should assume a responsible attitude and put aside strong emotions while you drive. Be courteous even if you happen to feel angry. Concentrate on driving safely.

Avoid Triggering Aggressive Driving

Put your angry feelings aside, or you may act in ways that cause other drivers to act aggressively. You can avoid doing so by practicing common courtesy. Here are some examples.

- Keep a safe distance from the vehicles ahead.
- Apologize with an appropriate gesture when you make a mistake.
- Always signal when changing lanes.
- Keep your cool. Don't make obscene gestures or flash your headlights.

◆ *Don't let your emotions get the better of you. Instead, learn ways to control your emotions.*

Identify Troublesome Situations

Identify situations that may upset or annoy you, and deal with them in a responsible way. When a situation is likely to bother you—an unexpected traffic jam, for example—take a few deep breaths; say to yourself, "I won't let this get to me"; and focus your attention on driving.

You know, for example, that traffic is heavy at rush hour. If you must drive then, you have a choice to make. You can grit your teeth and snarl at the traffic. Or you can tell yourself, "I know traffic is going to be slow now, but this won't last forever. I'm not going to let this bother me." Then you can drive safely and patiently.

Plan Ahead

Advance planning can reduce stress and avoid problems. Will your route take you near a stadium at the time that sports fans are crowding the roadways? You can leave home earlier. Will you be traveling on a highway that is partially closed for repair? Try to find an alternate route.

Always allow enough time to get where you are going—extra time if you know you'll be traveling in heavy traffic or bad weather.

Expect Mistakes from Others

Rather than let yourself get irritated by every instance of bad driving you encounter, accept the fact that everyone makes mistakes at one time or another. Drivers may be distracted, inexperienced, or even intoxicated. Never assume that other drivers will drive safely or obey all rules.

Don't Drive When Upset or Depressed

Anger or other strong emotions may be disturbing you. You may also have feelings of grief or intense anxiety that could last for several days. It may be dangerous to drive. Think twice and stay off the road until these feelings subside. It's better to wait until your feelings settle down and you're able to concentrate.

Don't Give In to Negative Peer Pressure

Peer pressure, or the influence of friends who are in your age group, can be very strong. After all, you want to be accepted. However, friends may sometimes encourage you to act in risky ways. For example, peer pressure can lead teens to believe risky driving is cool. Let your friends know that you think too much of yourself to give in to such pressure.

Train Yourself Always to Use Correct Procedures

Get into the habit of using safe driving procedures. Make such procedures automatic, no matter what your emotional state may be.

WHAT WOULD YOU DO?

You're already late. How will you deal with your emotions and with getting to your destination in this situation?

Lesson 1 Review

1. How can emotions affect your driving?
2. How can you control your emotions when you drive?

How Vision Affects Your Ability to Drive

Your sense of sight is the most important of the senses that affect your ability to drive. In fact, about 90 percent of the decisions you make while driving are based on information you gather with your eyes. If you are having trouble seeing, your ability to drive safely is in serious jeopardy.

Why Is Good Vision Critical to Driving Ability?

Being able to see well means more than simply having "20/20 vision." It means being able to see straight ahead and to the sides and being able to perceive depth as well as color.

If your ability to see clearly is impaired, you will have difficulty adjusting your car's speed and position to minimize risk. You will not be able to search the roadway far enough ahead to spot a threatening condition early. You will also have trouble identifying signs, signals, and roadway markings.

To check your ability to see clearly, you should be tested for **visual acuity** (clear vision) by a health care professional or by your local department of motor vehicles. The visual acuity test measures how well you can see and whether or not you need to wear glasses or contact lenses to improve your vision.

Field of Vision

When you are standing still and looking straight ahead, you can see what is directly ahead and also what is at an angle to your right and left. This is your field of vision.

Your vision is clearest in a narrow cone-shaped area directly in front of you, your **area of central vision.** Vision at angles to your right and left is called **peripheral vision.** This vision enables you to notice objects and movement to your sides. Your vision up and down, called your **vertical field of vision,** allows you to see traffic lights overhead and pavement

◆ *Have your vision tested regularly. Good vision is crucial to risk management. Traveling at 30 mph, with 20/20 visual acuity, you can read a 6-inch-high street sign from a distance of about 180 to 225 feet, or 4 to 5 seconds away. With 20/40 vision, you would have to be within 90 to 135 feet, or 2 to 3 seconds away, to read the same sign. With 20/100 vision, you would have less than 1 second to read and respond to the sign.*

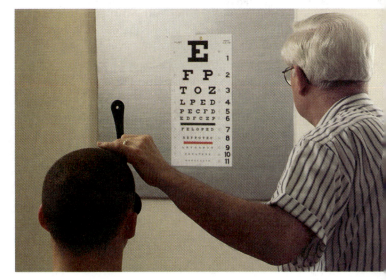

markings, such as crosswalks or arrows in turn lanes. When you are in forward motion as you drive, your field of vision narrows. You need to move your eyes from side to side and up and down to detect any potentially dangerous conditions.

How Can You Compensate for Vision Problems?

If you have a problem with depth perception, distance judgement, contrast sensitivity, color blindness, or night blindness, you can compensate for the problem when you drive.

Poor Depth Perception

Depth perception gives a three-dimensional perspective to objects. It helps you judge the relative distance between two objects. Whenever you look at an object far away, you are using depth perception. You use distance judgment to estimate the distance between yourself and the object.

Depth perception and distance judgment work together. They are especially important when you drive because they help you control your following distance and adjust your position in traffic.

To compensate for poor depth perception, give yourself extra margins of space and time. For example, you can increase your following distance. You can also compare the relative speeds of the cars coming toward you.

Contrast Sensitivity

Contrast sensitivity helps you see details in the driving environment. Any time you face the glare of headlights or drive when it is dark, you are using contrast sensitivity. If you have trouble seeing details because of glare or darkness, slow down and adjust your position in traffic.

Color Blindness

The most commonly used colors in traffic are red, green, and yellow. If you have normal color vision, you won't have

TIPS FOR NEW DRIVERS

Driving at Night

When you drive at night, you need to compensate for reduced visibility. Here are some steps to take.
- Drive more slowly than you would during the day. Adjust your speed to the range of your headlights. Increase your following distance to 3 or 4 seconds or more.
- Keep your eyes moving. Don't stare at brightly lit areas. Keep your attention on the street-level activities around you and in the direction in which you are heading.
- Make sure your windshield and headlights are clean.
- Use your headlights wisely. Use your high beams when possible, such as on long stretches of empty road. Switch to low beams for city driving and when following vehicles or meeting oncoming vehicles.
- Avoid driving near your usual bedtime. Your level of alertness is low at this time.

a problem recognizing these colors when you see them. Some people, however, have **color blindness.** These people are unable to tell the difference between red and green or between blue and yellow.

Color-blind people *can* drive safely. They can tell the meaning of signs and signals by their shape and position or by reading the words printed on them.

Night Blindness

Even if you have 20/20 vision, you do not see as well at night as you do during the day. At night your visual acuity, field of vision, depth perception, contrast sensitivity, and color vision are all reduced. For some people, seeing at night is even more difficult.

If seeing at night poses a particular problem for you, you may have a condition known as **night blindness.** Have your eyes checked, and avoid driving at night.

One of the biggest problems in night driving is glare caused by the sudden brightness of the headlights of oncoming vehicles. Whether you look directly at the approaching beams or not, the pupils of your eyes narrow to adjust to the brightness. Your eyes then take a moment to readjust to the darkness of night. During this time, you may be temporarily blinded.

Here are some ways to deal with the danger of glare.

- Do not look directly at the headlights of an oncoming car. Instead, look beyond them and direct your attention to the right edge of the roadway, keeping the approaching car in your peripheral vision.
- Reduce your speed if you are momentarily blinded by glare.
- Keep alert to possible glare situations that may arise, as on curved or hilly roadways. When you anticipate such a situation, turn your eyes slightly away from it, keeping it in your peripheral vision.

Lesson 2 Review

1. Why is good vision important to driving ability?
2. What can you do to compensate for poor depth perception? For night blindness?

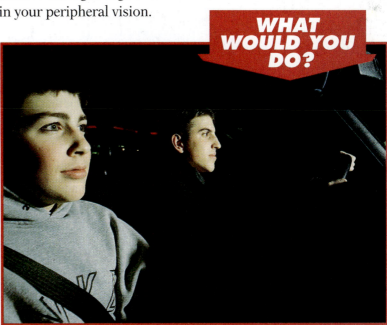

WHAT WOULD YOU DO?

You are driving at night and are having trouble seeing the road. How can you ensure the safety of yourself and your passengers?

OBJECTIVES

1. Describe how fatigue affects driving ability and how to fight fatigue.
2. Explain the ways that short-term illnesses and injuries may affect driving.

KEY TERM

carbon monoxide

Temporary Physical Conditions That Affect Your Ability to Drive

At times, you will have to decide whether or not you feel physically well enough to drive—or whether it is safe to ride with another driver. Conditions such as fatigue, a cold, the flu, or an injury may be temporary, but these conditions can affect your ability to make good decisions while driving.

You've already read about two important factors affecting a driver's ability to operate a vehicle: emotional state and vision. Various other physical factors can limit or impair driving ability.

In some instances, you can compensate for a limiting physical condition. At other times, your wisest course of action is not to drive at all.

TIPS FOR NEW DRIVERS

Fighting Fatigue

Fatigue is usually temporary and easily overcome. The best way to overcome fatigue is to stop doing whatever you are doing and get some rest.

Before You Drive

- Get plenty of rest.
- Avoid heavy, fatty foods.
- Do not drink alcoholic beverages.

While You Drive

- Make sure there is a good flow of fresh air in the car. If your car is overheated or poorly ventilated, you may become sleepy.
- Wear sunglasses to cope with glare from sun and snow.
- Take turns driving with someone else.
- Turn on the radio. Sing, whistle, or talk to yourself.
- Stop regularly, get out of the car, and walk, jog, or do other light exercise for a few minutes.

How Does Fatigue Affect Your Driving Ability?

Nearly everyone experiences fatigue at times. Fatigue may be brought on by lack of sleep, boredom, illness, or stress. Drivers often experience fatigue during a long, monotonous drive. Overeating, drinking alcoholic beverages, or riding in an overheated vehicle all compound the effects of fatigue.

Fatigue is dangerous if you're driving. It affects your body and your mind. Your senses are impaired. You are not as alert as you should be. You may not see objects clearly. You may miss critical information—signs, lights, sounds. You may misjudge speed and distance or take needless risks. You may drift into a state of "highway hypnosis" or even fall asleep at the wheel.

Lack of sleep is now recognized as perhaps the leading cause of traffic fatalities—even ahead of drinking. Combining too little sleep with alcohol consumption virtually guarantees a crash.

When you feel tired, you're clearly in no condition to begin a long drive. If you are already on the road and find yourself getting sleepy, you're better off pulling over than trying to continue driving. Although it is usually not a good idea to sleep in your car at the side of the road, here are some tips if you have no choice but to stop and rest.

- At night, stop at a well-lit roadside rest area. If you cannot find such an area, make sure you are as far off the highway as possible.
- Roll down a window just enough so that fresh air enters the vehicle but not enough that someone might be able to enter it.
- Turn off the engine to avoid being poisoned by **carbon monoxide,** a colorless, odorless gas.
- Lock all the doors.
- Leave your parking lights on, but turn off all other electrical equipment.
- Before you begin to drive again, get out of the car and make sure you are fully awake.

How Do Short-Term Illnesses or Injuries Affect Your Driving?

A temporary illness, such as a cold, the flu, or an allergy, can make it risky for you to drive. So can an injury, such as a broken bone or a pinched nerve. The discomfort or pain you experience can distract your attention from the road and lessen your ability to manage visibility, time, and space.

If you cannot avoid driving when you're ill, at least try to minimize the amount of driving you do. Allow extra time to get where you're going. Drive more slowly than you normally would, and keep your attention focused on driving, not on how you feel.

Be especially careful about driving if you are taking any medication. Always read the information that appears on medicine containers. Some labels specifically warn against driving. Indeed, some medications for common illnesses can cause drowsiness, nausea, headache, or dizziness—conditions that are extremely dangerous for the driver of a vehicle.

Lesson 3 Review

1. How can fatigue affect your driving? How can you fight fatigue?
2. What effect can temporary illness or injury have on your driving?

WHAT WOULD YOU DO?

Describe your driving strategy for the next few hours until you reach your destination.

OBJECTIVES

1. Describe the ways that hearing loss affects driving ability.
2. Identify several ways that drivers can compensate for physical disabilities.
3. Describe how aging and chronic illnesses can affect driving ability.

KEY TERM

driver evaluation facility

Long-Term Physical Factors That Affect Driving Ability

Some people face long-term or permanent physical challenges. Science and medicine, along with advances in technology, have greatly improved the driving potential of such individuals.

How Does Hearing Loss Affect Driving Ability?

◆ *Special devices enable many people to drive who would otherwise be unable to do so.*

Your sense of hearing is an important guide to conditions on the roadway and within your own car. The sound of a siren, horn, or train signal warns you of possible danger. You may hear the sound of a vehicle before you actually see the vehicle. Sounds from your own vehicle may alert you to engine, muffler, or tire trouble.

Drivers with a hearing loss may be able to compensate by wearing hearing aids. They can rely more on their vision, frequently searching the roadway and making good use of the rearview and sideview mirrors.

How Can Challenges Caused by Physical Disabilities Be Met?

A few years ago, it would have been virtually impossible for a person with cerebral palsy or a spinal cord injury to drive. Such challenges, called physical disabilities, often created obstacles that were impossible to overcome. With the development of modern science and technology, however, such disabilities are no longer permanent barriers. Although the severity of a person's physical disability still has an impact on driving ability, new types of equipment, such as joystick driving systems, voice-activated controls, and modified vehicles, can greatly increase his or her driving potential.

For example, many people who do not have full use of their legs are able to drive with the aid of such special devices as hand-operated brakes and gas pedals. People without arms can utilize special rings that are attached to the steering wheel, dashboard controls, door locks, radio controls, and so forth. Artificial limbs, called prosthetic devices, enable these drivers to grasp the rings and operate the vehicle.

Special vans are made for people who use wheelchairs. These vans are equipped with wheelchair lifts that can be operated from inside or outside the vehicle, as well as with extra space that permits the driver to smoothly transfer from a wheelchair to a special power seat.

Drivers who have no ability to turn their heads or shoulders can use extra-large rearview mirrors to extend their vision over a wider area.

Anyone with a physical disability who wants to drive a car, and is able to show that he or she can do so safely, can get a license. Usually, such individuals are required to undergo a comprehensive medical assessment that determines their potential to drive. A special center, called a **driver evaluation facility,** is designed specifically for this purpose.

Be especially careful when you see elderly pedestrians. People 75 years of age and older have the highest pedestrian death rates.

How Do Aging and Chronic Illnesses Affect Driving Ability?

Aging and chronic illnesses are other long-term physical factors that can affect a person's ability to drive.

◆ *Older drivers can call on their experience to help them manage risk.*

Aging

As a young person, your reaction time is likely to be faster and your sense of sight keener than that of an older person. Older people, however, can call on their driving experience to help them reduce risk and anticipate threatening conditions. They can also compensate for possible age-related limitations by reducing driving speed and by avoiding heavily traveled roadways.

As you encounter older drivers and pedestrians, be respectful of their age and experience. Slow down and be patient. Someone will do the same for you one day.

Sue MacNeil

Injury Prevention Specialist, Little World Road Safety and Injury Prevention, Kinburn, Ontario, Canada

To evaluate and manage risk, you have to be honest with yourself. Are you feeling upset or angry about something? Is your mind focused on some disturbing event that just occurred? If so, you may be wise to put off driving until you feel calmer and can better concentrate.

Sometimes events that upset you occur while you are driving. For example, another driver may cut in front of you. Resist the urge to let your emotions affect your driving. Don't let outside pressures interfere with your ability to manage risk.

Chronic Illnesses

A chronic illness is one that lasts over a long period of time or one that recurs often.

Some chronic illnesses, such as epilepsy, arthritis, diabetes, and asthma, can be treated and controlled by medication. However, the medication itself can result in such side effects as drowsiness, dizziness, headache, and nausea, that interfere with safe driving. To obtain a driver's license, people with chronic illnesses must furnish proof that the illnesses are under control and that medication won't cause side effects that impair driving ability.

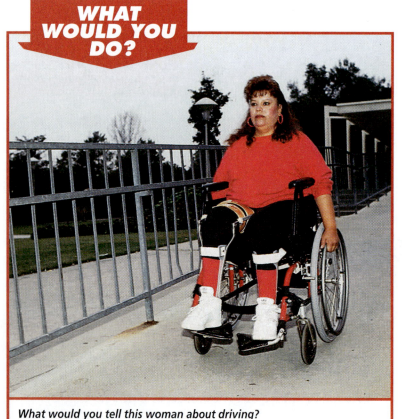

WHAT WOULD YOU DO?

What would you tell this woman about driving?

Lesson 4 Review

1. How can impaired hearing affect your ability to drive?
2. How can drivers who have a physical disability compensate for that disability?
3. What effect do aging and chronic illnesses have on driving ability?

Kitty O'Neil

Kitty O'Neil is 5 feet 3 inches tall and weighs only 98 pounds, but her accomplishments are giant-sized. She has held the women's world land speed driving record of 512 mph and has gone on to become the second-fastest human, with a land speed of 618 mph. Of course, both of these records were accomplished in specially designed cars driven at test sites and not on highways.

O'Neil has also set records as a champion drag boat racer and water-skier, and she is a former American Athletic Union national diving champion. She uses the skills that enabled her to set these records in her work as a movie stunt woman. Among other things, she has jumped off six-story buildings, pretended to be drowning, and been set on fire.

Why does Kitty O'Neil do these things? As she says, one reason is to prove that physically challenged people "can do anything." Kitty O'Neil has been deaf since she was four months old. She believes that she owes her will to succeed to her mother, a woman of Cherokee descent who died when Kitty was 21 years old. She taught Kitty how to talk and play the cello and the piano and rewarded Kitty whenever she perfected a new skill. O'Neil says that she would like to show others that her mother's encouragement and support "has paid off beyond anyone's hopes."

What Do You Think Now?

Does the story of Kitty O'Neil change or confirm your opinion of the capabilities of people who are physically challenged? Explain your answer.

KEY POINTS

Lesson One

1. Emotions such as joy, sadness, anger, and fear can cause you to be inattentive, interfere with your ability to concentrate, and hinder your ability to process information while driving.
2. You can make an effort to control your emotions by maintaining a responsible attitude and identifying situations that may cause you to become upset.

Lesson Two

1. You must have good vision in order to adjust your car's speed and position to minimize risk. Good vision also enables you to identify signs, signals, and roadway markings.
2. To compensate for poor depth perception, practice judging the distance between two objects; for color blindness, learn the meaning of signs and signals by their shape and position; for low-contrast situations and night blindness, drive more slowly than you would during the day.

Lesson Three

1. Fatigue impairs your senses. It could cause you to fall asleep while driving, miss critical information, take risks, or misjudge speed and distance. Fight fatigue by getting plenty of rest, avoiding alcoholic beverages and heavy foods, opening the windows to get fresh air, and taking turns driving with someone else.
2. Short-term illness or injury can cause pain or discomfort, which can distract your attention from the road and lessen your ability to manage visibility, time, and space.

Lesson Four

1. Hearing loss may prevent you from being aware of sounds that warn you of possible danger, such as the sounds of sirens or horns, and can prevent you from being aware of problems within your own car.
2. People without full use of their legs can drive with the aid of devices such as hand-operated brakes and accelerators. With the aid of prosthetic devices, people without arms can drive using special rings and dashboard controls. Those who use wheelchairs can use specially equipped vehicles.
3. Aging can affect a driver's reaction time and eyesight. Medications for chronic illnesses may have side effects that interfere with safe driving.

PROJECTS

1. Emotional factors play an important part in the way people drive. What are some ways that people could be reminded to maintain a responsible attitude and to be courteous and patient while driving?
2. While you are a passenger, close your eyes. Use your other senses to gather information. Can you identify the sounds you hear? Can you tell whether the car is speeding up, slowing down, or making a turn?

*inter*NET
CONNECTION

Use the Internet to investigate the problems of aggressive driving, which may also be called road rage.
www.glencoe.com/sec/driver.ed

CHAPTER TEST

Write the letter of the answer that best completes each sentence.

1. Strong emotions can
   a. affect your night vision.
   b. help you drive safely.
   c. interfere with your driving judgment.

2. If you are severely fatigued, you should
   a. avoid driving.
   b. drive with your high beams on.
   c. drive quickly to your destination.

3. A physical factor that may affect driving ability is
   a. the effects of medication.
   b. the color of your eyes.
   c. a feeling of sadness.

4. A person who cannot see well at angles to the left and right has difficulty with
   a. night vision.
   b. depth perception.
   c. peripheral vision.

5. One way to deal with headlight glare is to
   a. look right at the car's headlights.
   b. look at the right edge of the road.
   c. increase speed to get past the car quickly.

6. As a driver, it is your responsibility to drive
   a. your friends to school.
   b. only when you are able to concentrate.
   c. no matter how you are feeling.

7. Drivers who are unable to turn their head or shoulders can use
   a. revolving seats.
   b. extra-large rearview mirrors.
   c. a thickly padded seat cushion.

8. To control your emotions in traffic
   a. yell at other drivers.
   b. daydream about pleasant events.
   c. expect others to make mistakes.

9. If you use correct procedures, you will
   a. reduce risk no matter how you may feel.
   b. never have a collision.
   c. be able to drive without paying attention.

10. Most of the information you gather about traffic situations comes from
    a. other drivers.
    b. your vision.
    c. your sense of hearing.

Choose the phrase that best completes each sentence.

field of vision	wheelchair lifts
responsible attitude	lack of concentration
depth perception	sense of hearing

11. Your _____ helps you judge the distance between cars.

12. Having a(n) _____ means respecting others' well-being and an awareness of the consequences of your actions.

13. Your _____ includes what you can see directly in front of you, up and down, and at an angle to the sides.

14. Strong emotions can lead to a(n) _____ when you drive.

15. Modified vehicles for people who are physically disabled may include _____.

DRIVER'S LOG

In this chapter, you have learned about how emotional and physical factors can affect driving. Write at least two paragraphs giving your ideas on the following questions.
• What "sets you off" emotionally?
• How will you control these factors and your emotions?

CHAPTER *4*

Handling Social Pressures

As a driver, you will be responsible for your safety as well as that of your passengers and other roadway users. It is important to learn how to base your decisions on good judgment and not on a desire to "go along" with the crowd.

Alcohol's Effect on One's Health and One's Future

You are at an exciting, yet confusing, time in your life. Sometimes people treat you as an adult and at other times as a child. Learning to cope with this partial independence is a natural stage of growing up. It is the time when you are very vulnerable to peer pressure.

Peer pressure can influence the way you dress, your taste in music, and even the way you talk. This is usually harmless. However, peer pressure can also influence you in ways that can damage you and your future, such as influencing you to experiment with drinking alcohol. Understanding how alcohol can destroy your hopes, dreams, and ambitions can help you resist destructive peer pressure.

What Are the Effects of Alcohol?

Alcohol is a powerful and dangerous drug—it can change the way people act, think, and feel. Many people experiment with alcohol to overcome feelings of shyness, inhibition, or unhappiness or because it makes them feel like part of the group. Alcohol addiction can creep up slowly and take control of a person's life. School, work, friends, family, plans for the future become meaningless to the problem drinker. He or she becomes psychologically and physically dependent on alcohol.

Annually, fatalities associated with alcohol use claim five times more people than heroin, cocaine, marijuana, and all other illegal drugs combined. The high number of traffic fatalities involving young people is the reason why every state has passed laws to make it illegal for people under age 21 to buy, possess, or consume alcohol. In 1997, more than 16,000 people died in alcohol-related crashes in the United States.

For people age 21 or over, excessive drinking is no longer tolerated. Recently enacted laws that prohibit open containers of alcoholic beverages in vehicles, lower permissible blood alcohol levels, and increase fines and penalties encourage responsible drinking for people 21 and older.

What Are a Person's Responsibilities Regarding Drinking?

There is no such thing as responsible drinking for an underage person. There are, however, responsibilities that everyone has regarding alcohol drinking and drinkers.

No one is alone. If a person or someone he or she knows has a drinking problem, he or she can contact:

Alcoholics Anonymous
P.O. Box 459
Grand Central Station
New York, NY 10163

Alateen
P.O. Box 862
Midtown Station
New York, NY 10018

Both of these organizations have listings in local phone directories.

- People have a responsibility to protect themselves from the threat that drinking poses to their health and well-being. They also have a responsibility to protect themselves and others from the risk posed by people who drink and drive.
- If you are with someone who has been drinking, don't let that person drive. You can help by taking the car keys, driving yourself, calling your parents for a ride, calling a taxi, or making other arrangements.
- There are support groups to help problem drinkers and their relatives and friends. These groups keep any information confidential. Two such groups are Alcoholics Anonymous, or AA, and Alateen.

AA is an organization for people who feel or know that they may have a problem with alcohol and need help. Alateen is a support group for young people who have an alcoholic parent, sibling, or friend.

What Are the Symptoms of a Problem Drinker?

People must be able to recognize the signs of problem drinking. Look for changes in a person's behavior or life situation such as loss of initiative, frequent lateness and absences from school, behavior problems at school, a decline in grades, a change of friends, leisure activities that focus on alcohol, and trouble with the law. A person with a drinking problem often denies having a problem, drinks alone, has trouble sleeping, and may suffer from memory loss or blackouts.

Other symptoms can be seen in health problems that can afflict the problem drinker, such as liver failure, heart disease, cancer, brain damage, convulsions, and malnutrition.

Alcoholism is a disease. Its consequences are devastating and include loss of self-esteem, loss of friends and family, and even loss of life. The best defense against this disease is to say no when you are offered that first drink.

WHAT WOULD YOU DO?

You and a friend are offered a drink. You say no but your friend wants to try one. What will you say to your friend?

Lesson *1* Review

1. What can be the consequences of alcohol use?
2. What responsibilities do people have to themselves and to friends regarding drinking?
3. How would you recognize the signs of a problem drinker, and what might you do to help that person?

OBJECTIVES

1. Explain how alcohol affects driving ability.
2. Name the laws about and penalties for driving while intoxicated.

KEY TERMS

blood-alcohol concentration (BAC)
inhibitions
implied consent
driving while intoxicated (DWI)
driving under the influence (DUI)

Alcohol and Its Effects on Driving Ability

When you are behind the wheel of a motor vehicle, all of your senses must be on alert. You need to react quickly to potentially threatening conditions and then make split-second decisions. Being a good driver takes skill and judgment. No matter how good a driver you are, however, alcohol *will* decrease your skill and *will* damage your judgment.

How Does Alcohol Affect Driving Ability?

Even one drink might be enough to impair your ability to drive safely. From the moment alcohol enters your bloodstream, you begin to lose your ability to think clearly. Even a small amount of alcohol causes changes in your coordination. It should not come as a surprise that approximately 40 percent of all highway deaths are alcohol related.

Facts About Alcohol and Driving

These facts tell you why drinking and driving is a recipe for disaster.

- The 16,189 fatalities in alcohol-related crashes during 1997 represent an average of one alcohol-related fatality every 32 minutes.
- In 1997, 14 percent (7,670) of the 56,602 drivers who were involved in fatal crashes who had a 0.10 percent or greater **blood-alcohol**

CONNECTIONS

Social Studies

In 1981 a high school in Wayland, Massachusetts, lost two of its students in alcohol-related crashes in one week. From these needless deaths began a movement by Robert Anastas, the high school's health director, that resulted in the formation of **Students Against Driving Drunk** (SADD). Mr. Anastas wanted to find a way to help his students confront the dangers of drinking and driving. By the end of 1982, SADD had become a national organization.

Recently, SADD changed its name to Students Against Destructive Decisions. Why? SADD's message now includes viewpoints on issues affecting the health and safety of youth. While its biggest message is still about drinking and driving, SADD is also concerned with drugs and drug prevention, seat-belt use, teen pregnancy, suicide, and gangs. The new name better reflects all the issues SADD is now dedicated to helping.

concentration (BAC), or percentage of alcohol in the blood, were young drivers 15 to 20 years old.

- In 1997, 21 percent of young drivers 15 to 20 years old who were killed in crashes were intoxicated.
- More than 327,000 people were injured in crashes where police reported that alcohol was present—an average of one person injured about every 2 minutes.
- About three in every ten Americans will be involved in an alcohol-related crash at some time in their lives.

In spite of these terrible statistics, alcohol is the most widely used and abused drug in the world. Yes, it is a drug, and it is deadly.

Even one drink of alcohol causes changes in the body. That is because alcohol is not digested, as food is. Rather, it is absorbed into the bloodstream through the walls of the stomach and small intestine. Once in the bloodstream, alcohol is quickly carried to all parts of the body. Alcohol has the greatest effect on the brain because that is the organ that controls all body functions. A drinker's mental and physical abilities become diminished.

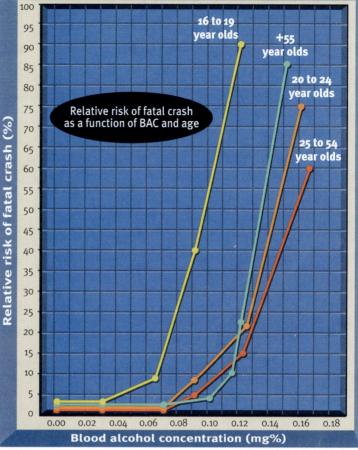

PROBABILITY OF A FATAL COLLISION

Relative risk of fatal crash as a function of BAC and age

16 to 19 year olds
+55 year olds
20 to 24 year olds
25 to 54 year olds

Relative risk of fatal crash (%)

Blood alcohol concentration (mg%)

◆ This graph shows how age, blood alcohol concentration (BAC), and the probability of being in a crash are related.

Myths and Facts About Alcohol

Alcohol is one of the most misunderstood and widely used drugs. The truth about alcohol is the best weapon against it.

There are plenty of myths about alcohol. Let's look at the facts.

Myth Beer is not as intoxicating as hard liquor.

Fact Not true! Sure, there is more alcohol in an ounce of liquor than in an ounce of beer. However, each of these standard drinks—a 12-ounce bottle of beer, a 5-ounce glass of wine, or a 1½ ounce shot of 80 proof liquor—contains about the same amount of alcohol.

Myth You can't get drunk on a full stomach.

Fact A full stomach just means the alcohol is absorbed into the bloodstream a little more slowly. *All* of that alcohol will still get into the bloodstream and travel to the brain and other parts of your body.

Myth Drinking and driving is not dangerous.

Fact Motor vehicle crashes are the single largest health risk for people under 28 and the number 1 killer of teenagers.

Myth You must drink because friends want you to even though you are the driver.

Fact Real friends would not want you to hurt yourself or others. Tell them the facts about alcohol.

Myth Black coffee, a cold shower, lots of exercise, or all three together can quickly sober up a drinker.

Fact No way! The body cannot burn up much more than ½ ounce of alcohol in an hour. Nothing can speed up the process.

Myth Alcohol makes you feel better when you're down in the dumps.

Fact Not really. Alcohol is a depressant, or "downer." It may make a person feel worse than before.

Myth Sometimes, because of peer pressure at a party, there is no other choice but to drink.

Fact You do have a choice. Don't drink. Abstinence is the only responsible action for anyone under 21.

The Physical Effects of Alcohol

Drinking drivers 16 to 19 years old have a higher fatal crash probability than any other age group. For instance, young drivers with a blood-alcohol concentration of between 0.08 and 0.10 percent are 40 times more likely to be involved in a fatal crash than a sober driver. Why does this occur?

The answer is that people who have little or no driving experience have a higher risk of being involved in a fatal crash.

◆ *An intoxicated driver will have difficulty focusing on the pen as the officer moves it.*

Reaction time After two or more drinks, a driver becomes physically slower and less alert. In fact, for some people, reaction time may be impaired after only one drink.

Coordination Movement gets sloppy and uncoordinated. Drivers who have been drinking are less able than others to make critical decisions. They have trouble steering and may step on the brake pedal too late or miss it entirely.

Distance (depth) perception Alcohol affects the ability to judge distance, or depth. Drinking drivers may perceive something as farther away than it really is. They cannot tell where the vehicles around them really are or how far away road signs or signals are.

Speed perception Drinking drivers often cannot tell how fast another vehicle is approaching. Such drivers also have a distorted sense of how fast they are going, which is not surprising when you consider that alcohol severely dulls the senses.

Vision Alcohol affects the reflex action of the eyes that causes pupils to become smaller in bright light and larger as light diminishes. Drinkers' eyes are not protected against headlight glare because pupils don't return to normal size quickly enough once the headlights have passed. Temporary blindness results. Alcohol also impairs side, color, and night vision, eye focus, and it may cause double vision.

◆ *Blurred or double vision is often the result of a driver's having had too much to drink.*

The Mental Effects of Alcohol

Alcohol doesn't just affect the part of your brain that controls your physical reactions. It also affects the part of the brain that controls the ability to reason.

As if that isn't bad enough, alcohol affects your judgment and, consequently, can make you feel as if you are thinking more clearly than usual. This false message makes drinking drivers even more dangerous because they do not have the judgment to realize that something is wrong. A driver in this condition is apt to make poor decisions—even fatal ones.

Alcohol affects your **inhibitions,** the elements of your personality that stop you from behaving without regard to possible consequences. In drivers, the loss of inhibition can be very dangerous and can cause them to take chances they would normally avoid.

What Are the Laws, Tests, and Penalties for Drinking and Driving?

Drinking and driving causes countless tragedies. All states have laws regulating the minimum drinking age and laws against drinking and driving. In all states, it is illegal for people under age 21 to buy, possess, or drink alcoholic beverages.

Implied Consent Laws

When you use public roads, you agree to give law enforcement officials permission to test you for alcohol use if you are arrested on suspicion of drinking and driving. This permission is known as **implied consent,** and it is the law in all 50 states. The test will determine your blood-alcohol concentration (BAC).

Most states and the District of Columbia have enacted administrative license suspension (ALS) laws. A driver's license can be suspended if a person refuses to take a test for blood-alcohol concentration or if a person fails the test. This is in addition to any fines or penalties connected with conviction for driving while intoxicated or under the influence.

In many states, adult drivers with a BAC of 0.10 percent or higher can be charged with **driving while intoxicated (DWI).** Some states call this **driving under the influence (DUI).**

Tests for Intoxication

Chemical analysis of blood or urine can measure a person's BAC, or a breath-testing device can measure the percentage of alcohol in the breath. In an increasing number of states, a reading of 0.08 percent or higher is enough to convict adult drivers of DWI or DUI and to take away their license. In most states, teenage drivers with any BAC over 0.00 up to 0.02 percent violate 21-year-old minimum drinking age laws—sometimes referred to as zero tolerance laws.

Even if a driver's BAC is lower than the legal limit, he or she can still be charged with DWI or DUI. The police can stop anyone whose driving appears to be impaired. They can give a field sobriety test by asking the driver to perform simple tasks, such as standing on one leg or walking a line.

If you are ever stopped for suspicion of DWI or DUI, be courteous and cooperate with the police officer. Drivers who refuse to submit to a chemical test for BAC can have their licenses suspended whether they are convicted or not.

Penalties and Consequences

The penalties for DWI or DUI differ in each state. A license can be suspended, a fine can be assessed, and a jail term can be imposed. If injury or death results from a collision in which the driver has been drinking, the driver can be prosecuted for more serious offenses, such as vehicular homicide. Drivers convicted of DWI or DUI pay higher insurance premiums once their licenses are restored, and may have to attend education and counseling programs.

In addition to legal penalties, there may be other consequences. Drunk drivers involved in crashes have to live with the emotional consequences of having caused injury or death. Civil suits, permanent physical disabilities and long-term health problems to both the driver and passengers may also result.

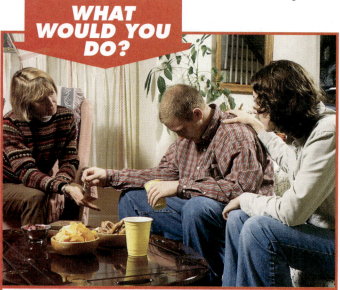

WHAT WOULD YOU DO?

The driver has been drinking steadily. How can his companions get home? What is their responsibility to the driver?

Lesson **2** Review

1. How does alcohol affect a driver?
2. What should you know about the laws, tests, and penalties for driving while intoxicated?

How Other Drugs Affect Driving Ability

OBJECTIVES
1. Describe some kinds of drugs other than alcohol.
2. Explain how these drugs affect driving ability.

Alcohol is not the only drug that can impair your ability to drive. Almost any drug can have a harmful effect on your driving skill.

There are many different kinds of drugs. Some can be bought only by prescription. Others can be bought over the counter without a prescription. Some drugs are against the law but can be bought illegally.

What Drugs Affect Driving Ability?

How a drug affects you depends on the drug itself. Some drugs can decrease your ability to make sound decisions and respond well to situations. Other drugs can change the way you think. It is important that you know about these drugs and their effects on driving. Once you understand the danger of combining drugs and driving, you can take steps to avoid putting yourself and others at risk.

Synergism

Synergism is the interaction of one drug with another to enhance the effect of one or both. For example, if a person drinks alcohol and takes a depressant, the combination could produce an effect on the person greater than the individual effects of either substance when taken alone. Even a nonprescription drug such as an antihistamine can be dangerous when mixed with alcohol. It is very important, therefore, to avoid combining alcohol and other drugs or combining any drugs unless prescribed by a physician.

TIPS FOR NEW DRIVERS

Under the Influence

Be aware of signs that other drivers on the road may be under the influence of alcohol or other drugs. Various signs indicate possible problems.

Traveling at Erratic Speeds—Either Too Fast or Too Slowly
Alcohol-impaired drivers often have trouble driving at a steady speed.

Running over Curbs or Turning into the Wrong Lane
Alcohol-impaired drivers are often unable to turn smoothly.

Weaving from Side to Side
Alcohol-impaired drivers suffer from loss of coordination and attention, which affects their ability to steer smoothly.

Ignoring or Overshooting Traffic Signs
Alcohol-impaired drivers suffer impaired reflexes and vision loss.

If you find yourself on the same roadway as a driver who shows any of these signs, increase the amount of space between your vehicles. Be alert to the fact that there is an impaired driver sharing the roadway with you. If possible, inform a police officer of what you have noticed.

◆ *Many of the capsules, tablets, and syrups commonly found in medicine cabinets are over-the-counter drugs.*

Over-the-Counter Drugs

Over-the-counter drugs are drugs that can be purchased legally without a doctor's prescription. You may not even think of them as drugs. They are used for colds, flu, headaches, allergies, and other everyday ailments. It's important to read the package label of these drugs, which may warn that their use may "cause drowsiness or dizziness," or "Do not drive after using." Pay attention to these warnings! It is your responsibility as a driver to know what side effects any medications you are taking might cause.

Prescription Drugs

You can buy prescription drugs at a pharmacy if your doctor prescribes them for you. Remember to ask your doctor or the pharmacist if you can drive safely while you are taking any prescription medication.

Many prescription drugs have warnings on the package or the bottle. Look carefully. It is your responsibility as a driver to know what drugs you are taking and what effects they can have.

Depressants

Depressants slow down, or depress, the central nervous system. Doctors order depressants for patients who are experiencing a great deal of tension, who are very anxious, or who are being treated for high blood pressure.

While depressants can help with these symptoms, they also slow down the patient's mental and physical activity. Like alcohol, which is also a depressant, these drugs slow down reflexes and have a harmful effect on coordination.

DRUGS THAT AFFECT DRIVING ABILITY

Narcotics	Depressants	Stimulants	Hallucinogens
Heroin	Alcohol	Amphetamines (speed)	Marijuana
Codeine	Barbiturates		LSD
Morphine	Methadone	Cocaine (crack or rock)	PCP (angel dust)
	Sleeping pills		Hashish
	Tranquilizers		

Stimulants

Stimulants speed up, or stimulate, the central nervous system. Some drivers misuse these drugs and take them to keep awake when driving long distances.

Stimulants can give users a false feeling of well-being and make them think that they are superalert. These drugs often cause drivers to take foolish and life-threatening risks. When the effect of stimulants wears off, which can happen very suddenly, users can become very tired quickly. Many stimulants are illegal.

Hallucinogens

Hallucinogens are so dangerous that selling or using them is against the law. They are called mind-altering drugs for a good reason. Hallucinogens change the way a person thinks, sees, and acts.

Marijuana Marijuana may make a user drowsy. It can affect people's awareness of how fast or slow they are driving and their ability to judge time and space. People who use marijuana may just sit and stare and be completely unaware of anything that is going on around them. No one really knows when the effects of marijuana wear off. The chemicals in this drug can stay in the body for as long as four to six weeks. Drivers may think that the effects have worn off when they are still under the influence of marijuana.

LSD and PCP The strongest hallucinogens are LSD and PCP (angel dust). While using LSD or PCP, people can forget who they are, where they are, and what they are doing. These drugs can cause drivers to lose the ability to judge space and the speed at which they are driving.

Narcotics

Narcotics have a strong depressant effect. They can cause stupor, coma, and even death.

Lesson 3 Review

1. What are some other kinds of drugs besides alcohol?
2. How do these drugs affect your ability to drive?

FYI

Marijuana masks the feeling of nausea that accompanies intoxication. Drinkers who mix marijuana and alcohol may not realize how much alcohol they have consumed. They may continue drinking until they suffer alcohol poisoning, which can result in coma or even death.

WHAT WOULD YOU DO?

You are taking a prescription medicine. Can you drive your sister to the movies? How will you decide if it is safe for you to drive?

OBJECTIVES
1. Name some distractions that increase driving risk.
2. Describe how these distractions can hinder your driving ability.

Distractions Can Increase Driving Risk

There is much to pay attention to when you drive. You have to see what is going on around you. You need to be sure that other drivers know where you are and what you plan to do. You have to keep adjusting your speed and vehicle position to driving conditions. You have to be alert to any surprises that might turn into emergencies.

With all of this going on, you need to be sure that no distractions inside your vehicle will take your attention away from your driving and increase your risk.

SAFETY TIPS

When driving with infants and small children, be sure they are in safety seats and that the seats are securely fastened in place in the backseat. Do not allow small children to ride in the front seat of vehicles equipped with passenger-side air bags. The powerful force of an inflating air bag can injure or kill small children.

How Can Distractions Hinder Your Driving Ability?

Imagine that you are driving along a busy highway. Suddenly you see an antique car driving beside you. You have never seen a vehicle like this before, so you take your eyes off the road ahead for just a second to get a closer look. Just then another vehicle pulls ahead of you, and you have to brake hard. You have let yourself become distracted from your driving responsibilities. You almost crashed into another vehicle.

Many events can distract you as you drive. It is important to be aware of these distractions so that you can be a safe and responsible driver.

A Vehicle Audio System Can Distract You

Most vehicles have radios, cassette players, or CD players, but do not become so interested in the music that you forget to pay attention to your driving. Remember, too, that loud music can mask useful information.

A radio can be distracting if it is too loud. Keep volume at a reasonable level. Your concentration must be focused on driving. Looking for and changing tapes or CDs is also distracting—and very dangerous. Risk is increased anytime you take your eyes off the road or drive with only one hand on the wheel.

Headphones Can Be Dangerous

In most states, it is against the law to wear stereo headphones while you drive. You need information when you drive—and that includes roadway sounds.

If you're wearing headphones, you may not be able to hear another vehicle honking its horn at you. You may lose your concentration if you're too absorbed in what you're hearing. Put them away. Your job now is to pay attention to your driving.

Cellular Phones Can Distract You

Using a cellular phone while driving is not recommended. Statistics show that cell phones are distracting and increase the risk of a crash. Dialing and talking divert a driver's attention away from controlling the vehicle and watching the road.

Cellular phones *can* provide some safety benefits for a motorist. You can, for instance, use a cell phone to get help if your vehicle malfunctions or to report a crash.

Keep your phone in the glove compartment with the ringer off. If you must place or receive a phone call, even in an emergency, do so only when stopped, preferably in an off-road location. Never try to talk while driving. Remember that you need to give driving your full attention.

Passengers Can Distract You

Sometimes the people in your vehicle want you to pay more attention to them than to your driving. They may ask you to turn around and look at what they're doing. Sometimes they can be talking loudly. They may try to roughhouse in the vehicle or hang out the windows.

You are responsible for the safety of your passengers, and it is your responsibility to tell them to sit still or be quiet. You're not being rude— you're being a safe, responsible driver.

Little children can become bored or restless on long trips. They may start fighting with each other or try to take off their safety belts. You can make sure that children behave by telling them the rules before you start driving and by keeping them quietly occupied.

Make sure you have some tape cassettes for them to listen to or quiet games for them to play in the vehicle. You can also stop more often than you normally would and let the children get out and stretch their legs.

Other Distractions

Driving with animals in your vehicle can be dangerous. A dog may suddenly jump on your lap, or a cat may crawl under your feet and land on the gas pedal. You have to plan ahead if you are going to take an animal in

◆ *If you talk on a cellular phone while you are driving, you increase your chances of having an accident, because your full attention is not on driving.*

◆ *Don't let passengers distract you. Tell them how you expect them to behave before they enter your car.*

William F. Cullinane
Executive Director, Students Against Destructive Decisions (SADD)

Most young people have rejected the social pressure to drink and drive. Next, they must reject the pressure to use alcohol and other drugs. They must realize that to solve this problem, they first have to see themselves as part of it.

For young people to recognize their involvement in the problem, they need to receive honest feedback from others who care. SADD students across the country are providing alcohol-free and drug-free alternatives for their peers. They are offering a caring hand, not an enabling one.

your vehicle. Think about putting the animal in a carrying case, or ask a friend to come with you and hold the animal by its leash. If you travel with pets frequently, you should be aware that pet safety belts are available at specialty shops.

Many drivers become distracted in traffic jams. They get stuck for a long time and lose their concentration. Remember, even when you are stopped, that it is important to pay attention to everything that is going on around you.

When you are driving on a toll road, you will need change to pay the toll. Make sure you know how much change you will need, and look for change *before* you start out on your trip. Plan ahead. Have a container with plenty of change in it within reach so that you don't have to search through your pockets when you should be concentrating on driving.

Drivers who smoke are distracted when they search for or light cigars, cigarettes, or pipes. A lit cigarette falling on the seat or in the driver's lap is dangerous. Don't smoke and drive—especially in a closed vehicle, where passengers can inhale the smoke.

Remember, your job is to concentrate on your driving. Being prepared to handle distractions is part of that job.

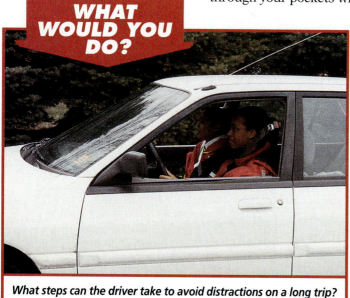

WHAT WOULD YOU DO?

What steps can the driver take to avoid distractions on a long trip?

Lesson 4 Review

1. What distractions can increase your driving risk?
2. How can these distractions hinder your driving ability?

Using the Mileage Chart

Suppose you are planning to drive from Abilene to El Paso. How many miles would you be traveling? One way to find out would be to use a mileage chart such as the one on this page. Using a mileage chart is easy.

First look at the names of cities down the left side of the chart. Find Abilene, and put your left finger over it.

Then look at the cities across the top of the chart. Put your right finger on El Paso.

Now move your left finger across the chart until it reaches the box below El Paso. The number in the box is the distance in miles between Abilene and El Paso. The distance is 450 miles. That's quite a trip.

To estimate how long it will take you if you drive at an average speed of 55 miles per hour, divide 450 by 55. The trip will take between 8 and 9 hours. But don't forget to add in some time for rest stops. Therefore, you can figure on about a 10-hour trip.

Try It Yourself

1. How many miles is it between San Angelo and Eagle Pass?
2. If you are traveling at 55 miles an hour, how long will it take you to drive from El Paso to Pecos?
3. Which trip would be longer—one from Odessa to Houston or one from Lubbock to San Antonio?

MILEAGE CHART	Abilene	Amarillo	Dallas	Eagle Pass	El Paso	Houston	Lubbock	Midland	Odessa	Pecos	San Angelo	San Antonio
Abilene		273	180	302	450	355	171	148	180	245	92	250
Amarillo	273		351	517	421	597	134	237	258	330	310	513
El Paso	450	421	646	479		751	345	312	289	210	415	555
Lubbock	171	134	318	394	345	530		121	142	219	202	406
Odessa	180	258	352	301	289	507	142	20		75	132	345
San Angelo	92	310	262	215	415	374	202	113	132	210		215

KEY POINTS

Lesson One

1. Drinking alcohol can change a person's actions, thoughts, and feelings. It can become addictive so that the need for alcohol becomes more important than friends, family, and future plans.
2. People's responsibilities include protecting themselves from the hazards that drinking poses to their health and well-being, as well as protecting themselves and others from the threat of people who drink and drive.
3. Some symptoms that indicate a problem drinker are loss of initiative, frequent lateness and absence from school, trouble with the law, sleeplessness, and memory loss.

Lesson Two

1. Some ways that alcohol affects driving ability are that it reduces inhibitions, reduces ability to react quickly, impairs coordination, and has a negative effect on a driver's judgment.
2. When people use public roads, they agree to give law enforcement officials the right to test them for alcohol use if they suspect the drivers of drinking and driving. This is the law of implied consent. In many states, a driver over age 21 is considered intoxicated if his or her blood-alcohol concentration is 0.08 percent or greater. Most states have enacted lower BAC limits (0.00 percent to 0.02 percent) for people under age 21. Penalties for DWI or DUI may include driver's license suspension, assessment of a fine, and a term in jail.

Lesson Three

1. Over-the-counter drugs, prescription drugs, depressants, stimulants, hallucinogens, and narcotics can affect driving ability.
2. Depressants slow down the central nervous system; stimulants speed it up. Hallucinogens are illegal mind-altering drugs. Narcotics are illegal drugs that have a strong depressant effect.

Lesson Four

1. Distractions can hinder your driving ability by drawing your attention away from the road.
2. Distractions include radios, tape decks, CD players, stereo headphones, cell phones, noisy passengers, disruptive children, animals, traffic jams, toll payments, and smoking.

PROJECTS

1. Many organizations work to educate drivers about the dangers of drinking and driving. Besides SADD, Mothers Against Drunk Driving (MADD) is probably the best known. Find information about MADD.
2. Refer to your state driver's manual or interview a police officer. Discover the circumstances under which a teenage driver can be convicted of DUI or DWI in your state. Find out about the penalties for conviction as well.

*inter*NET CONNECTION

Explore the Web for other statistics on drinking and driving.
www.glencoe.com/sec/driver.ed

CHAPTER TEST

Write the letter of the answer that best completes each sentence.

1. Distractions can
   a. slow reflexes.
   b. decrease risk.
   c. increase risk.

2. Drinking alcohol
   a. does not affect your mental abilities.
   b. often helps you think more clearly.
   c. slows down the part of your brain that controls muscles and reflexes.

3. Over-the-counter drugs
   a. may be used when driving short distances.
   b. may impair driving ability.
   c. must be ordered for you by a doctor.

4. You can reduce the effects of alcohol if you
   a. take a very cold shower.
   b. exercise.
   c. allow several hours to pass.

5. Implied consent means that you
   a. agree to be tested if you are suspected of drinking and driving.
   b. agree to obey the rules of the road.
   c. have the right to be uncooperative if you are stopped by police.

6. You can reduce distractions while driving by
   a. putting on a set of stereo headphones.
   b. looking at the scenery.
   c. keeping radio volume low and asking passengers to speak quietly.

7. To get help with a drinking problem
   a. drink just once a week.
   b. drink only beer.
   c. join a support group.

8. Alcohol is
   a. a harmless substance.
   b. a powerful drug.
   c. nonaddictive.

9. In most states, drivers over age 21 are considered intoxicated if their BAC is greater than
   a. 0.10 percent.
   b. 0.07 percent.
   c. 0.04 percent.

10. Even a small amount of alcohol can affect your
    a. long-term memory.
    b. ability to judge distance and speed.
    c. hearing.

Write the word or phrase that best completes each sentence.

| prescription | stimulants | concentration |
| depressants | inhibitions | peer pressure |

11. _____ stop you from behaving without regard to possible consequences.

12. Drugs that slow down the central nervous system are called _____.

13. _____ drugs must be ordered by a doctor.

14. _____ often give drivers a false sense of self-confidence and cause them to take foolish and life-threatening risks.

15. The influence of your friends is called _____.

DRIVER'S LOG

In this chapter, you have learned about how social pressures can cause you to behave in ways that will put you and others at risk. Imagine that a friend has been drinking and wants to drive you home. Your friend says, "Don't worry, I'm just fine." What will you say? How might your friend respond? Write a dialogue showing what might happen.

This review tests your knowledge of the material in Chapters 1–4. Use the review to help you study for your state driving test. Choose the answer that best completes each statement.

1. The best way to fight fatigue is to
   a. use a stimulant.
   b. rest.
   c. look at the scenery.
   d. drink coffee.

2. *BAC* stands for
   a. brain alcohol content.
   b. blood-alcohol concentration.
   c. basic automobile collision.
   d. body alcohol content.

3. In 1 hour, the adult human body can burn
   a. about ½ ounce of alcohol.
   b. about 1 ounce of alcohol.
   c. about 2 ounces of alcohol.
   d. about 3 ounces of alcohol.

4. Traffic laws are enforced by
   a. the CIA.
   b. state and local police.
   c. the department of motor vehicles.
   d. United States marshals.

5. Over 39 percent of all occupant fatalities
   a. involve more than one vehicle.
   b. involve only one vehicle.
   c. are "fender-benders."
   d. involve pedestrians.

6. Marijuana remains in the body for
   a. up to one week.
   b. up to two weeks.
   c. up to six weeks.
   d. up to ten weeks.

7. A visual acuity test measures
   a. how well you can see.
   b. pupil dilation.
   c. convex vision.
   d. headlight power.

8. Over-the-counter medications
   a. never affect driving ability.
   b. sometimes produce side effects.
   c. improve concentration.
   d. must be prescribed by a doctor.

9. The area of vision directly ahead of a person is called
   a. side vision.
   b. convex vision.
   c. the area of central vision.
   d. peripheral vision.

10. The second stage of the graduated driver licensing (GDL) system is
    a. an intermediate/probationary license.
    b. supervised driving at all times.
    c. a learner's permit.
    d. full driving privileges.

11. Each year, a driver's chance of being involved in a collision is
    a. 1 in 15.
    b. 1 in 9.
    c. 1 in 3.
    d. 1 in 2.

12. The influence of one's friends is called
    a. maturity.
    b. peer pressure.
    c. HTS.
    d. SIPDE.

13. One way to reduce driving risk is to
    a. anticipate the actions of others.
    b. always use high-beam headlights.
    c. join a support group.
    d. close the windows.

14. Through driver education, students learn
    a. how to maneuver and control a vehicle.
    b. the traffic laws of all 50 states.
    c. how to drive without paying attention.
    d. how to join a support group.

15. If you are temporarily blinded by headlight glare, you should
    a. look down.
    b. see a doctor.
    c. reduce your speed.
    d. close your eyes.

16. Some people with physical disabilities are able to drive by using
    a. prosthetic devices.
    b. a breathalyzer.
    c. peripheral vision.
    d. narcotics.

17. To be eligible for Stage 1 of the GDL program, a teen should
    a. complete six months' supervised driving.
    b. have a parent's written permission.
    c. be at least 18 years old.
    d. pass the road test.

18. Alcohol affects
    a. judgment.
    b. traffic laws.
    c. the HTS.
    d. the automotive industry.

19. A person who is feeling angry or upset should
    a. let someone else drive.
    b. turn on the radio.
    c. talk to passengers.
    d. sing.

20. You must provide a vehicle for the
    a. Smith System.
    b. knowledge test.
    c. in-vehicle test.
    d. visual acuity test.

21. Playing loud music will reduce your ability to sense
    a. a pedestrian crossing in front of you.
    b. warning signs of danger such as sirens.
    c. 90 percent of your driving decisions.
    d. the relative distance of two objects.

22. To prove your identity at the department of motor vehicles, you can take
    a. a birth certificate.
    b. your parent's tax return.
    c. a phone bill.
    d. a report card.

23. Make sure that the vehicle you use to take your in-vehicle test
    a. has a standard shift.
    b. is registered and insured.
    c. is the school's driver-training vehicle.
    d. has a working stereo system.

24. As of 1995, maximum speed limits on highways are set by
    a. local police.
    b. the federal government.
    c. the individual states.
    d. the Uniform Vehicle Code.

25. Roads are part of the
    a. highway transportation system.
    b. Smith System.
    c. administrative system.
    d. uniform vehicle network.

26. Stimulants
    a. improve concentration.
    b. impair judgment.
    c. depress the central nervous system.
    d. improve reflexes.

27. One problem common to night driving is
    a. moon blindness.
    b. pedestrians.
    c. headlight glare.
    d. color blindness.

28. To make wise driving decisions, use
    a. the SIPDE process.
    b. the Uniform Vehicle Code.
    c. an HTS.
    d. risk.

UNIT 2

Learning the Basics

The fundamentals of driving are second nature to good drivers. These basics should become second nature to you as well. This unit will help you learn the first steps toward becoming a good driver.

CHAPTER 5

Signs, Signals, and Markings

Good drivers understand the role of communication. The signs, signals, and markings you see on the roadway are a vital means of communication. It is important that you understand the messages that they communicate.

LESSON ONE
Understanding Regulatory and Warning Signs

LESSON TWO
Guide and International Signs

LESSON THREE
Understanding the Purpose of Pavement Markings

LESSON FOUR
Responding to Traffic Control Signals

OBJECTIVES

1. Identify and describe the purpose of regulatory signs.
2. Describe the actions to take at regulatory signs.
3. Identify the purpose of warning signs.
4. Describe how to respond to warning signs.

KEY TERMS

regulatory sign
yield sign
warning sign

Understanding Regulatory and Warning Signs

Highways and streets would be difficult to use without signs that give drivers information and warnings and tell them what to do and what not to do. If there were no signs, how would you know you were on the right road? Imagine how difficult it would be to manage risk if there were no speed limits or rules regulating when or where to yield. Roadway signs provide important information about where you are, where you are going, and what rules or laws to follow.

What Are Regulatory Signs?

◆ *Stop signs are most frequently placed at one or more corners of an intersection.*

A **regulatory sign** regulates or controls the movement of traffic. These signs tell you and other drivers what you must do and what you must not do when you drive. Regulatory signs are red, white, black, green on white, or white on black. Most regulatory signs have square, vertical rectangular, or horizontal rectangular shapes. A red circle with a red slash on any of these signs means *NO*. You can recognize regulatory signs by their color and shape.

What Actions Should You Take at Regulatory Signs?

Regulatory signs give commands or set limits. When you see a stop sign, you must stop. When you see a **yield sign,** you must slow and yield (give way) to traffic on the crossroad or the road onto which you are merging. A speed limit sign indicates the maximum speed you may drive under ideal conditions.

Stop Signs

Most often you will see a stop sign at the intersection of two roadways. There may be stop signs on all four corners or on only one or two corners of an intersection. In

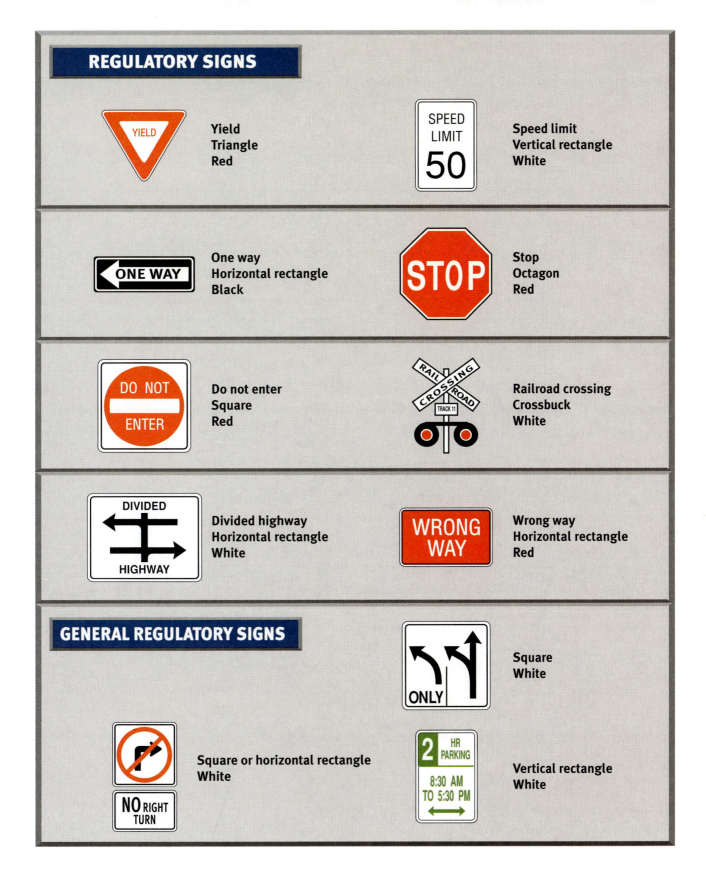

REGULATORY SIGNS

Yield
Triangle
Red

Speed limit
Vertical rectangle
White

One way
Horizontal rectangle
Black

Stop
Octagon
Red

Do not enter
Square
Red

Railroad crossing
Crossbuck
White

Divided highway
Horizontal rectangle
White

Wrong way
Horizontal rectangle
Red

GENERAL REGULATORY SIGNS

Square
White

Square or horizontal rectangle
White

Vertical rectangle
White

WARNING SIGNS

Intersections

Changes in width

Traffic

Crossings

Conditions

Curves

Construction

RIGHT LANE ENDS

12'-6"

R R

DIP

END CONSTRUCTION

DETOUR

some places, stop signs are located in the middle of the block; these indicate crosswalks.

You must come to a full stop at a stop sign. Often a white stop line is painted on the pavement in line with the sign. There may be two white lines indicating a pedestrian crosswalk just beyond the stop line, or there may be walk lines and no stop line. You are required to stop in front of the first white line you come to. If there are no lines, stop just in front of or in line with the sign.

After you stop, if there is no traffic from the right or left you may proceed. When there is traffic on the other roadway, you must decide what to do. If there are stop signs for cross traffic and another vehicle has reached its stop sign before you reach yours, you must let it go first. If you and the other vehicle arrive at the same time, the driver on the left must let the vehicle on the right go first. If you are the driver of the vehicle on the right, make sure the driver of the vehicle on the left is going to wait. Then proceed cautiously.

Yield Signs

At a yield sign, you move from one roadway onto or across another one. As you approach the yield sign, slow down and check oncoming traffic and the traffic behind you. Search right and left for cross and oncoming traffic. If a vehicle is coming toward you, you'll have to judge its distance and speed and decide whether you can safely enter or cross the road. You may need to stop and wait until the roadway is clear of traffic before you proceed.

Speed Limit Signs

Speed limit signs show the maximum, or fastest, speed allowed on a roadway. Driving faster than the posted speed is illegal. Some speed limit signs also post minimum speeds. These signs are usually on expressways. You should not travel more slowly than the minimum speed posted, unless road or weather conditions make it unsafe to travel at that speed.

Railroad Crossbuck

A railroad crossing crossbuck is located where railroad tracks cross the roadway. On multiple-lane roadways and in heavy traffic areas, signal bells, flashing red lights, and railroad gates may also warn and protect drivers. Regardless of whether or not lights or gates are present, if a train is coming, you must stop.

◆ *Yield signs and speed limit signs are two examples of regulatory traffic signs.*

What Are Warning Signs?

A **warning sign** alerts you to changes in the condition or use of the road ahead. Warning signs include those that tell you about road construction and maintenance, school zones and crossings, railroad crossings, curves, intersections, changes in road width, and deer crossings. All warning signs are either yellow or orange with black symbols or letters, and most are diamond-shaped.

◆ *A railroad advance warning sign is placed well before a railroad crossing crossbuck.*

What Actions Should You Take at Warning Signs?

When you see a warning sign, increase your level of alertness to changes in the roadway, in traffic, or in environmental conditions. Always proceed with caution. Be especially careful when you see a school zone sign or a railroad advance warning sign.

School Area Signs

When you see a school zone or school crossing sign, you must slow down and proceed with caution. Children may be playing nearby and may dart into the street. At a school crossing sign, stop and wait for children to cross the roadway.

Railroad Advance Warning Signs

Be especially careful when you come to a railroad advance warning sign. Slow down before you reach the tracks, and be prepared to stop. Look in both directions to see if a train is approaching.

WHAT WOULD YOU DO?

The symbol on this sign is called a chevron. What does the sign mean? What would you do in this situation?

Lesson 1 Review

1. How can you tell which roadway signs are regulatory signs?
2. What should you do when you see a stop sign? A yield sign? A railroad crossbuck?
3. How do you know which signs are warning signs?
4. How should you proceed at school zone or school crossing signs and railroad advance warning signs?

Guide and International Signs

Highway signs do more than just warn you and tell you what you can and cannot do. Signs can provide information about where you are, where you are going, how to get there, how far you have to go, and what services and sites are available to help make your trip comfortable and enjoyable.

As you drive, you will see signs that convey information through color, shape, and symbols instead of words.

What Are the Functions of Guide Signs?

As you travel along the roadways, you'll see four kinds of guide signs. A **guide sign** gives information about roadways and routes; the mileage to certain destinations; roadside services such as rest stops, service stations, and campsites; and recreational areas and nearby points of interest.

Route Markers

Routes are the numbered roadways that crisscross the continent. Interstate routes that lead *into* cities have three digits and begin with an odd digit (195, 395, and so on). If a three-digit route begins with an even digit (295, 684), the route goes *around* a city or connects to interstate highways at both ends.

Destination and Mileage Signs

You will often see destination and mileage signs mounted over highway lanes. They tell you where you are, which lane to take to get to your destination, what exits are coming up, and how far away the exits are. Smaller

ROUTE MARKERS

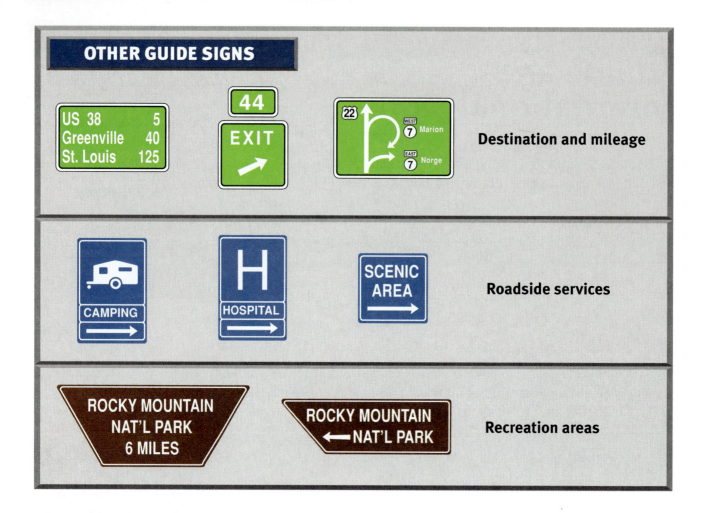

OTHER GUIDE SIGns

US 38 — 5 / Greenville — 40 / St. Louis — 125 · 44 EXIT → · 22 WEST 7 Marion EAST 7 Norge	**Destination and mileage**
CAMPING → · H HOSPITAL → · SCENIC AREA →	**Roadside services**
ROCKY MOUNTAIN NAT'L PARK 6 MILES · ← ROCKY MOUNTAIN NAT'L PARK	**Recreation areas**

INTERNATIONAL TRAFFIC SIGNS

No entry for cycles

Falling rocks

No U-turn

First aid station

Telephone

Gas station

One of the most important traffic safety devices is the automatic traffic signal. It is responsible for the orderly movement of millions of vehicles and pedestrians in today's cities and towns. The three-way traffic signal was invented in 1923 by Garrett A. Morgan. He sold the rights to his invention to the General Electric Company for $40,000.

Morgan earned a far more important reward for another of his safety devices. In 1916, two dozen men were trapped by an explosion in a tunnel 228 feet below Lake Erie near Cleveland, Ohio. The tunnel was filled with smoke, natural gases, dust, and debris. The situation seemed hopeless because no one could survive going down into the tunnel to rescue the trapped men. However, by using his new invention—the gas inhalator, an early gas mask—Morgan was able to lead a rescue party to reach the men and to save the lives of many of them. In 1963, the city of Cleveland awarded this courageous African American a gold medal for his heroism.

signs on the side of the road also tell you how far you are from different places. Destination and mileage signs are either white or green.

Roadside Services

When you want to stop for gas or food or make a phone call, look for blue signs with white lettering.

Recreational Areas

Some informational signs are brown with white lettering. These signs guide you to state and national parks, historic sites, and other places of interest.

What International Signs Are Used in the United States?

An **international sign** is one that you can understand without knowing another language. The meaning is conveyed by colors, shapes, symbols, and numbers.

Lesson 2 Review

1. Which signs are guide signs?
2. What kinds of international signs are used in the United States?

What does the sign mean? What should you be alert to when you see this sign?

OBJECTIVES

1. Identify the meaning of yellow and white road-way lane markings.
2. Describe the meaning of arrows and other non-lane roadway markings.

KEY TERM

shared left-turn lane

Understanding the Purpose of Pavement Markings

You have probably noticed lines, arrows, and words painted on streets and highways. These markings give drivers and pedestrians important information, directions, and warnings about roadway travel. You need to understand pavement markings in order to control and reduce risk.

What Do Yellow or White Lines on the Roadway Mean?

Yellow and white roadway lines provide directions or warnings for drivers. Yellow lines divide traffic traveling in opposite directions. White lines parallel to the roadway separate same-direction traffic into lanes. White lines perpendicular to the roadway indicate crosswalks, railroad crossings, and stop signs at intersections.

◆ *Double broken yellow lines mark lanes in which traffic changes direction at different times of the day.*

Yellow Lines

Traffic that is traveling in opposite directions on a roadway is separated by a broken yellow line, double solid yellow lines, or a combination of broken and solid yellow lines. On divided highways, a single solid yellow line marks the left edge of the roadway.

If the solid line of the combination solid-broken yellow lines is the first one to your left, you may not cross it to pass another vehicle. If the broken yellow line is the first one to your left, you may cross it (and the solid yellow line) to pass a vehicle

when it is safe to do so. When two solid yellow lines divide a road, neither you nor drivers traveling in the opposite direction can cross them to pass another vehicle. You may, however, turn left across them to turn into a driveway.

White Lines

White lines that are parallel to the roadway mark the lanes for traffic moving in the same direction. If the lines are broken, you can move from lane to lane when it is safe to do so. Single white lines between lanes of traffic moving in the same direction are meant to discourage passing at high-risk locations but do not prohibit passing.

Solid white lines are used to indicate the right side of the roadway. These lines are especially helpful at night because they mark the outer edges of the road, which are otherwise hard to see. A solid white line may also mark a bicycle or breakdown lane on the right side of the roadway.

◆ You may not pass on a two-way road divided by solid yellow lines.

◆ The broken white lines indicate that you may change lanes or pass. This solid white edge line marks a breakdown lane. You should not travel in a breakdown lane.

◆ *Other roadway markings include lines, arrows, symbols, and lettering that help guide drivers and pedestrians.*

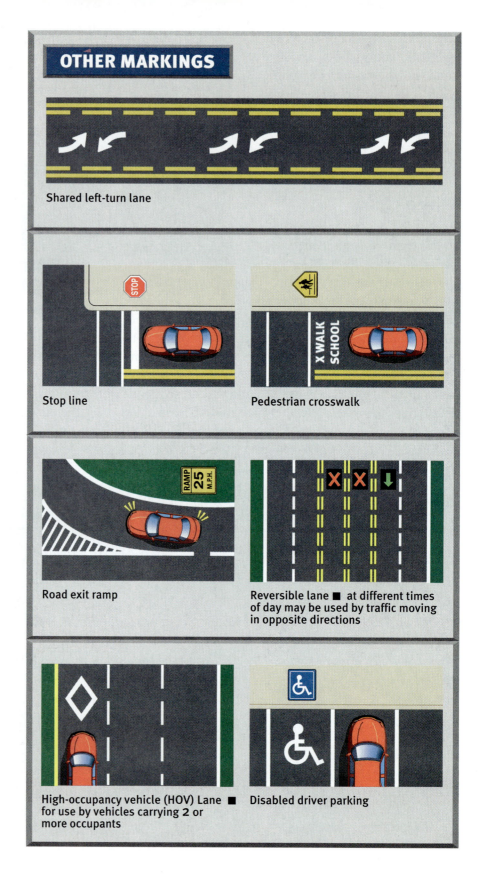

OTHER MARKINGS

Shared left-turn lane

Stop line

Pedestrian crosswalk

Road exit ramp

Reversible lane ■ at different times of day may be used by traffic moving in opposite directions

High-occupancy vehicle (HOV) Lane ■ for use by vehicles carrying **2** or more occupants

Disabled driver parking

What Do Other Markings on the Roadway Mean?

Other roadway markings may include lines, arrows, symbols, and lettering designed to guide drivers and pedestrians.

Arrows

White arrows on the roadway identify lanes from which you can drive straight ahead or turn right or left. On some three-lane roadways, the center lane is marked by parallel solid and broken yellow lines with white arrows that point alternately left and right. This lane is called a **shared left-turn lane.** Vehicles moving in either direction can use these lanes to make left turns onto another road or into an entrance. Drivers who want to make left turns onto the roadway can also move into the shared left-turn lane and wait for a gap in traffic.

Other Markings

On the opposite page are other pavement markings whose meaning and purpose you should know.

Lesson 3 Review

1. Which pavement markings let you know that it is legal to pass? That it is illegal to pass?
2. How is a shared left-turn lane marked? How would you use it?

WHAT WOULD YOU DO?

You are driving alone. Are you allowed to use this lane? Why or why not?

Responding to Traffic Control Signals

A **traffic control signal** keeps traffic moving in an orderly manner. Except in large cities, most signals operate automatically, using a timer system to change the lights through the green-yellow-red sequence. In many large cities, signals are linked electronically to and are controlled by computer. This sets up a gridwork that allows traffic to move smoothly and adjusts to changes in traffic volume.

How Do You Know When to Stop or Move Your Vehicle Through Traffic?

As a user of the highway transportation system, your movement, whether you're a driver or pedestrian, is controlled by a series of traffic signals, arrows, flashing lights, pedestrian signals, or the directions of a traffic officer.

Traffic Signals

Traffic signals are usually located at intersections where the level of risk increases. Special-use signals may operate during specific hours or on demand at school zones, fire stations, or factories. Traffic signals may be vertical or horizontal, and may have one to five or more separate lenses that give information to roadway users. The most common lenses are red, yellow, and green circles.

At a flashing signal you must either stop or slow down, depending on the color of the light. If you see a flashing red signal this means that

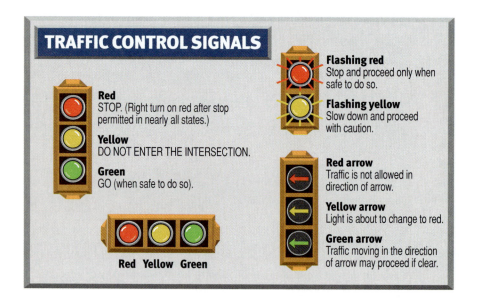

TRAFFIC CONTROL SIGNALS

Red
STOP. (Right turn on red after stop permitted in nearly all states.)

Yellow
DO NOT ENTER THE INTERSECTION.

Green
GO (when safe to do so).

Red   Yellow   Green

Flashing red
Stop and proceed only when safe to do so.

Flashing yellow
Slow down and proceed with caution.

Red arrow
Traffic is not allowed in direction of arrow.

Yellow arrow
Light is about to change to red.

Green arrow
Traffic moving in the direction of arrow may proceed if clear.

PEDESTRIAN SIGNALS

Steady WALK
Pedestrians may proceed across street.

Steady DON'T WALK
Pedestrians should not enter street.

Flashing DON'T WALK
Pedestrians in street may proceed across street; others should not start.

LANE-USE LIGHTS

Red X
Never drive in a lane under a red X signal.

Green arrow
Drivers are permitted to drive in a lane under a green arrow.

Yellow X
A steady yellow X indicates the driver should safely vacate this lane, because it soon will be controlled by a red X.

Flashing yellow X
A flashing yellow X indicates the lane is to be used, with caution, for left-turn movements only.

you must come to a full stop, just as you would at a stop sign. You must slow down at a flashing yellow signal.

Pedestrian Signals

In the city, you'll find pedestrian signals at busy intersections. Some are also located in the middle of the block. They may have either words or signals telling **pedestrians,** or people on foot, how to proceed.

If you're driving and the pedestrian signal starts to flash an orange "Don't walk," you can expect that your traffic signal is going to turn from green to yellow to red. However, don't just watch the pedestrian signals. Pay attention to the pedestrians and the traffic signal controlling vehicle traffic.

Traffic Officer's Signals

Keep in mind that a police officer can take the place of and overrule traffic control signals. Thus, when an officer *is* present and directing traffic, you should follow the officer's signals even if they go against those of an automatic traffic signal or stop sign.

Energy Tips

Save fuel by letting up on the accelerator well in advance of a red light, stop sign, or yield sign.

James E. Weaver
Highway Engineer, Traffic Control Division, Federal Highway Administration

Highway and traffic engineers design traffic control devices to convey a uniform, clear, and simple message to all highway users. It is your responsibility as a driver to recognize and fully understand the meaning of these devices by their color, shape, legend, and placement. This is important so that you will be able to respond properly and take the actions needed to maneuver your car safely in different traffic, terrain, and weather conditions.

Are There Signals That Let You Know Which Lanes You Can Use?

On heavily traveled multiple-lane roadways, you may see **lane-use lights** mounted above the roadway. It is important for you to know what to do in response to these signals because they are used when lane traffic is reversed during rush hours. Lane-use lights indicate which lane(s) you can use at any given time.

Lesson **4** Review

1. What are the colors and the meanings of the colors of traffic signals?
2. What are the meanings of the different colors of lane-use lights?

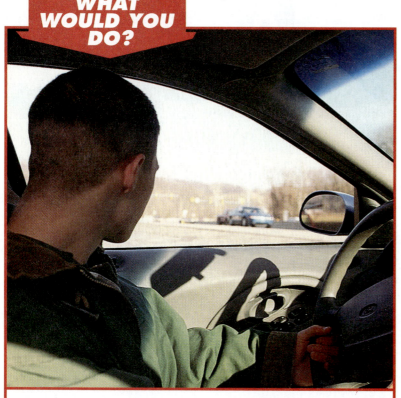

WHAT WOULD YOU DO?

You are stopped at a red light and want to turn right. Should you make the turn now?

Reading and Interpreting a Bar Graph

A bar graph presents information in a way that makes it easy to compare quantities.

The bar graph below shows the number of licensed vehicle drivers in different years. The numbers along the vertical axis, going up the left side of the graph, stand for tens of millions. So 1 equals 10 million, 5 equals 50 million, and so on.

The years in which the number of drivers are being compared are written along the bottom of the graph, on the horizontal axis.

Try It Yourself

1. About how many licensed drivers were there in 1962? In 1997?

2. About how many more licensed drivers were there in 1975 than in 1955? About how many more were there in 1975 than in 1962?

3. Which year shown on the graph had the smallest increase in the number of new drivers from the previous year?

4. Between which two years shown did the number of licensed drivers nearly double?

5. What is the approximate average number of new licensed drivers each year? (Figure the difference between the last and the first years shown. Then divide by the number of years.)

6. If the trend in numbers of licensed drivers continues, about how many would you expect in the year 2010?

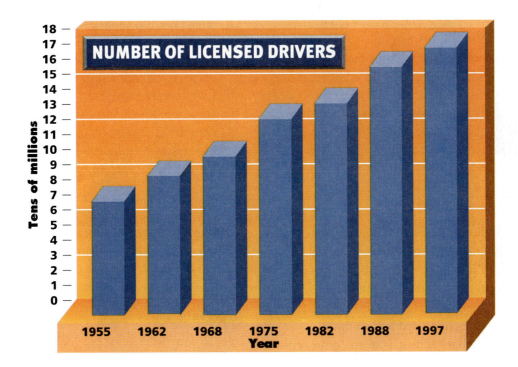

NUMBER OF LICENSED DRIVERS

Tens of millions

Year: 1955, 1962, 1968, 1975, 1982, 1988, 1997

KEY POINTS

Lesson One

1. Regulatory signs control the movement of traffic. They can be red, white, black, green on white, or white on black. A red circle with a red slash on any of these signs means *NO*.

2. You must come to a full stop at stop signs, yield to cross traffic at yield signs, drive no faster than the limit posted on speed limit signs, and be prepared to stop at railroad crossbuck signs.

3. Warning signs alert you to changes in road conditions. They are black on yellow or orange and are usually diamond-shaped. Some warning signs are construction, school area, and railroad advance warning signs.

4. Respond to warning signs by increasing your level of alertness, slowing down, and proceeding with caution.

Lesson Two

1. Informational, or guide, signs include route signs, destination and mileage signs, roadside service signs, and recreational area signs.

2. International signs communicate their meaning by symbols. Some international signs used in the United States are First Aid Station and Telephone.

Lesson Three

1. Yellow lane markings divide traffic moving in opposite directions. White lane markings separate traffic traveling in the same direction. If the first line on the pavement to your left is a yellow or white broken line, you may pass another vehicle when it is safe to do so. If the line is solid, you may not pass.

2. Arrows direct drivers into lanes from which they can turn. Other road markings include lines, symbols, and words to guide drivers and pedestrians.

Lesson Four

1. Traffic signals have from one to five or more lenses. Those with three lenses can be either vertical or horizontal. The most common lenses are red (Stop), yellow (Do not enter intersection), and green (Go when safe to do so).

2. A red X signal indicates that you should not drive in that lane. A green arrow indicates that you are permitted to drive in that lane. A steady yellow X indicates that you should vacate the lane as soon as possible, and a flashing yellow X indicates that the lane may be used with caution to make left turns.

PROJECTS

1. Find out how intersections in your state are marked where right turns on red lights are prohibited. Describe what you believe to be the advantages and disadvantages of allowing right turns on red lights. Find intersections where right on red is prohibited. Determine what each one has in common.

2. Do you find certain signs, signals, or pavement markings confusing? How would you improve them? How would you change their location, shape, size, color, symbols, lettering, numbering, timing, and how often they appear?

*inter*NET
CONNECTION

Take a trip to the Web to find more information on international traffic signs.
www.glencoe.com/sec/driver.ed

CHAPTER TEST

Write the letter of the answer that best completes each sentence.

1. White lines parallel to the road separate
   a. traffic moving in the same direction.
   b. traffic moving in opposite directions.
   c. vans from trucks.

2. When a police officer is giving hand signals at an intersection, you should
   a. always follow the officer's directions.
   b. follow the traffic signals.
   c. proceed with caution.

3. A yield sign indicates that a driver
   a. has the right of way.
   b. may need to stop and wait until the roadway is clear of traffic before proceeding.
   c. must move to a different lane.

4. When you approach a stop sign and observe no other vehicles around, you should
   a. slow down but continue moving past the sign.
   b. come to a full stop at the sign.
   c. blow your horn and increase your speed.

5. Two solid yellow lines on a roadway indicate that
   a. passing is permitted in either direction.
   b. the left lane may be used only for left turns.
   c. no passing is permitted in either direction.

6. When approaching a flashing red traffic signal, you should
   a. slow down and proceed with caution.
   b. respond as if it were a stop sign.
   c. immediately turn right.

7. A steady yellow X posted above a highway lane indicates that
   a. vehicles should move slowly.
   b. vehicles should move to a different lane.
   c. the lane will become an exit ramp.

8. Blue signs with white lettering indicate
   a. roadside services.
   b. roadway conditions.
   c. construction areas.

9. Shared left-turn lanes are marked by
   a. solid yellow lines.
   b. white arrows that point in the same direction.
   c. parallel broken yellow lines with white arrows that point left and right.

10. A red arrow indicates
    a. a detour.
    b. a one-way street.
    c. traffic is not allowed in the direction of the arrow.

Write the word or phrase that best completes each sentence.

advance warning   regulatory
pavement markings   breakdown lanes
high-occupancy vehicle

11. You may be permitted to drive in _____ lanes if your vehicle has two or more occupants.

12. A(n) _____ sign indicates what a driver must or must not do.

13. Traffic signals, signs, and _____ provide drivers with information.

14. A railroad _____ sign is round and yellow with black markings.

DRIVER'S LOG

In this chapter you have learned about the signs, signals, and pavement markings that communicate information to drivers. Take 5 minutes to list all that you can remember and explain what they mean. Which ones did you leave out? Write about how you will remember them in the future.

CHAPTER 6

Rules of the Road

Drivers belong to the society of roadway users. In a smoothly running society, members agree to follow the rules. It is important that you learn the rules of the road in order to be a responsible member of the roadway community.

LESSON ONE
Each State Has Administrative Laws

LESSON TWO
Right-of-Way Rules Are Essential

LESSON THREE
Speed Limits Help in Reducing Risk

LESSON FOUR
If You Are Involved in a Collision

OBJECTIVES

1. Identify the procedures that are regulated by administrative laws.
2. Describe how to comply with administrative laws.

KEY TERMS

administrative laws
suspend
revoke
point system

Each State Has Administrative Laws

Rules and laws are vital to society. Traffic laws and ordinances are important for a variety of reasons.

They provide rules for the behavior of drivers and help drivers predict what others on the road will do. They serve as a guide to police and courts, promote the orderly flow of traffic, and help prevent collisions.

What Are Administrative Laws?

Each state has laws that enable state officials to control the operation of the state's highway transportation system. Among the laws are **administrative laws,** which establish the procedures for issuing driver's licenses and learner's permits and registering motor vehicles. Other procedures cover the financial responsibilities of vehicle drivers and owners and the minimum safety equipment and care of a vehicle.

How Do You Comply with Administrative Laws?

To drive and own a vehicle, you must obey your state's motor vehicle laws—beginning with obtaining a license to drive.

Getting a Driver's License

Granting a license to operate a motor vehicle is a function of state government. To obtain a license, you must pass a series of tests. Each state tests vision; knowledge of signs, signals, and markings; traffic laws; and safe driving practices. Tests may be verbal, written, or computerized.

In most states, the last test is a road or in-vehicle test. This test demonstrates your basic vehicle control skills. If you pass these tests and pay the necessary fees, you will receive your license. If your state has a graduated driver licensing system, you may need to take more than one driving test.

States also have the power to take licenses away. States can **suspend,** or take away, licenses for a specified period of time—usually for 30 to 90 days, but fewer than 365 days. States can also **revoke** licenses. This means states can take licenses away for a year or more, after which the person whose license has been revoked can apply for another license.

Energy Tips

Excessive speed causes crashes and can cost you points. Excessive speed also wastes fuel. Be responsible!

Violations and the Point System

How does a state decide when to take away a person's driver's license? Most states use a **point system.** Various traffic violations "cost" a number of points, depending on their seriousness. When a driver is ticketed for violating a traffic law and is convicted, a report is sent to the state's department of motor vehicles. The points are then put on the driver's record.

If a driver whose license has been suspended continues to get points when the suspension is lifted, the license can be revoked. Some violations are so serious that offenders can lose their licenses immediately upon conviction. These violations include driving under the influence of alcohol or other drugs, leaving the scene of a collision in which there has been an injury, and using a motor vehicle in the commission of a crime.

Certificate of Title

States issue a certificate of title when you buy a motor vehicle. This proves that you own the vehicle. The state keeps a copy of this title. Anyone selling a motor vehicle must supply a certificate of title to the buyer. The certificate lists the name of the owner and the make, style, vehicle identification number (VIN), and engine number of the vehicle.

Vehicle Registration

When purchasing a vehicle, you must register it with the state. You'll receive a registration form and license plate(s). If liability insurance is required, you must provide the name of your insurance company. Registration must be renewed every year or two. Keep your registration in the vehicle.

Insurance

Part of driving is the ability to prove financial responsibility. You must show that you can pay for damages you may cause if you are in a crash that results in death, injury, or property damage to others. You will learn more about automobile insurance in Chapter 16.

Lesson 1 Review

1. What administrative laws does every state have?
2. What do administrative laws require you to do?

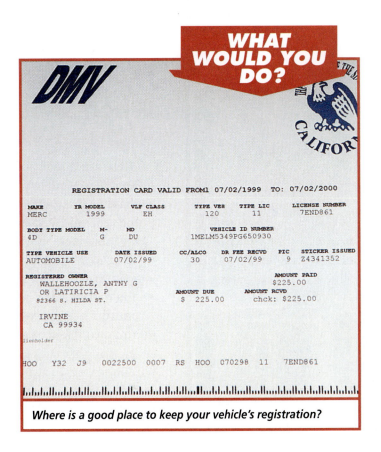

WHAT WOULD YOU DO?

Where is a good place to keep your vehicle's registration?

OBJECTIVES

1. Define the meaning of the term *right-of-way.*
2. Identify when you should yield the right-of-way.

KEY TERM

right-of-way

Right-of-Way Rules Are Essential

When you drive, sometimes one or more drivers or pedestrians will want to use the same roadway space at the same time that you do. How can you avoid a collision? You can determine who should go first and who should wait. To do so, you need to know the rules about right-of-way.

What Is Right-of-Way?

As a good driver, you will sometimes have to yield the **right-of-way,** or let others go first. Never assume that you have the right-of-way. Right-of-way is *always given* by someone. Right-of-way laws are very clear in identifying who shall yield to whom in almost every situation. However, human beings make mistakes. The rule that you must yield the right-of-way in order to avoid a collision overrides all the other rules.

Right-of-way laws of all states are based on the Uniform Vehicle Code. Therefore, the laws about when drivers should yield the right-of-way are the same from state to state.

When Should You Yield the Right-of-Way?

Here are three situations in which you must yield the right-of-way.

- You must yield to any emergency vehicle, such as an ambulance, that has its sirens on and its lights flashing. Move to the far right of the road and stop if you are on a two-way, two-lane roadway or on a multiple-lane highway going in the same direction as the emergency vehicle. If you are going in the opposite direction on a multiple-lane road, you do not have to stop, but you should move to the right.
- You must yield to people who are blind and are carrying a white cane or using a guide dog, no matter where they cross.
- You must yield to any pedestrians at crosswalks.

On the following pages, you will find some of the right-of-way situations that occur most often. In each picture, the red car is required to yield. In all these situations, drivers must yield to pedestrians who are crossing at crosswalks.

At STOP signs, yield to traffic on the through street.

At intersections not controlled by traffic signs or signals, yield to vehicles already in the intersection. Drivers on the left must yield to those on their right.

At traffic lights, yield to vehicles still in the intersection when the light changes.

At four-way stops, yield to vehicles that arrive first. If you arrive at the same time, yield to a vehicle from the right.

When you are turning left at an intersection, yield to all oncoming vehicles until you have the time and space to make a turn.

When you are on a side street approaching a well-traveled road, stop at the intersection even if a stop sign is not present. Proceed when you are sure you have enough time and space to do so.

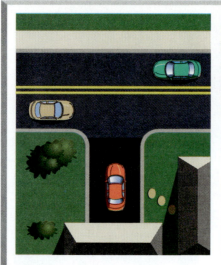

Coming out of a driveway or alley, yield to all vehicles in the roadway.

At all YIELD signs, yield to all vehicles on the cross street.

One of the most common violations in fatal collisions involving more than one car is a driver's failure to yield the right-of-way. Remember, just because you are on a major street or are on the right at a four-way stop, do not assume that others will yield to you. Be alert! Sometimes it is safer to yield even if the other driver is required by law to yield. To manage risk, you should remember that others will not always obey traffic signs and signals. Make yourself visible, and identify an escape route in case something goes wrong.

When signaling a move left or right into a lane being used by other drivers, you must yield to any vehicle that is passing or appears to be so close that it presents a danger.

On a nondivided highway, all drivers must stop when meeting or overtaking a school bus that is loading or unloading children. Laws vary from state to state, so it is important to know the school bus laws for states in which you will be traveling.

WHAT WOULD YOU DO?

To whom would you yield? Why?

Lesson 2 Review

1. What does right-of-way mean?
2. In which situations should you yield the right-of-way?

Speed Limits Help in Reducing Risk

The most important requirements for safe driving are visibility, time, and space. Together they determine the speed at which you can travel safely. What is a safe speed? Posted maximum speed limits give guidelines to answer this question, but they only apply under ideal conditions.

Speed limits are chosen to protect you and other drivers. Traffic engineers study road conditions and evaluate the road surface, the average amount of traffic, and any hidden dangers. They also know how many collisions have happened at any given location. A speed limit is decided upon only after all these factors have been taken into consideration. Further studies may also be conducted to see if limits should be lowered as congestion increases.

OBJECTIVES

1. Define the meaning of the following kinds of speed limits: fixed, advisory, and day and night.
2. Explain under what conditions posted speed limits do not apply.

KEY TERMS

fixed speed limit
advisory speed limit

What Kinds of Speed Limits Are There?

All states post speed limits on their roadways. These speed limit signs reflect the *maximum* speed at which you can drive under the best of conditions. For example, you would not drive at the maximum allowable

CONNECTIONS
Social Studies

CULTURAL CROSSROADS

If you drive in Mexico or Canada, you will see signs in Spanish or French. In both countries, another "language" is used on signs as well. It is the "language" of the metric system of measurement.

Distances on destination signs in Mexico and Canada are given in kilometers rather than in miles. Similarly, speed limit signs refer not to *miles per hour* but to *kilometers per hour.* The speed limit sign you see here means 100 kilometers per hour (km/h), or about 65 miles per hour. You can figure out whether you are traveling

within the allowable speed limit by converting kilometers per hour to miles per hour. To make a rough estimate, take half of the posted speed limit and add a little more. Half of 100 is 50, and a little more is 60 or 65. For a closer estimate, take ⅝ of the posted speed limit. Then check your speedometer to see whether you are traveling between 60 and 65 miles per hour.

When you are driving in another country, make sure you know whether or not that country uses the metric system of measurement. To help you out, the speedometers in many vehicle models record speeds both in miles per hour and in kilometers per hour.

◆ *Note the advisory speed limit sign. You should not exceed 15 mph on this curve.*

speed in the middle of a snowstorm, but you might do so on a clear day.

Posted speed limits do not tell you at what speed to drive. They only say you cannot safely go faster or, in special cases, more slowly than the speed shown. All states also have basic speed limits that mean you cannot drive at speeds slower or faster than conditions safely permit. What does this mean to you as a driver?

Fixed Speed Limit

A **fixed speed limit** is the maximum and minimum speed that a vehicle may be driven on a particular roadway. Drivers may never legally travel at a speed faster than the maximum posted speed. Drivers whose speed is greater than the posted maximum speed can be arrested and, if convicted, made to pay a fine.

Drivers can also be arrested and ticketed for driving too slowly. A vehicle traveling below the minimum posted speed limit can be dangerous to other drivers who must suddenly slow down when they approach this vehicle. Slow drivers can also make other drivers nervous or angry and in addition cause traffic tie-ups and congestion.

Advisory Speed Limit

All roads are not straight and flat. There are hills, curves, and other changes in the roadway. Drivers need to adjust their speed for these changes. An **advisory speed limit** interrupts normal driving speed for a limited time. It provides guidelines for adjusting speed.

For example, a warning sign is usually posted before a sharp curve and before an exit ramp. If the curve is very sharp, a square yellow advisory speed sign may be posted beneath the warning sign to advise you of the maximum safe speed for that curve. In addition, chevron-shaped markings may be used to emphasize the risk. Like all speed limits, advisory limits are based on ideal road conditions.

Day and Night Speed Limits

Some states have lower speed limits at night. Night driving is much more

---

TIPS — FOR NEW DRIVERS

Being Pulled Over

What should you do if you are pulled over by the police?
- Stay calm.
- Remain in your vehicle, keeping your hands visible.
- Produce requested documents quickly and efficiently.
- Be courteous. Do not argue with, insult, or touch the officer.
- Do not lie, cry, or make excuses.
- *Never* try to bribe the officer. Bribery is illegal!

dangerous because it is hard to see in the dark. Driving at a lower speed gives drivers more time to search for visual clues and to identify objects or conditions that could increase risk.

What Are Basic Speed Laws?

No matter what speed limit is posted, all states have a basic speed rule in their traffic laws that says: Always drive at a speed that is reasonable and proper for existing conditions.

A safe speed at any particular time is determined by the type and condition of the road and by such factors as the traffic, weather, and light. Your ability to manage visibility, time, and space also determines what is a safe speed at any given time.

By law, drivers must go more slowly than the minimum posted speed if poor road or traffic conditions make that speed unsafe. In such cases, the arresting officer must show that the driver was going too fast for the weather, road, or traffic conditions at that time.

Driving faster than the posted speed limit is never safe or reasonable and is always illegal.

Take note of these facts about speed. The higher the speed:

- the less time the driver has to spot dangerous situations and take action.
- the greater the time and distance it takes to stop a vehicle.
- the greater the chance the vehicle will skid or roll over on a turn.
- the greater the force of impact will be in a collision.
- the greater the personal injuries and property damage will be in a collision.

Drivers can also be arrested for driving too slowly. In these cases, the officer must show that the speed was so slow that it caused danger to other drivers going at a reasonable speed.

◆ *A few interstate roads have speed limits as high as 75 mph. This speed may not be reasonable or proper in bad weather.*

WHAT WOULD YOU DO?

Snow is on the ground and you see this sign. At what speed would you drive? Why?

Lesson 3 Review

1. What are the different kinds of speed limits?
2. What are the basic speed laws?

If You Are Involved in a Collision

No matter how good a driver you are, there is no guarantee that you can always avoid a collision. Human suffering, loss of time, legal problems, and great expense can result from a collision regardless of who is at fault.

What Should You Do If You Are in a Collision?

After a collision, some people may panic or react in strange ways. They may also be in a state of shock. If you are in a collision, you should try to remain calm. Remember that the collision scene is no place to begin arguing with the other driver or with the police. Do not accuse anyone of causing the collision and do not admit fault yourself. Sign only forms given to you by the police. Do not sign any other statements at the scene of the accident. You have the legal right to consult an attorney before making any statement.

If you are involved in a collision, you should do the following.

◆ *Collisions are frightening, but knowing what to do if you are involved in one can help you to stay calm.*

Stop immediately. Drivers who do not stop when involved in a collision are breaking the law. Unless someone was seriously injured or killed, and if you can still drive your vehicle, try to move it off the roadway and out of traffic. Turn off the ignition to prevent the risk of fire.

Warn others if possible. If you cannot move your vehicle out of traffic, you must do everything you can to notify other drivers that there is a problem ahead. Turn on your hazard flashers. If you have flares or reflecting triangles, set them up at least 100 feet ahead of and behind the collision scene. If you don't have them, ask someone, possibly another driver who offers to help, to stand at the side of the road out of traffic and wave a flashlight or light-colored cloth to warn oncoming traffic.

Give aid to the injured. Check for injured persons. Try to make them comfortable, but do not move them unless you know what you are doing. Moving an injured person can result in more serious injury. Do what you can to provide first aid. (You will learn more about first aid in Chapter 15.)

Try to get medical help. If you or someone who has stopped to help has a cellular phone or a CB (citizens-band radio), use it to call the police, who will ensure that other emergency services are also notified. Use 911 or other emergency numbers if available. Or try to flag down another driver to go for aid or to call the appropriate emergency services.

Call the police. By law, a collision resulting in injury, death, or property damage above a given dollar value must be reported to the police. A few states require that all collisions be reported no matter what the damages are.

Exchange information. Drivers involved in collisions should exchange information with the other driver and any passengers. You should exchange drivers' and passengers' names and addresses, driver's license information, names of insurance companies, and vehicle registration information. If you are involved in a collision with a parked car, you should try to locate the owner. If you cannot, leave a note under the windshield wiper blades containing the same information that you would exchange at any other collision scene. For your records, write down a description and the license number of the vehicle that was struck, plus the date, time, and place.

Get names and addresses of witnesses. You have already exchanged information with the other driver and passengers. If there are witnesses at the scene, write down their names and addresses too. You might need them to verify your account of the collision.

Stay at the scene. If you are uninjured, remain at the scene of the collision until your help is no longer needed. If people have been seriously injured or killed, remain at the scene until the police allow you to leave.

Make accident reports. Drivers involved in any collision that results in injury should make a written report to the police and to the department of motor vehicles. States have different laws about reporting property damage under certain amounts. Know what your state law requires. Check your state driver's manual or contact your motor vehicle department to get this information. If you do not file a report, your driver's license could be suspended

Death rates are higher for occupants of small pickup trucks and small utility vehicles than for any other type of passenger vehicles, including the smallest cars.

◆ *Make a written accident report to the police, even if you have talked with them at the collision scene.*

William Coar
Traffic Safety Technician, AAA, National Office

Driving is a risky business. Every year in the United States more than 40,000 people are killed and over 3 million are injured in motor vehicle crashes. Speeding is one of the biggest contributors to these crashes. Other factors include: inattention, failure to obey stop signs and signals, failure to yield the right-of-way, and driving under the influence.

To reduce risk, drivers must effectively manage visibility, time, and space. This can be accomplished by looking well ahead of your vehicle, maintaining a proper following distance, and controlling your speed.

regardless of whether or not the collision was your fault. Of course, you should also inform your insurance company.

See a doctor. Even if you have been treated at the scene of the collision, be sure to see your own doctor. Some injuries do not appear right away. Be safe and get yourself checked out thoroughly.

Legal consequences of a collision can be very serious. If a collision is the result of your having broken a traffic law, you may, depending on the severity of the crash:

WHAT WOULD YOU DO?

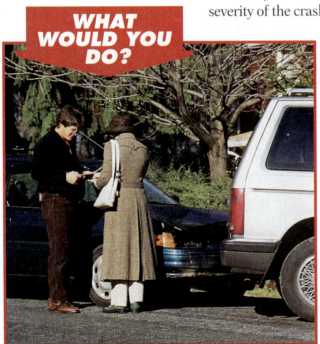

You have had a collision. The other driver says that there's no need to get the police involved. What would you tell the driver?

- be fined and have to pay court costs.
- have your license suspended or revoked.
- be sent to jail.

If it is found that you were intoxicated or under the influence of other drugs at the time of a collision, the penalties are even more severe.

If you pass a collision scene and help appears needed, you should stop well off the roadway and offer whatever assistance that you can. However, if the situation appears under control, keep going. Stopping at the scene of a collision when it is unnecessary for you to do so can cause additional hazards for others who are using the roadway.

Lesson **4** Review

1. What are your responsibilities if you are in a collision?
2. What may be the legal consequences of a collision?

Using Coordinates

You want to find Port Allen, Louisiana, on the map. How can you do that quickly?

First find Port Allen on the map index. It is listed alphabetically. Beside the name, you will see H-12. These are coordinates.

Look at the map. There are letters along the left side and numbers along the bottom. Find the H and put your left finger on it. Now find the 12. Move your left finger straight across the map until it is above the 12. Port Allen is in that area.

Notice the ⊙ beside Port Allen. This means it is a county seat. A ◯ stands for a town, a ▢ stands for a city, and ✪ stands for the state

capital. If you scan the map quickly, you can see that the names of cities and towns are written in different-size type. The larger the type, the greater the population.

Try It Yourself

1. Find Denson on the map. Is its population greater or less than the population of Port Allen?
2. Find Franklinton and Watson. Which is a county seat?
3. Find Baton Rouge and New Orleans. Which is the capital of Louisiana? Which has the smaller population?

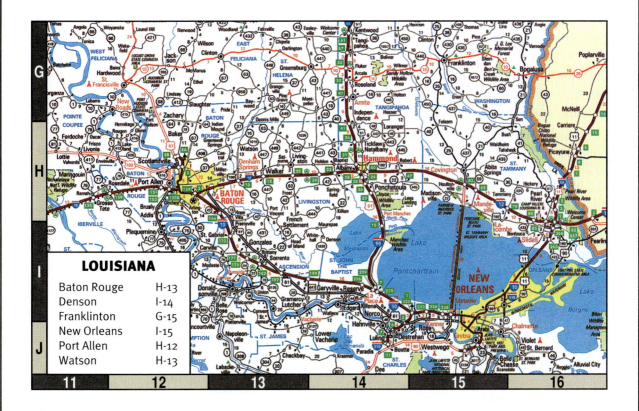

LOUISIANA

Baton Rouge	H-13
Denson	I-14
Franklinton	G-15
New Orleans	I-15
Port Allen	H-12
Watson	H-13

KEY POINTS

Lesson One

1. Every state has administrative laws that set standards for issuing driver's licenses and learner's permits, certificates of title, motor vehicle registration, and financial responsibility requirements.

2. To comply with the administrative laws, drivers must obtain a driver's license, maintain an acceptable driving record, obtain a certificate of title when buying a car, register their vehicle, and prove financial responsibility by obtaining vehicle insurance.

Lesson Two

1. Right-of-way means that one driver is required to yield when making a move in traffic.

2. You must yield the right-of-way to emergency vehicles, people who are blind, and pedestrians in crosswalks. At intersections not controlled by signals or signs, yield to vehicles already in the intersection. At stop or yield signs, yield to traffic on the cross street. At traffic lights, vehicles still in the intersection when the light changes must be given the right of way. When moving into a lane used by other drivers, yield to passing vehicles. Stop when a school bus stops to pick up or discharge students.

Lesson Three

1. Fixed speed limits are the maximum and minimum speeds that a vehicle may be driven on a particular roadway. Advisory speed limits provide guidelines when an adjustment in speed is needed, such as when approaching a sharp curve in the road.

2. Always drive at a speed that is reasonable and proper for existing conditions.

Lesson Four

1. Drivers involved in a collision must stop immediately and turn off the ignition, give aid to the injured, try to get medical help, call the police, exchange relevant information, get names and addresses of witnesses, stay at the scene, make accident reports, and see a doctor.

2. The legal consequences of a collision can be serious. If the collision is the result of your having broken a traffic law, you may, depending on the severity of the crash, be fined, have your license suspended or revoked, or be sent to jail.

PROJECTS

1. Find out the location of your area's department of motor vehicles. Visit it or write a letter asking for a copy of your state's driver's manual. Do the same with two neighboring states. Report on laws that are the same as the laws in your state and those that are different.

2. Ask at least four drivers if they can name five facts about roadway speed. Prepare a report on your findings. You may want to compare your report with the reports of others in your class and put together a combined report on drivers' attitudes and knowledge about speeding and speed laws.

inter NET CONNECTION

Search the Glencoe Web site for information on how to fill out an accident report form.
www.glencoe.com/sec/driver.ed

CHAPTER TEST

Write the letter of the answer that best completes each sentence.

1. If you are in a collision and the other driver is injured, you should
   a. go home and call an ambulance.
   b. stay at the scene until the police arrive.
   c. run away as fast as you can.

2. Posted speed limits
   a. tell you at what speed you must drive.
   b. are only on interstate highways.
   c. indicate you cannot safely go faster or slower than specified speeds.

3. The higher the speed, the more likely it is that a vehicle will
   a. develop engine problems.
   b. roll over on a turn.
   c. get excellent gas mileage.

4. Administrative laws set standards for
   a. rules of the road.
   b. minimum speed allowed.
   c. motor vehicle registration.

5. On a two-lane street, an ambulance is coming from behind with its siren blaring and lights flashing. You should
   a. pull over to the left and stop.
   b. pull over to the right and stop.
   c. increase your speed.

6. At an intersection, a person with a guide dog steps off the curb. You
   a. tap your horn and continue forward.
   b. stop to yield the right-of-way.
   c. drive around the person.

7. Your driver's license can be revoked if you
   a. are convicted of DUI or DWI.
   b. get into a collision.
   c. drive below the minimum speed limit.

8. Two drivers who have been in a collision should
   a. avoid any contact with each other or with witnesses.
   b. split the cost of any damages.
   c. exchange names and other information.

9. Right-of-way rules determine
   a. minimum speed limits in each state.
   b. procedures for turning right.
   c. who should yield the right-of-way.

10. You must pass a series of tests in order to
    a. increase your number of driving points.
    b. obtain a driver's license.
    c. obtain a certificate of title.

Write the word or phrase that best completes each sentence.

vehicle registration information
Uniform Vehicle Code   point system
accident report   basic speed rule

11. The _____ states that you should always drive at a speed that is reasonable and proper for existing conditions.

12. If you are involved in a collision, you should make a(n) _____.

13. Most states use a(n) _____ to keep track of traffic violations by individual drivers.

14. All states have right-of-way laws that are based on the _____.

DRIVER'S LOG

In this chapter, you have learned about the rules and laws that govern the roadways and the motorists who use them. Write about the five rules you think you will have the most trouble remembering. Explain what you will do to jog your memory.

CHAPTER 7

Getting to Know Your Vehicle

It is important for you to know and understand your vehicle's systems and the checks you should make before you start driving. Understanding the function and purpose of each system and what the lights and gauges can tell you will help you manage risk. To manage risk when driving, you must be able to quickly locate, read, understand, and operate all controls and switches without taking your eyes off the road ahead for more than one second at a time.

OBJECTIVES

1. Describe four devices that help make you comfortable in a vehicle.
2. List six devices that enable you to control a vehicle, and explain what each one does.

KEY TERMS

gear selector lever
gearshift
overdrive
power steering
accelerator
cruise control
brake pedal
power brakes
parking brake

Comfort and Control Systems and Risk Management

Suppose you're driving along and suddenly you see a light blink on your control panel. What does it mean? If you don't know the answer, it means that you don't know your vehicle. Not knowing puts you, your passengers, and other drivers at risk.

Vehicles are equipped with a variety of comfort and control devices. You have to know what these devices do, where they are located, and how they operate. For specific information, refer to the owner's manual.

What Devices Help Make You Comfortable in a Vehicle?

You must concentrate while driving, and being uncomfortable can distract you from the driving task. Vehicles have comfort devices to help you, but you have to know how to use them to their best advantage. Some comfort devices help reduce muscle strain. Others control the interior climate of your car and make driving less tiring.

Seat-Position Controls

The driver's seat must be comfortable, and it must suit the driver. It should provide good visibility and access to the controls.

Many vehicles have power seat-adjustment controls, which allow you to adjust the seat up or down, forward or back, or tilt the seat to better fit the vehicle to the driver.

In vehicles without power seats, the seat-adjustment lever is usually located on the lower left side or front of the driver's seat. Pulling back or up on the lever allows the driver to adjust the seat forward or back for better access to vehicle controls and switches.

In a vehicle with a steering wheel air bag, adjust the seat so you are at least 10 inches from the steering wheel.

Steering Wheel

The top of the steering wheel should be no higher than the top of the driver's shoulders. Many vehicles have an adjustable (tilt wheel)

SAFETY TIPS

Cruise control should not be used when driving where grip between the tires and road is low or where frequent speed adjustments are necessary.

steering wheel. Drivers can adjust the steering wheel to a position that provides maximum comfort and control. In vehicles that do not have a tilt wheel, a driver may need to use a wedge-shaped driving cushion.

Air Conditioner and Heater

Use the air conditioner to cool the vehicle and lower the humidity, and use the heater to warm the vehicle interior and clear fogged windows. Never overheat your vehicle. An overheated vehicle can cause drowsiness.

Air Vents

Adjustable vents allow outside air to flow into the vehicle. They are usually located on the dashboard or on the front lower left and right sides.

How Can You Control the Movement of Your Vehicle?

The parts of a vehicle's control system enable you to start and stop the vehicle and control its speed and direction.

Ignition Switch

Inserting and turning the key in a vehicle's ignition switch starts the engine. This switch is usually found on the steering column. The ignition switch normally has five positions: Accessory, Lock, Off, On, and Start.

Selector Lever for Automatic Transmission

On vehicles that have automatic transmissions, you choose the gear you want by moving the **gear selector lever.** This lever is located either on the steering column or on the floor to the right of the driver's seat.

A vehicle with an automatic transmission will start only in Park or Neutral. Usually drivers start from Park, because Park is the gear in which they leave the car. In this position, a vehicle will not roll. A car in Neutral *will* roll on an incline.

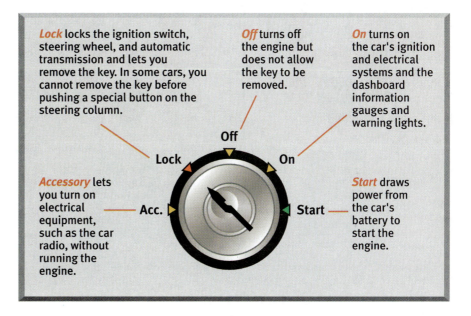

Lock locks the ignition switch, steering wheel, and automatic transmission and lets you remove the key. In some cars, you cannot remove the key before pushing a special button on the steering column.

Off turns off the engine but does not allow the key to be removed.

On turns on the car's ignition and electrical systems and the dashboard information gauges and warning lights.

Accessory lets you turn on electrical equipment, such as the car radio, without running the engine.

Start draws power from the car's battery to start the engine.

Off   **Lock**   **On**   **Acc.**   **Start**

FYI

CULTURAL CROSSROADS

The refrigerated truck was patented in 1949 by Frederick McKinley Jones, an African-American inventor. Until that time, fresh produce and other perishable food had to be transported by railroad. The refrigerated truck made it possible for towns not on railroad routes to receive regular deliveries of these products.

Gearshift for Manual Transmission

On vehicles that have manual transmissions, you choose the gear you need by stepping down on the clutch pedal and moving the **gearshift** (or stick shift). The gearshift is usually located on the floor to the right of the driver's seat, although occasionally you'll find the gearshift on the side of the steering column.

The gearshift may have three, four, or five speed positions, plus a reverse position. The fifth gear serves as an **overdrive** gear, which allows the engine to run more slowly and fuel efficiently at high speeds.

Clutch Pedal

Cars with manual transmissions have a clutch pedal located to the left of the brake pedal. In Chapter 8 you will read more about how to operate the clutch pedal and the gearshift.

Steering Wheel

You control the direction of your front wheels by turning the steering wheel. In cars equipped with **power steering,** it takes little effort to turn the wheel.

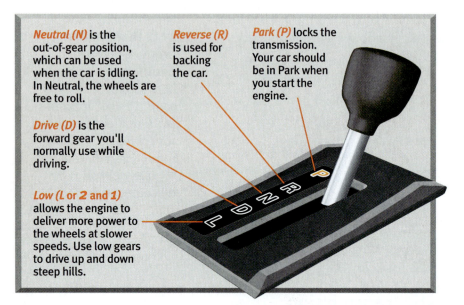

Neutral (N) is the out-of-gear position, which can be used when the car is idling. In Neutral, the wheels are free to roll.

Drive (D) is the forward gear you'll normally use while driving.

Low (L or 2 and 1) allows the engine to deliver more power to the wheels at slower speeds. Use low gears to drive up and down steep hills.

Reverse (R) is used for backing the car.

Park (P) locks the transmission. Your car should be in Park when you start the engine.

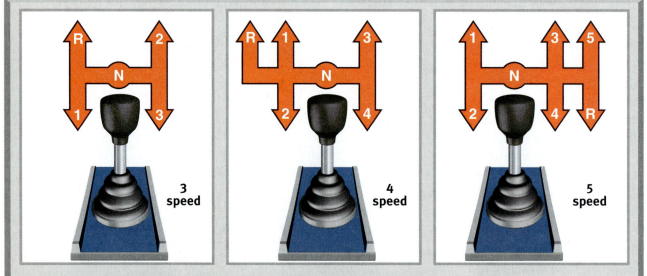

3 speed

4 speed

5 speed

Cars with a manual transmission have a gearshift instead of a selector lever. The gearshift can have 3, 4, or 5 speeds.

Accelerator (Gas Pedal)

You move the vehicle and control its speed by pressing on the **accelerator,** or gas pedal, with your right foot. The greater the pressure you put on the accelerator, the more fuel the carburetor or fuel injectors feed to the engine. The more fuel that flows into the engine, the faster the vehicle will go.

Cruise Control

Cruise (or speed) **control** is an optional vehicle feature that lets you maintain a desired speed without keeping your foot on the accelerator. Cruise control is intended for highway driving, in situations where you can maintain a constant rate of speed.

To use cruise control, first accelerate to the speed of the traffic, then reduce speed by 2 or 3 mph. Set the control button or switch located on the turn-indicator arm or on the steering wheel. You can switch off cruise control whenever you choose, or you can cancel it by tapping the brake pedal.

Although cruise control is a convenience, think when you use it. Cruise control may lead you to be less alert than you should be.

FYI

When a vehicle with power steering stalls, the power steering is lost. If the vehicle cannot be started and needs to be rolled off the road, the steering wheel will be very difficult to turn.

Brake Pedal

You slow or stop the vehicle by pressing down on the **brake pedal. Power brakes** require less foot pressure to operate than non-power brakes. However, power brakes do *not* shorten the distance needed to stop the vehicle.

Parking Brake

The **parking brake,** frequently called the emergency or hand brake, is used to keep a parked vehicle from rolling. The parking brake control can be a small pedal located to the left side of the floor panel, a hand lever located under the left side of the dashboard, or a floor-mounted hand lever located to the right of the driver's seat.

Lesson 1 Review

1. What equipment is designed to make drivers comfortable?
2. What devices control the vehicle? What does each device do?

WHAT WOULD YOU DO?

You are driving in the right lane at 50 mph. What actions will you take to minimize risk? What vehicle controls will come into play?

OBJECTIVES

1. Name at least five aids to visibility.
2. Describe four features that are designed to protect you and your passengers from injury.
3. Name three antitheft devices.

KEY TERMS

defroster
blind spot
passive safety device
air bag
head restraint
antitheft device

◆ *Glancing often in your rearview and side-view mirrors helps you to scan all around your car.*

The Visibility and Protective Systems of Your Vehicle

Some safety features reduce driving risk by aiding visibility. Others reduce or control risk by protecting the driver and passengers from injury. Still others guard the vehicle against theft.

What Devices Aid Visibility?

Seeing and being seen are critical to controlling risk and making driving easier and safer. A vehicle's visibility system better enables you to see the roadway and maximizes the ability of others to see you.

Lights

Using your headlights helps other roadway users to see you both at night *and* during the *day*. Headlights help you see better at night, in dim light, and in bad weather. Taillights and side-marker lights better enable drivers and other highway users to see your vehicle.

Headlights can be switched to either low beams or more intense high beams. Most of the time you'll be using the low beams.

The switch to turn on your headlights is either on the dashboard or on a stem on the left side of the steering column. You either pull the lever toward you or push it away to change to high or low beams. In some older vehicles, the switch is a button located on the left side of the floor panel.

When you turn on your headlights, your taillights and side-marker lights also come on. In addition, the dashboard gauges, dials, and controls light up. You can dim or brighten these dashboard lights by turning a knob located on the instrument panel or turn-indicator lever.

In many vehicles, the same light switch knob used to turn on exterior lights can also control the brightness of the dashboard lights and turn on the interior dome light.

Windshield Wipers and Washer

Vehicles normally have two-, three-, or variable-speed windshield wipers. Some vehicles also have a wiper in the rear window.

Variable-speed wipers allow the driver to set the wipers to move at a very slow or very rapid rate. This feature is useful when only an occasional wipe is needed to keep the window clear, as during a light drizzle. It is also helpful during a driving rain when a faster rate is needed.

The windshield washer squirts water or an antifreeze solution onto the windshield. The liquid is stored in a container under the hood.

Sun Visors

Sun visors can be moved up and down and turned to the side to prevent the sun from shining in the driver's eyes. However, be careful not to let the visors interfere with your view of the roadway or traffic to the side.

Defroster (Defogger)

Use the **defroster**—sometimes called the defogger—to clear moisture or frost from the front, rear, and side windows. Heat from the defroster can also make it easier to scrape ice from the windows. In most vehicles, front and rear defrosters have separate controls.

Rearview and Sideview Mirrors

Your vehicle's rearview and sideview mirrors provide vision to the rear and sides of the roadway. Even when correctly adjusted, however, they cannot eliminate all **blind spots**—areas of the road that you cannot see in the mirrors. You must make a final check to the sides before you make any lateral move. Turning your head to use the side mirrors or to check over your shoulder should be limited to a quick glance to detect the presence of objects and not to gather detailed information.

◆ *Look over your shoulder for traffic in your blind spots before changing lanes, and try never to travel in another driver's blind spots.*

What Features Protect You and Your Passengers from Injury?

Your vehicle's protective features help reduce risk by guarding you and your passengers against injury in case of a collision or sudden emergency maneuver.

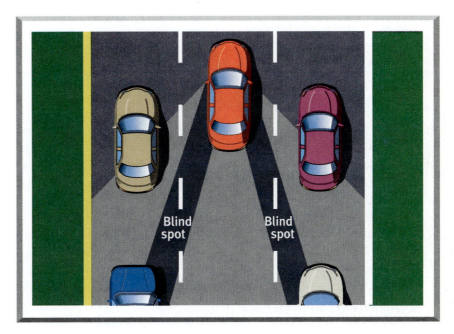

Some safety features, such as air bags, are passive safety devices. **Passive safety devices** operate without the user having to do anything. Other features, such as manual safety belts, require drivers and passengers to take some action to protect themselves.

Safety Belts

Drivers and passengers should always wear safety belts—preferably, shoulder-lap belts—whenever the vehicle is in motion. If you are wearing a shoulder-lap belt at the time of a crash, your risk of being killed is reduced by about 50 percent, and your risk of serious injury is reduced by 70 percent.

Properly worn safety belts protect the wearer against injury in a collision. They lessen the chance that you or your passengers will be thrown against the dashboard, through the windshield, or out a door that has sprung open in a crash. In addition, safety belts help keep you behind the wheel and in control of the vehicle if you have to swerve or brake abruptly or are struck by another vehicle.

Forty-nine states have passed laws that require the driver and front-seat passengers to wear safety belts. All 50 states have laws requiring very young children to ride only in special safety-tested and approved child safety seats.

Air Bags

Almost 79 million vehicles are now equipped with **air bags,** which inflate automatically in a frontal crash, then deflate again in a fraction of a second. Some vehicles also have air bags that inflate in a side collision. Air bags are very effective in preventing injuries, but they do not reduce the need for wearing a safety belt.

CONNECTIONS

Science

When you are planning to change lanes, you must be certain your blind spots are clear. One way you can reduce the size of blind spots is by adjusting your rearview and sideview mirrors 15 degrees outward.

Adjust the inside rearview mirror to take in as much as possible. You should be able to use this mirror with a shift of the eyes, not a turn of the head. Drivers 6 feet tall or more may find it helpful to turn the mirror 180 degrees so that the day/night switch is on the top of the mirror. This action raises the mirror about 2 inches and eliminates a blind spot to the front.

Adjust the sideview mirrors to reduce side and rear blind spots as much as possible. To adjust the driver's side mirror, place your head against the window and set the mirror so you can just see the side of the car. For the passenger's side mirror, position your head in the middle of the car and adjust the mirror in the same way, so you can just see the side of the car. Remember, though, that even properly adjusted mirrors will not eliminate all blind spots. You will still need to check over your shoulder. See the illustration on page 119.

Head Restraints

Head restraints are standard equipment on front-seat backs and optional on the rear seats of some vehicles. These padded restraints protect against whiplash (neck injury), especially when your vehicle is hit from behind. To get the maximum benefit from head restraints, make sure that they are properly adjusted. Head restraints should be high enough to make contact with the back of your head, not the base of your skull.

Door Locks

Keep vehicle doors locked. Locked doors not only are unlikely to open in a crash, but they also help prevent uninvited people from entering your car when you're stopped.

FYI

Nearly one out of seven recovered stolen vehicles still have the keys in them!

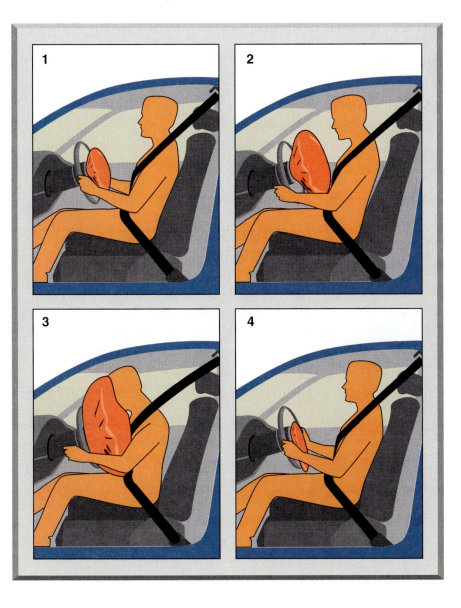

◆ *In less than one second, airbags (1) begin to inflate on impact, (2) become fully inflated, (3) cushion the driver from the frontal blow, and (4) deflate.*

Structural Features

Automotive manufacturers build a wide range of safety features into their vehicles. These features include tempered safety-glass windows, impact-resistant bumpers, protective padding on the dashboard and interior roof, energy-absorbing steering columns, and childproof door locks that are controlled by the driver. Factors such as a vehicle's size and weight also help determine how well occupants are protected in a crash.

What Devices Guard Against Vehicle Theft?

Vehicle theft is a nationwide problem. Various devices help protect your vehicle against thieves and vandals.

Ignition Buzzer

When your key is in the ignition switch and you open the driver's door, you will hear a buzz or other sound to remind you to take your key with you when you leave the vehicle.

Locks

Vehicles are now equipped with various locks, including door locks, a steering-column lock, and locks on the trunk, hood, and gas tank.

Alarms and Other Antitheft Devices

A wide range of **antitheft devices** are available for vehicles, ranging from elaborate alarm systems to disabling devices that keep the vehicle from starting or prevent the steering wheel from turning. Some vehicle security systems can be turned on or off by remote control using a key chain transmitter.

WHAT WOULD YOU DO?

What is this driver doing wrong? What would you tell him?

Lesson 2 Review

1. What vehicle devices aid your ability to see and be seen?
2. What features help protect you and your passengers from injury in the event of a collision?
3. What devices might prevent the theft of a vehicle?

Information and Communication Systems

As you drive, you gather information about other roadway users, the roadway itself, and off-road conditions by searching in all directions. You get information about the workings of your own vehicle by checking the instruments, gauges, and lights on the dashboard.

While you gather information, you are letting other roadway users know where you are and what you intend to do.

What Devices Provide Information About Your Vehicle?

Drivers need to know how fast they are going, how far they have gone, and how their vehicle systems are working. The instruments, gauges, and lights on your dashboard can give you this information.

Speedometer and Odometer

The **speedometer** shows, in miles per hour and kilometers per hour, how fast your vehicle is moving.

The **odometer** keeps track of the total number of miles the vehicle has been driven. Some vehicles also have a separate trip odometer, which can be reset to zero at any time.

Fuel Gauge

Your fuel gauge shows how close to full—or empty—your fuel tank is. Your owner's manual tells you how many gallons of fuel your tank holds.

Alternator Gauge or Warning Light

Your vehicle's **alternator** provides electricity to keep the engine running, recharge the battery, and operate such equipment as lights and radio. If the alternator does not produce enough power, the electricity stored in your battery will be drained. The alternator gauge will indicate "discharge" or a red warning light will come on.

When the alternator does not work properly, turn off unnecessary electrical devices and check with a mechanic as soon as possible. If you delay, your battery will die.

◆ *It is time to refuel when the needle on your fuel gauge reaches the red area.*

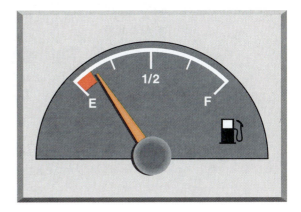

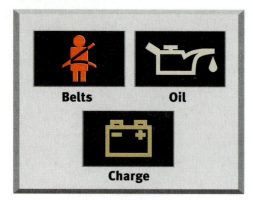

◆ *The safety-belt light turns red when you start the car to remind you to buckle up.*

Temperature Gauge or Warning Light

The temperature gauge or light lets you know if your engine temperature is too high. Overheating can damage your engine. Get off the road as soon as possible, turn off the engine, and have the problem checked.

Oil-Pressure Gauge or Warning Light

The oil-pressure gauge warns you when the pressure at which oil is being pumped to the engine is low. This means that the engine is not being lubricated properly. To avoid serious engine damage, stop driving immediately and consult a mechanic.
Note that the oil-pressure gauge or light does not indicate how much oil is in the engine. You need to check the oil dipstick for that information.

Brake Warning Light

Most vehicles have a brake warning light. When it goes on, you might be low on brake fluid, the fluid is leaking, or the brakes are not working properly. Check with a mechanic immediately.

Other Dashboard Lights

Your parking-brake light reminds you to release the parking brake before moving the vehicle. A daytime running light indicator shows when your daytime running lights are on. A high-beam indicator light shows when your vehicle's high-beam headlights are on, and a safety-belt warning light and buzzer remind you to fasten your safety belt. There is also an air bag light and an antilock brake system (ABS) light.

How Can You Communicate with Other Roadway Users?

Other drivers need to know where you are and what you are planning to do. You cannot talk to them verbally, but your vehicle has a number of devices that you can use to communicate with other roadway users.

Taillights

Like headlights and side-marker lights, taillights help others see your vehicle. Taillights also help communicate your intentions.

In addition to red taillights, the back of your car is equipped with red brake lights, white backup lights, and red or amber turn indicators. All vehicles manufactured since 1986 also have a third centered high-mounted brake light located at the bottom or above the top of the rear window.

Brake lights go on when you step on the brake, to warn others that you are slowing or stopping. The backup lights signal that you've shifted into Reverse and intend to back up.

One other light on the back of your vehicle is the license-plate light, which comes on with headlights and parking lights. This light is required by law and aids in identifying vehicles.

Directional (Turn) Signals

Your flashing red or amber **directional,** or turn, **signal**—sometimes called a blinker—shows that you plan to turn or change lanes. To operate the signal, move the turn-indicator arm up for right and down for left.

Normally, the signal lever clicks into position, then clicks off when you straighten the wheel. If the signal doesn't stop flashing, move the lever back manually.

Emergency Flashers (Hazard Lights)

The emergency-flasher switch is usually located on the steering column or dashboard. **Emergency flashers** make all four turn-signal lights flash at the same time. Use your flashers to warn other drivers that your vehicle is stopped on or near the road or that you are moving very slowly.

Parking Lights

In addition to low- and high-beam headlights, your vehicle is equipped with parking lights. Use parking lights (or emergency flashers) to help other drivers see you when your car is stopped along the side of the road. Parking lights are *not* designed to light the roadway when your vehicle is in motion. In some states it is illegal to drive with parking lights on.

Horn

Use your vehicle's horn to alert drivers, pedestrians, or cyclists to your presence or to warn them of danger.

The horn is generally located on the steering wheel. Before driving any vehicle, it is wise to locate and try the horn.

Lesson 3 Review

1. What devices provide information about your vehicle?
2. What devices enable you to communicate with other roadway users?

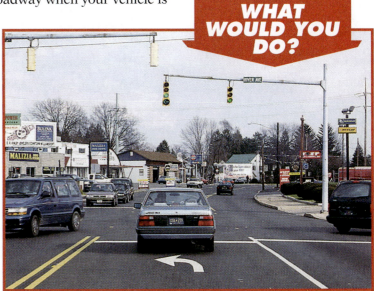

WHAT WOULD YOU DO?

You want to turn left, then pull over to the right side of the road. How will you communicate to others what you plan to do?

OBJECTIVES

1. Describe six checks you should make before entering your vehicle.
2. Describe five checks you should make after entering your vehicle.

Checks and Procedures to Use Before Driving

If you were a pilot, you wouldn't dream of taking off without thoroughly checking your airplane first. Safety and equipment checks are equally important when you're about to drive a motor vehicle. The best time to find out about a problem or potential problem is *before* your vehicle is moving.

What Should You Check Before Entering Your Vehicle?

You should inspect the vehicle and the area around it before you enter your vehicle. If you need to step into the roadway, check carefully for approaching traffic.

◆ *Check under your car for leaks, objects, and animals every time you plan to drive.*

Surrounding Area

- Look for children playing nearby. Each year about 200 children under the age of six are killed while playing in the family driveway.
- Look for animals that may be hiding under or walking or sleeping near the vehicle.
- Look for objects in the area of the vehicle and on the roadway that may interfere with safe movement or damage the tires.
- Check under the vehicle for fresh stains that could be indications of fluid leaks.

Wheels

- Check for underinflated tires and for tire wear or damage.
- Note which way your front wheels are turned. This is the direction in which your vehicle will go as soon as it begins moving.

Car Body

- Check for damaged or missing parts, and make sure that all lights and windows are clean and undamaged.
- In winter, scrape off snow and ice.

Under the Hood

- At least once a week or when you stop for gas, check the engine oil, radiator coolant, battery charge, brakes, transmission, and windshield-washer fluids.
- Check the battery connections. Are the cables tight? Are the terminals free from corrosion?

Getting into the Vehicle

Now you are ready to get into your vehicle. Do it safely.

- Load packages and have passengers enter from the curbside.
- Look carefully for approaching traffic before stepping into the roadway. Have your keys in hand.
- Walk around the front of the vehicle, facing oncoming traffic.
- Wait for a break in traffic before opening the door, and open it only far enough and long enough to allow you to get into the vehicle.

◆ *Adjust mirrors and seats, fasten your safety belt, and lock the doors before you move into traffic.*

What Should You Check After Entering the Vehicle?

Get into the habit of making safety checks and adjustments as soon as you get into the vehicle. In addition to observing the following guidelines, consult your owner's manual for further information.

Inside-the-Vehicle Checks and Procedures

- Close and lock all doors.
- Place the key in the ignition.
- Adjust the seat so that you can clearly see the roadway and comfortably reach the floor pedals and other vehicle controls.

Charles A. Butler
Director, Safety Services, AAA

How well you manage risk is determined by what you do before you start driving. Make sure all vehicle system devices are working properly, and know how to use and adjust them—especially mirrors, seat, lights, steering wheel, and occupant restraints. Vehicle system devices improve visibility and improve your ability to steer, accelerate, and brake. They also protect you in the event of a crash. Good risk managers always make predriving vehicle systems checks.

- Adjust the head restraint. Have passengers adjust theirs.
- Adjust rearview and left sideview mirrors so that you can use them with just your eyes and do not need to move your head. Adjust the right sideview mirror for the best vision with the least head movement.
- Check the inside of the windows. Then clean, defog, or defrost as necessary.

- Make sure there are no objects inside the vehicle that will block your view or tumble about as you drive.
- Familiarize yourself with the controls for any devices you may need to use. While moving, minimize the time you take to use any of these devices. Make any adjustments when traffic and roadway conditions do not pose a threat.
- Fasten your safety belt and make sure all passengers have fastened theirs.

WHAT WOULD YOU DO?

You have never driven this vehicle before. What checks and procedures will you use before entering and driving it?

Lesson 4 Review

1. What should you check before getting into your vehicle?
2. What should you check once you are inside the vehicle?

Making a Circle Graph

A poll is a way of finding out what a group of people think about a certain topic. You've probably seen or heard of polls showing what people think about political events, celebrities, and economic situations.

Conduct a poll to find out what members of your class think are their chances of being involved in a collision.

Try It Yourself

Follow these steps.

1. Count the number of people in your class. This number represents 100 percent of the class.
2. Ask each person this question: *What do you think the chances are of your being in a collision?* Then ask each person to choose one of the following as a response:
   a. 1 in 5, **b.** 1 in 10, **c.** 1 in 50, **d.** 1 in 100, **e.** 1 in 500, **f.** 1 in 1,000, **g.** don't know

3. Tally the number of responses to each choice.
4. Divide the number of responses to a choice by the total number of people in the class to get the percentage of people who responded to that choice. For example, if four people said "1 in 10" and there are 27 people in the class, the fraction would be $\frac{4}{27}$, or about 15 percent.
5. Make a circle graph to show the results. A full circle represents the whole class, or 100 percent. First divide the circle into fourths. Each fourth represents 25 percent. Then mark segments of the circle to show the approximate percentage of people who responded to each choice.
6. Your finished graph might look something like the one below.
   The chances of being in a traffic collision in any given year are actually 1 in 5. In a poll of 1,506 people, only 1 person out of 10 chose that rate. How does your class compare?

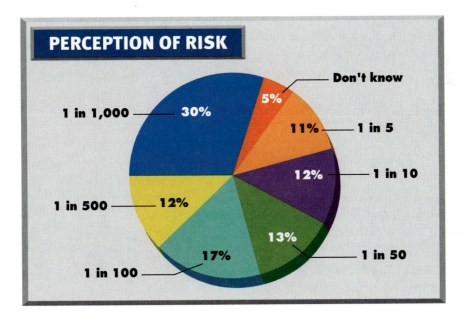

PERCEPTION OF RISK

- Don't know — 5%
- 1 in 5 — 11%
- 1 in 10 — 12%
- 1 in 50 — 13%
- 1 in 100 — 17%
- 1 in 500 — 12%
- 1 in 1,000 — 30%

CHAPTER 7 REVIEW

KEY POINTS

Lesson One

1. Devices that help make you comfortable in a vehicle include seat-position controls, adjustable steering wheel, heater, air conditioner, and air vents.
2. Devices that enable you to control a vehicle include the ignition switch, the gear-selector lever or gearshift, the steering wheel, cruise control, the accelerator, the brake pedal, and the parking brake.

Lesson Two

1. Devices that aid visibility include lights, windshield wipers and washer, sun visors, defroster, and rearview and sideview mirrors.
2. Car features that protect you and your passengers from injury include safety belts, air bags, head restraints, door locks, and various structural features such as safety-glass windows, impact-resistant bumpers, and protective padding on the dashboard.
3. Devices such as locks, alarms, and the audible key reminder can help prevent the theft of a vehicle.

Lesson Three

1. The speedometer, odometer, fuel gauge, alternator gauge, temperature gauge, oil-pressure gauge, brake warning lights, and various dashboard lights provide information about your vehicle.
2. Taillights, directional signals, emergency flashers, parking lights, and horn let you communicate with others.

Lesson Four

1. Before entering your vehicle, you should check the surrounding area for children, animals, objects, or fluid leaks; check the condition and direction of the tires; inspect the body of the vehicle for damage and clean the lights and windows; and regularly check the fluid levels and battery connections.
2. After entering the vehicle, lock the doors; adjust the seat, head restraint, and mirrors; clear the windows; reposition any objects inside the car that may block your view or tumble about; familiarize yourself with all controls; fasten your safety belt; and make sure passengers have fastened theirs.

PROJECTS

1. Obtain a vehicle owner's manual and read through the contents. Find the sections that deal with the various kinds of systems you've read about in this chapter. What information can you obtain from an owner's manual that you won't find in a textbook?
2. Research and report on the comparative safety of different makes and models of motor vehicles. Try to find out specific reasons why some vehicles are safer than others. Your librarian can help you identify sources of information.

You may also want to discuss this subject with insurance agents, mechanics, and other knowledgeable people.

*inter*NET CONNECTION

For the latest news on air bag safety, visit Glencoe's Web site.
www.glencoe.com/sec/driver.ed

CHAPTER TEST

Write the letter of the answer that best completes each sentence.

1. Three features that improve visibility are
   a. sun visors, bucket seats, and headlights.
   b. defroster, windshield wipers, and side-view mirrors.
   c. sunroof, air bags, and brake lights.

2. Head restraints should make contact with
   a. the base of your skull.
   b. the top of your head.
   c. the back of your head.

3. Cruise control
   a. increases your control of a vehicle.
   b. may lead you to be less alert.
   c. is best used in heavy inner-city traffic.

4. An odometer indicates
   a. the distance a vehicle has traveled.
   b. the speed at which a vehicle is traveling.
   c. the amount of current in your battery.

5. Three devices that control the speed and direction of your vehicle are the
   a. gearshift, brake pedal, and steering wheel.
   b. engine, battery, and accelerator.
   c. tires, air conditioner, and ignition switch.

6. Ice has formed on your windshield. You should
   a. pull the sun visor into the "up" position.
   b. turn on the air conditioner.
   c. turn on the defroster.

7. Each year approximately 200 children under the age of six are killed while playing
   a. on highways.
   b. in driveways.
   c. on sidewalks.

8. Taillights, emergency flashers, and parking lights
   a. are parts of a vehicle's communications system.
   b. cannot be activated with the ignition in the "off" position.
   c. are parts of a vehicle's information system.

9. Using a safety belt will
   a. protect you from getting whiplash.
   b. increase your chances of surviving a collision.
   c. decrease your chances of surviving a collision.

10. Directional signals
    a. are controlled by the turn-indicator arm.
    b. are controlled by a button on the dashboard.
    c. become activated whenever you turn the steering wheel.

Write the word or phrase that best completes each sentence.

safety check	blind spots	air bags
antitheft devices	automatic	manual

11. You should look over your shoulder when turning to detect anything in your _____.

12. Vehicles that have a(n) _____ transmission require you to use a clutch pedal.

13. _____ are considered passive safety devices because they operate automatically.

14. A(n) _____ enables you to find out about a problem before your vehicle is moving.

15. Alarm systems and audible key reminders are examples of _____.

DRIVER'S LOG

In this chapter, you have learned about the different systems of your vehicle and checks you should make before and after entering your vehicle. When you become a driver, what will you do to be sure that you do not forget to make these checks—even if you feel you're in too much of a hurry to take the time? Write a paragraph telling what you will do.

CHAPTER 8

Starting, Steering, Stopping

Basic driving procedures are second nature to good drivers. It is important that you learn these procedures so that you can manage them safely and smoothly. Mastering the basics is crucial to the driving task.

LESSON ONE
Basic Operating Procedures:
Automatic Transmission

LESSON TWO
Basic Operating Procedures:
Manual Transmission

LESSON THREE
Acceleration, Deceleration, and Speed

LESSON FOUR
Learning How to Steer the Vehicle

◆ *When you follow the steps for starting your car, warning lights come on briefly.*

Basic Operating Procedures: Automatic Transmission

In Chapter 1, you learned a basic principle of responsible driving: To reduce risk, you need to manage visibility, time, and space. Your ability to put this principle into practice depends on how well you can control your vehicle. You control a vehicle through a set of gears called a **transmission.** The transmission enables you to move your vehicle forward or backward. The gear you select determines the direction.

Whether you drive a vehicle with an automatic transmission or one with a manual transmission, the key to becoming a skilled driver is the same: *practice.*

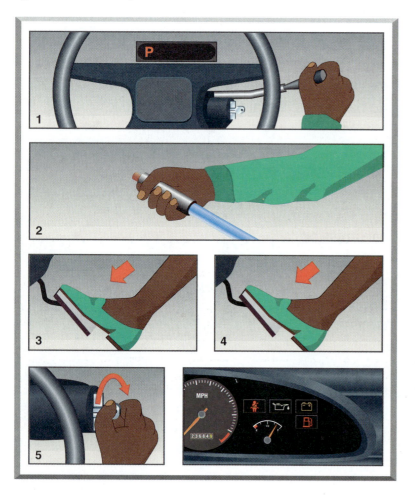

How Do You Start and Move a Vehicle with an Automatic Transmission?

It is important to start your vehicle's engine properly to avoid damaging the starter system or wasting fuel.

To start the engine of a vehicle with an automatic transmission, follow the steps below, one at a time. Practice doing these steps until they become habit.

1. Make sure the gear selector lever is in Park. If the selector lever is in Neutral, the car may roll if the parking brake has not been set.
2. Check that the parking brake is set.

   Note: If your car has an electronic fuel-injection (EFI) system or if the engine is warm from driving or very cold from the weather, Steps 3 and 4 may vary or may not be required at all. Check your vehicle's owner's manual for details.

3. Set the automatic choke by pressing the accelerator (gas pedal) once to the floor and releasing it.
4. Press the accelerator lightly with your right foot and hold it.
5. Turn the ignition key to the Start position. Release the key *as soon as* the engine starts.
6. As the engine **idles** (runs with no pressure on the accelerator), check the gauges and warning lights to be sure that the oil-pressure system and other systems are working properly.

Putting the Vehicle in Motion

Once your engine is running and you've checked the gauges, you're ready to put the vehicle in motion. Follow these steps.

1. Press down firmly on the brake pedal. While most drivers use their right foot to brake, some use their left foot. Follow the advice of your driving instructor.
2. Use your right hand to shift the gear selector lever to Drive or Reverse, depending on which way you intend to move.
3. Release the parking brake.
4. Check for traffic in your rearview and sideview mirrors. Be prepared to accelerate into the desired lane once the roadway is clear.
5. Turn on your directional signal to indicate the direction in which you want to move.
6. Look over your shoulder to check blind spots.
7. Remove your foot from the brake, and gradually apply pressure to the accelerator.

Working the accelerator properly takes practice if you use your right foot for both accelerating and braking. For best control of both the accelerator and brake pedals, rest the heel of your right foot on the floor in a position that lets you keep it there while

◆ *To put a car in motion, accelerate gently to avoid "jackrabbit" starts.*

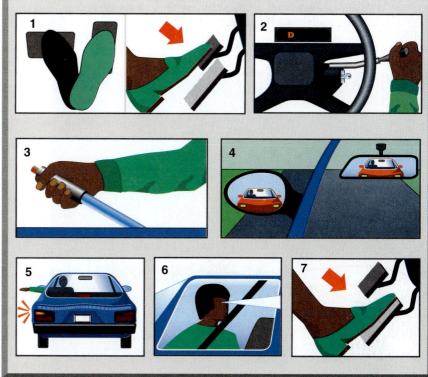

pivoting back and forth between the two pedals. The forward part of your foot should fall comfortably on both pedals.

Moving forward after stopping on an uphill grade requires extra practice. To keep from rolling back, use your left foot to press the brake pedal while gently accelerating with your right foot. As soon as the vehicle starts to pull forward, take your left foot off the brake. (An alternative is to hold the vehicle in place by setting the parking brake, then releasing the brake as you accelerate.)

How Do You Slow and Stop a Vehicle with Automatic Transmission?

You will often have to slow down and stop your vehicle under both planned and unexpected circumstances. Red lights, stop signs, pedestrians running across streets, vehicles cutting in front of you—these and countless other situations will require you to apply your brakes.

Braking

For smooth braking, you need to develop a sense of timing and get a feel for applying the right amount of pressure on the brake pedal. Your goal is to stop in time, neither overshooting nor undershooting your desired stopping point. Moreover, whenever possible, you want to stop your vehicle gradually, not abruptly.

♦ **Identify in advance the need to stop by using the SIPDE process.**

The amount of foot pressure required to brake to a stop depends on the size and weight of the vehicle, its type of brakes, your maneuvering space, and the road surface. As you practice driving and become more experienced, you'll become increasingly skilled at judging the distance needed to bring your vehicle to a smooth stop.

For effective control of brake pressure, position the heel of your foot between and in front of the accelerator and brake pedal. In this way, you'll be able to apply pressure with your toes, and you can easily increase or decrease pressure as needed. (See illustration on page 135.)

Follow these steps when preparing to brake to a stop.

1. Check your mirrors for any vehicles that may be following. Lightly tap the brake pedal: your flashing brake lights will warn following drivers that you intend to stop.

2. Apply smooth, steady, firm pressure to the brake pedal, easing up slightly as you come to a halt.

3. Leave the transmission in Drive if you plan to move ahead within a minute or so, as when you're stopped for a red light. If you'll be stopped longer, follow the parking procedures described in Chapter 10, and turn off your engine.

Emergency Braking

The procedures for stopping under emergency conditions differ slightly. If a driver or pedestrian suddenly enters your path of travel, you may need to stop the vehicle as quickly as possible. However, you don't want to slam on the brakes so hard that the wheels lock (stop turning). Locked wheels can increase your stopping distance and can also cause you to lose steering control and go into a skid.

To prevent the wheels from locking, press, or "squeeze," the brake pedal firmly to a point just *before* the wheels lock, and hold it there. This is called **threshold braking.** If the wheels start to skid, reduce pressure very slightly, then add pressure again as needed. Release pressure as the vehicle comes to a stop. For additional guidelines on braking and skid control, see Chapter 14.

When purchasing a vehicle, consider buying one that has antilock brakes. An **antilock brake system (ABS)** is made to keep the wheels from locking when the driver brakes abruptly.

Lesson 1 Review

1. What steps would you follow to start and move a vehicle with an automatic transmission?

2. How would you use your brakes to slow and stop a vehicle with an automatic transmission? How would you stop in an emergency?

WHAT WOULD YOU DO?

How can you enter the flow of traffic safely and smoothly?

OBJECTIVES

1. Explain how manual and automatic transmissions differ.
2. Describe how to start and move a vehicle with a manual transmission.
3. Explain how to use each forward gear.

KEY TERMS

manual shift
clutch
friction point
downshift

Basic Operating Procedures: Manual Transmission

Many people drive vehicles with manual transmissions because they enjoy shifting gears. Others prefer manual transmission vehicles because they usually cost less than the same models with automatic transmissions and, when properly driven, may reduce fuel consumption.

How Do Manual and Automatic Transmissions Differ?

In manual transmissions, there are usually three to five gears in forward and one in reverse. The choice of the forward gear determines the power delivered by the engine to the drive wheels.

An automatic transmission set in Drive will shift the forward gears for you. When you operate a manual transmission, or **manual shift,** you must shift the gears by moving the gearshift (or stick shift) by hand. You start in Low, or First, gear and shift to higher gears as you pick up speed. As you slow down, you shift back down from high to low.

To change gears, you break the connection between the engine and the transmission by pressing the **clutch** pedal to the floor. When the clutch pedal is up, the engine is again engaged to the transmission.

◆ *Below are the gearshift positions for 4-speed and 5-speed manual transmissions.*

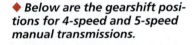

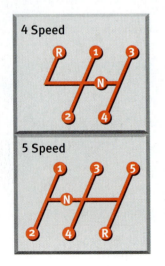

How Do You Operate a Vehicle with a Manual Transmission?

Learning to drive a vehicle equipped with a manual transmission is easier if you already know how to operate a vehicle with an automatic transmission. The key to driving a manual-shift vehicle is mastering the clutch, which you'll use each time you shift gears.

Starting the Engine

As when starting a vehicle with an automatic transmission, make sure the parking brake is set. Press the clutch pedal to the floor with your left foot, press the brake pedal with your right foot, and then shift

◆ *You use both feet when you shift and move a car with a manual transmission.*

1

2

3

4

5

6

7

8

into Neutral. (There is no gear position equivalent to Park on the gearshift for a vehicle with a manual transmission.) Now turn the ignition key to start.

Putting the Vehicle in Motion

To get a manual-shift vehicle to move—and to keep it moving—you must learn to coordinate the use of the clutch with that of the gearshift and the accelerator. Reading about how to do this will help you understand the process. Only through actual practice, however, can you gain the experience needed to master stick-shift driving.

Clutching and shifting actions should come to feel so natural to you that you

◆ *It takes plenty of practice to use the clutch pedal to shift smoothly.*

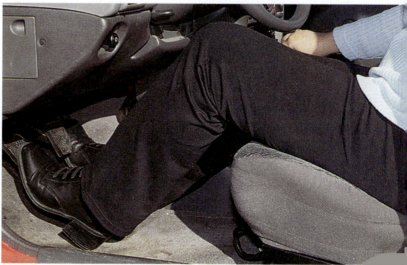

scarcely need to think about them. After all, once you're on the roadway, you can't be looking down at your feet and hands.

The key to smooth clutch operation is learning to sense the **friction point.** This is the point when, as you let up the clutch pedal, the engine and the transmission engage. As you continue to let up the clutch, you must match the forward (or backward) motion of the vehicle with an increase in pressure on the gas pedal.

The easiest way to get a feel for the friction point is to practice by using Reverse gear. Because Reverse is a lower gear than First, you'll find it easier to sense the friction point.

Follow these steps to put the vehicle in motion.

1. Press the brake pedal with your right foot. With your left foot, press the clutch pedal to the floor.
2. Shift into First gear.
3. Release the parking brake.
4. Switch on your turn signal to indicate the direction you plan to move.
5. Check for traffic in your rearview and sideview mirrors. Look over your shoulder to check blind spots.
6. With your your right foot on the brake, slowly let the clutch up to the friction point. Look at the roadway, not down at your feet or hands!

7. Move your right foot from the brake to the accelerator.
8. Pressing down gently on the accelerator, slowly let the clutch pedal up.

If the car jerks forward, you either released the clutch too abruptly, or you pressed too hard on the gas pedal. If the vehicle lurches and the engine stalls, you have not fed the engine enough gas. Keep practicing until you can coordinate clutch and accelerator.

How Can You Use Each Forward Gear?

Your selection of gears depends on the power and speed you need for various driving tasks.

Low, or First, gear gives the power needed to set a vehicle in motion.

Second gear lets you go as fast as 15 to 25 mph, depending on the horsepower of

---

the engine and on whether the transmission is a 3-, 4-, or 5-speed one. You can also use Second gear to start on ice or to drive in heavy snow.

Third gear, in vehicles with 3-speed transmissions, is used for all speeds over 25 mph. If a vehicle has a 4- or 5-speed transmission and a small engine, Third is used at speeds up to 30 or 40 mph.

Use Fourth gear for driving above 35 mph on flat roadway. When you are driving uphill, you may have to achieve 40 mph or more before shifting to Fourth or Fifth gear.

Keep in mind that power, speed, and the gear in use are strictly related. At a given speed, the power of an engine is greater in lower gear. For example, when starting up a steep grade, you generally shift to a lower gear to maintain power. When the roadway levels out, you can shift to a higher gear and keep up the same speed with less power.

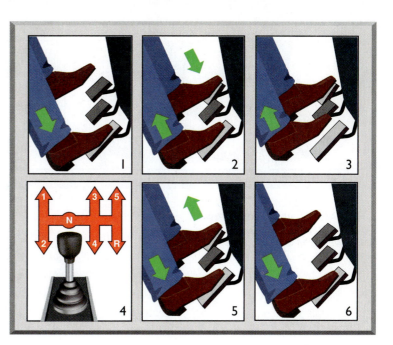

◆ *Coordinate using the clutch, gearshift, and gas pedal to shift gears.*

Shifting to a Higher Gear

To shift to a higher gear, follow these steps.

1. Accelerate to a speed appropriate for the gear you want to be in.
2. Press the clutch pedal to the floor.
3. Release the accelerator.
4. Shift to the next higher gear.
5. Press again on the accelerator. Release the clutch pedal slowly through the friction point.
6. Let the clutch pedal up all the way.

Downshifting

There are several reasons to **downshift,** or shift from a higher to a lower gear: to gain power, to accelerate, to steer effectively, to brake the vehicle on a downslope (except when the road is slippery), and to slow down or stop.

To shift to a lower gear, follow these steps.

1. Release the accelerator. (If you also want to slow down, press the brake pedal.)
2. Press the clutch pedal to the floor.

3. Shift to the next lower gear. (Sudden decrease in speed may require shifting to an even lower gear—as when braking sharply and downshifting from Fourth gear to Second.)

4. Release the clutch pedal to the friction point. Press down on the accelerator as necessary.

◆ To downshift, brake. Then press the clutch to the floor, shift to the next lower gear, and press the accelerator.

Note that you do not have to downshift through each lower gear as you slow down or stop. In fact, routinely downshifting to stop will cause unnecessary wear on the clutch, an expensive part to replace.

It is easy to downshift from Fifth, Fourth, and Third gears to lower gears, but it is difficult to shift from Second to First. To downshift to First gear, you have to bring the vehicle almost to a complete stop.

Stopping

To stop from a low gear, follow these steps.

1. Check mirrors for traffic behind you.
2. Tap the brake pedal to flash your brake lights and signal drivers behind you that you intend to stop.
3. Press the brake pedal to reduce speed to 10 to 15 mph. Then press the clutch pedal to the floor to keep the vehicle from stalling.
4. Apply smooth, steady brake pressure to bring the vehicle to a stop.
5. Keep your foot on the brake pedal and shift to Neutral.

To make an emergency stop, press the clutch pedal to the floor, and use threshold braking.

Lesson 2 Review

1. How is a manual transmission different from an automatic transmission?
2. What steps would you follow to start and move a vehicle with a manual transmission?
3. How would you use the forward gears of a vehicle that has a manual transmission?

WHAT WOULD YOU DO?

What actions will you take with the brake, the clutch, and the gearshift as you approach, then pass through, this intersection?

Acceleration, Deceleration, and Speed

OBJECTIVES

1. Define acceleration and deceleration.
2. Explain how these terms are related to speed.

KEY TERMS
acceleration
rate of acceleration
deceleration
rate of deceleration

To minimize driving risk, you must be able to maneuver your vehicle safely. To do so, you have to know your vehicle's capabilities and limitations. When changing lanes or passing, for example, you need to judge how much time and distance your vehicle will require to move ahead of other vehicles. Learning about acceleration, deceleration, and speed can help you judge time and space more accurately, thus helping you to be a safe driver.

How Are Acceleration, Deceleration, and Speed Related?

Speed and acceleration are closely linked. When drivers say their vehicle has good **acceleration** (or "pickup"), they mean the vehicle is able to increase speed relatively quickly. The time it takes to accelerate from one speed to another is the **rate of acceleration.**

Deceleration, on the other hand, refers to decreasing speed, or slowing down. The time it takes to decelerate from one speed to another is the **rate of deceleration.**

Several factors affect a vehicle's acceleration, including the power of the engine, the transmission and differential gear ratios, adhesion between the drive wheels and the road surface, and the weight the engine is pulling. Your ability to drive safely and effectively depends in large part on the knowledgeable use of your vehicle's acceleration.

CONNECTIONS

Math

A speedometer tells you how fast you're traveling at a given moment, but to find out your average speed for a particular distance, you'll need to do a little math.

Average speed equals total distance traveled divided by total time traveled. Suppose, for example, the distance from your home to the beach is 70 miles. One afternoon, it takes you an hour and a half to drive there. Your average speed equals 70 (total miles driven) divided by 1½ (total time), or just over 46 miles per hour.

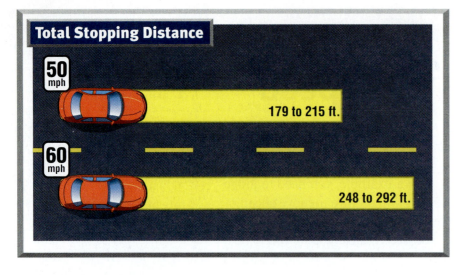

Total Stopping Distance

50 mph — 179 to 215 ft.

60 mph — 248 to 292 ft.

◆ *The greater the speed, the greater the distance needed to brake the car to a stop. Here the total stopping distance—which is the distance traveled from perception to response—for a car traveling at 50 mph ranges from 179 feet to 215 feet.*

Acceleration and Deceleration Rates Vary

Rate of acceleration varies with speed. At higher speeds, a vehicle's rate of acceleration will be lower. As a result, it will generally take more time to accelerate from 45 mph to 55 mph than from 20 mph to 30 mph.

Understanding this principle is important for risk management. For example, the lower acceleration rate at high speeds means you must allow more time to pass when traveling at 50 mph than when moving at 30 mph.

Equally important to keep in mind is that deceleration rates, like acceleration rates, vary with speed. At higher speeds, your vehicle's rate of deceleration is lower. So a vehicle traveling at 60 mph needs a great deal more time and space to slow and brake to a stop than the same vehicle traveling at 30 mph.

A vehicle's rates of acceleration and deceleration also vary with weight. A heavy truck, for example, needs much more time and distance to accelerate or decelerate than does a passenger vehicle.

Maintaining a Constant Speed

The ability of vehicles to maintain a given speed varies greatly. Large passenger vehicles with high-horsepower, 6- or 8-cylinder engines and mid-size and sport sedans with turbo-charged small engines generally have good acceleration and can maintain their speed climbing a hill. An under-powered subcompact vehicle, however, may not be able to hold its speed because of its small engine.

Many large vehicles also have difficulty maintaining their speed. Tractor-trailer rigs and inter-state buses have huge engines, but these large vehicles accelerate very slowly.

Monitoring Your Speed

New drivers find it difficult to control the speed of their vehicle simply by observing the

TIPS   **FOR NEW DRIVERS**

Accelerating

- For best control when accelerating, rest the heel of your foot on the floor, and press the pedal gently with your toes.
- As a general rule, accelerate gradually. Beginning drivers sometimes make errors when they increase speed quickly. Accelerating gradually also saves fuel.
- No two cars accelerate exactly the same way. When driving an unfamiliar vehicle, allow yourself time to get used to the feel of the gas pedal and to the vehicle's acceleration capability.

speed of traffic around them. As a result, they frequently check the speedometer. Such checks should be made with quick glances, as traffic conditions permit.

With experience, you'll become more aware of clues to your vehicle's performance and speed. You'll notice, for example, that as speed varies, there's a difference in the vehicle's vibration and in the level of sound from the tires, the wind, and the engine. Drivers of vehicles with manual transmissions must make a special effort to learn to judge speed because they have to make speed-related decisions about shifting gears.

Note that it is harder to estimate your vehicle's speed immediately after you've made a sharp change in speed. If, for example, you've been driving at 20 mph and rapidly accelerate to 45 mph, you'll feel as though you're moving faster than you actually are.

On the other hand, if you've been traveling at highway speeds and suddenly enter a 25-mph zone, your tendency may be to slow down less than you should because you've become accustomed to moving at higher speeds. The best way to prevent yourself from speeding in such an instance is to check your speedometer.

◆ *New drivers often increase speed without realizing it, so check your speedometer frequently.*

Lesson **3** Review

1. What is acceleration? How are acceleration and speed related?
2. What is deceleration? How is deceleration related to speed?

WHAT WOULD YOU DO?

Which vehicle probably needs more time and distance to accelerate: the truck or the car? How would knowing this help you manage time and space to reduce risk?

OBJECTIVES

1. Describe the procedures for steering straight ahead and when turning.
2. Explain how to steer in Reverse gear.

KEY TERMS

tracking
hand-over-hand steering
push-pull-feed steering

Learning How to Steer the Vehicle

Many new drivers assume that they know all they need to know about steering a vehicle. After all, they think, they've been steering bicycles and sleds since they were children. Such activities do share elements in common with steering a motor vehicle. However, there are important differences new drivers must learn.

For one thing, unlike a bicycle or sled, a motor vehicle has power independent of the driver's own efforts—a great deal of power. Moreover, steering is not simply a matter of pointing the vehicle in the direction you want to go. Steering is a basic means of risk management.

The average driver takes ½ to ¾ of a second to step on the brake after identifying a dangerous situation. Thus, even at 20 mph, your vehicle would travel at least 20 feet before you could step on the brake.

How Can You Steer Your Vehicle Forward and Through Turns?

Suppose you're about to drive through an intersection. Suddenly another vehicle crosses in front of you. The best way to avoid a collision is to brake your vehicle, right? Not necessarily.

It often takes less time and space to steer away from an object than to brake to avoid hitting it. (Of course, to avoid a collision by steering, you must have previously identified an area into which you can safely steer.)

Steering plays a particularly important part in risk management when you're traveling at speeds over 25 or 30 mph. At such speeds, steering may often be your only way to avoid a collision, because higher speeds increase the distance and time needed to stop the vehicle.

Holding the Steering Wheel

When steering in a straight line or through a moderate curve, grasp the steering wheel firmly with your fingers. Many experienced drivers place their hands at 9 o'clock and 3 o'clock or at 8 o'clock and 4 o'clock positions. Others position their hands on the lower part of the wheel, in the 7 o'clock and 5 o'clock positions. Follow the recommendations of your instructor. No matter which hand position you use, your thumbs should rest on the wheel.

Tracking and Steering

Keeping your vehicle moving on the path of travel that you have chosen is called **tracking**. Tracking requires a driver to make whatever steering adjustments are needed to hold the desired course.

To track smoothly, learn to direct your attention to points 20 to 30 seconds ahead along your intended path of travel. Choose these points on the basis of where you want to go and traffic conditions.

If you're like many new drivers, you'll find steering a vehicle more challenging than you'd anticipated, particularly when traveling on winding roads. At first, you may not notice small changes in your vehicle's position in a traffic lane. You may fail to adjust your steering in time and then tend to overcorrect, causing the car to zigzag rather than move in a straight line. You'll tend to look at the right edge marker or center line while driving through curves. Doing so will also cause the vehicle to zigzag. However, with practice and concentration, you'll learn to look through curves and well ahead of your vehicle along your path of travel. You'll soon improve your ability to keep your vehicle on track with only minor steering adjustments.

◆ *Think of the steering wheel as the face of a clock so that you can position your hands correctly.*

Steering in a Straight Line

The steering adjustments you must make on a straight road are small but critical. Be on the alert for gradual changes in the position of your vehicle. It should not "wander" in its lane.

Steer toward a point in the center of your path of travel, looking well ahead as you drive. When you look to the point where you will steer, you will automatically steer in the proper direction.

As you drive, check your mirrors whenever you spot anything along your intended path of travel that could cause you to change speed or position.

To look in your rearview mirror, move just your eyes. To look in your sideview mirror, turn your head only slightly.

◆ *Always look and steer toward a point in the center of your intended path of travel.*

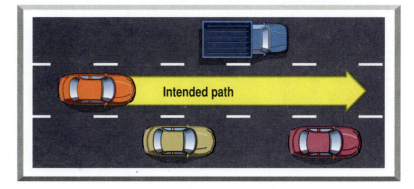

Intended path

Steering to Turn

Steering through a turn requires more steering-wheel movement than does lane positioning. To turn corners smoothly and safely, you need to develop a good sense of timing and make a habit of searching a wider area.

When steering through a turn, keep in mind that your vehicle's rear wheels do not follow the same path as the front wheels. They have a smaller turning radius, so you must allow ample space along the path you're turning. Without this space, your rear wheels may hit the curb or other objects.

Two specific steering techniques are effective for turning the wheel: hand-over-hand and push-pull-feed. The following procedures describe how to make a right turn; to make a left turn, reverse the movements.

Hand-over-hand steering To turn right using **hand-over-hand steering,** use your left hand to push the steering wheel up, around, and down. At the same time, bring your right hand across your left forearm to grip the wheel on the far side. Then use your right hand to pull the side of the wheel up, around, and down. Repeat this series of movements as often as needed to complete the turn, making any left or right steering corrections that may be required.

Hand-over-hand steering provides effective vehicle control when you're steering through tight-radius turns, such as hard turns and hairpin turns.

◆ *If you are not too tall or somewhat stout, you may find push-pull-feed steering more comfortable.*

Push-pull-feed steering Grasp the steering wheel with the right hand resting between 3 and 5 o'clock and the left hand between 7 and 9 o'clock. One hand pushes the wheel up toward 12 o'clock. (Use the left hand for right turns and vice versa.) At the same time, the other hand slides up to 1 o'clock for the right turn (or 11 o'clock for the left turn), grasps the wheel, and pulls it down. While the pulling hand goes down, the pushing hand releases its grip and returns to its original position to continue the process as needed.

Push-pull-feed steering lets you keep both your hands on the steering wheel at all times. The positioning of your hands causes less fatigue on longer drives and gives you better steering control in an

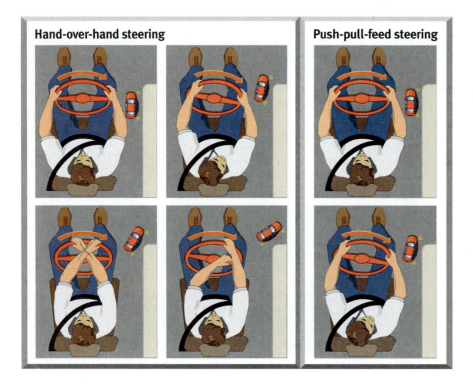

Hand-over-hand steering

Push-pull-feed steering

emergency. Also, you can sit farther from the steering wheel. Since your arms never cross over the face of the steering wheel, there is less chance of injury if the driver's side air bag deploys.

Whichever steering method you choose, use the following guidelines when making a turn.

- Look beyond the turn to the point you want to reach. Identify this point before you start to turn.
- Always use your directional signal. Check the roadway ahead and both mirrors before starting to turn. Check the mirrors again after completing the turn, waiting if possible until you've straightened the wheels.
- On a hard turn, slow down to maintain control as you enter the turn. Accelerate gently about halfway through to pull out of the turn.
- With your eyes on the point you want to reach, start to steer back to the straight-ahead position when you're about midway through the turn. Do this by reversing the hand-over-hand or push-pull-feed movements.

How Do You Steer in Reverse?

When steering in Reverse gear, you have to learn where to look and how to control direction and speed. Always back slowly. When you steer left or right while backing, the vehicle's movements are more abrupt.

When you are backing a vehicle, visibility through the rear window is limited. Head restraints and passengers may further block your view. Backing while looking into the rearview mirror restricts your view even more.

To maximize your ability to see, turn your head and shoulders so that you can look back in the direction you want to move. When you move backward, the rear of your vehicle moves in the direction that you turn the steering wheel, while the front swings in the opposite direction.

Note, too, that when you back a vehicle, the two points most likely to hit something are the rear side of the vehicle in the direction in which you are turning and the front side of the vehicle opposite the direction in which you are turning.

◆ *Don't forget to look over both shoulders when you steer to the rear.*

Steering to the Rear

Follow these steps when backing a vehicle.

1. With your foot on the brake, shift into Reverse gear. If you are backing straight, place your left hand on the top of the

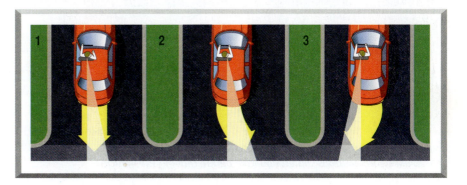

Ron Hales

Professor of Safety Education, Central Safety Center, Central Washington University

When preparing to stop, always check your inside mirror for vehicles that are following you. Maintaining adequate space around your vehicle is very important, and knowing what is behind you is critical to your safety and that of your passengers.

When stopping behind another vehicle, maintain an adequate space cushion in front of your vehicle. The best way to do this is to make sure that from the driver's seated position, the rear tires of the vehicle ahead and a small portion of the roadway are completely visible to you.

steering wheel and your right arm across the top of the seat. Look over your right shoulder. If you are backing to the right or left, keep both hands on the wheel and look over your shoulder in the direction you want to move.

2. Ease pressure off the brake slowly. Give yourself plenty of time to monitor the rear and front of your vehicle. To move the vehicle slowly, apply only slight pressure, if any, to the accelerator.

3. Look at the point where you want to go so that you can identify and correct steering errors early. Turn the wheel as needed.

4. Concentrate your visual search out the rear window, with quick, repeated glances to the front. Keep alert to ensure that the vehicle is moving in the right direction and that the front end is not about to strike anything.

5. Continue to look out the rear window as you bring the vehicle to a stop.

WHAT WOULD YOU DO?

What procedures would you follow to back out of this driveway? What safety precautions should you take before moving the vehicle?

Lesson 4 Review

1. What procedures would you follow to steer a vehicle straight ahead? To turn?
2. How do you back a vehicle?

Understanding Roadway Classifications

Maps help you get where you are going. They also tell about the kinds of roads you can use to get there. Most maps have a key such as this one. Find 🛡91 at coordinates D, 5 on the map. The map key indicates that this is a no-toll, limited-access highway. See the dots along Route 2? The key tells you that this is a scenic route. Find Route 9. The key tells you that Route 9 is a paved secondary road that is not divided.

Try It Yourself

1. What can you tell about Route 7 between Pittsfield and Stockbridge?
2. What kind of road connects Adams and Savoy Center?
3. Describe the different kinds of roads you can take from Southampton to Pittsfield.

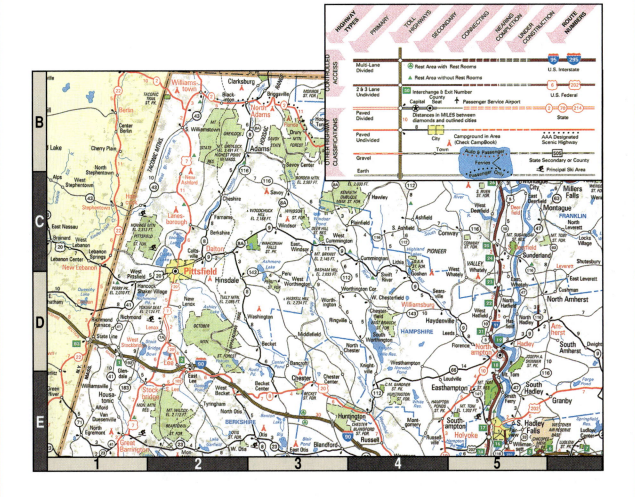

KEY POINTS

Lesson One

1. To start a vehicle with an automatic transmission, put the gear selector in Park. Set the automatic choke if it applies to your vehicle. Then press the accelerator and turn the key. To move the vehicle, step on the brake and shift to Drive or Reverse. Release the parking brake, take your foot off the brake, and accelerate gradually.

2. To slow and stop a vehicle with an automatic transmission, check your mirrors, tap your brake pedal, and apply steady pressure to the brake pedal, easing up slightly as you come to a halt.

Lesson Two

1. You need to change forward gears by manually shifting up or down in a manual transmission. An automatic transmission set in Drive will shift the forward gears for you.

2. To start a vehicle with a manual transmission, set the parking brake. Press the clutch to the floor, step on the brake, shift into Neutral, and turn the key. To move the vehicle, shift into First and release the parking brake. As you let the clutch up, move your right foot from the brake to the accelerator and press gently. To stop the vehicle, press the clutch to the floor, and move your right foot to the brake. Apply smooth pressure until the vehicle stops.

3. First gear sets the vehicle in motion. Second gear is used for speeds up to 15 to 25 mph or to start on ice or to drive in heavy snow. Third gear is used for speeds over 25 mph (3-speed transmissions) or speeds up to 30 or 40 mph (4- or 5-speed transmissions). Fourth or Fifth gear is used for driving at higher speeds.

Lesson Three

1. Acceleration is an increase of speed. Deceleration means a slowing down.

2. The rate of acceleration or deceleration varies with speed. At higher speeds, a vehicle's acceleration and deceleration rates are lower.

Lesson Four

1. To steer your vehicle straight ahead, steer toward a point in the center of your path of travel. When steering to turn, look beyond the turn to the point you want to reach. Use the hand-over-hand or push-pull-feed steering method.

2. When backing, look over your right shoulder, place your left hand at the top of the steering wheel, and steer in the direction you want the vehicle to move. Proceed slowly and carefully, monitoring both the rear and front of your vehicle.

PROJECTS

1. Talk to someone who has been driving for several years. Ask what lessons this driver has learned through experience and what tips he or she might offer you as a beginning driver.

2. Demonstrate the difference between the hand-over-hand and push-pull-feed steering. Which technique seems easier to you? Why? Survey several drivers to find out which method they use and why.

interNET CONNECTION

Use the Internet to download information on how antilock brakes work. Investigate the advantages and disadvantages of an antilock brake system.
www.glencoe.com/sec/driver.ed

CHAPTER TEST

Write the letter of the answer that best completes each sentence.

1. You can set an automatic choke by
   a. pumping the brake pedal.
   b. pressing the gas pedal to the floor once and then releasing it.
   c. turning the ignition key to "on."

2. One advantage of push-pull-feed steering is that
   a. your hands are on the wheel at all times.
   b. your hands are free to adjust the mirrors.
   c. you can back more easily.

3. With a manual transmission, the speed of the vehicle determines
   a. the tightness of the vehicle's turning radius.
   b. the choice of forward gear.
   c. the need for an occasional fuel injection.

4. A vehicle's rate of acceleration is lower at
   a. warmer engine temperatures.
   b. high speeds.
   c. low speeds.

5. To avoid rolling backward when starting on an uphill grade, you should
   a. set your parking brake firmly.
   b. lock the brakes.
   c. start the engine in third gear.

6. As you drive, you will develop the ability to estimate your speed by
   a. sensing the vehicle's friction point.
   b. riding the clutch.
   c. sensing a difference in the vehicle's vibrations.

7. To start a vehicle with an automatic transmission,
   a. first shift into Second gear.
   b. keep your foot on the brake pedal.
   c. make sure the gear selector lever is in Park.

8. To change gears in a vehicle with a manual transmission, you must
   a. press the clutch pedal to the floor.
   b. engage in threshold braking.
   c. rapidly decelerate.

9. When turning, always
   a. sound your horn.
   b. use your directional signal.
   c. shift into Reverse.

10. When driving around a curve, you should focus
    a. beyond the turn, on the point you want to reach.
    b. on the road directly in front of you.
    c. on objects in your rearview mirror.

Write the word or phrase that best completes each sentence.

acceleration	manual transmission
tracking	automatic transmission
clutch	rate of deceleration

11. _____ means an increase of speed.

12. A vehicle's _____ can have four or five forward gears.

13. The key to smooth _____ operation is sensing the friction point.

14. _____ means keeping your vehicle moving on the path that you have chosen to travel.

15. The time it takes for a vehicle to slow down is the _____.

DRIVER'S LOG

In this chapter, you have learned about the basic procedures you need to know to operate a vehicle. Write at least two paragraphs giving your ideas about why these procedures are almost second nature to experienced drivers and why they should become second nature to you.

CHAPTER 9

Basic Driving Skills

Minimizing risk on the roadway depends on drivers' mastery of basic driving skills, such as passing, changing lanes, and moving to and from curbs. Understanding how to safely execute these skills is vital to all drivers.

LESSON ONE

Moving from a Curb into Traffic and out of Traffic to a Curb

LESSON TWO

Managing Power and Speed on Hills and Mountains

LESSON THREE

Managing Visibility, Time, and Space When Changing Lanes

LESSON FOUR

Passing Another Vehicle and Being Passed

OBJECTIVES

1. Describe procedures for steering away from the curb and entering traffic.
2. Describe procedures for steering out of traffic and moving toward a curb.

Moving from a Curb into Traffic and out of Traffic to a Curb

Basic driving skills include moving your vehicle away from the curb and into traffic, as well as moving the vehicle out of traffic and to the curb.

Anytime you are moving into or out of the flow of traffic, not with it, you face increased risks. You have to make judgments about visibility, time, and space. For example: Can you see well enough to make this move safely? How fast are other vehicles moving? Is there time enough and space enough to make the move?

What Is the Procedure for Leaving a Curb and Entering Traffic?

◆ *As with any driving maneuver, you must plan ahead before leaving a curb and entering traffic.*

When you leave a curb, you are going from a stopped position to a moving position. This procedure involves planning how you will move, then actually making the move.

Advance Planning

Visibility, time, and space are important factors in planning your move away from a curb.

Visibility Check your view of oncoming traffic and also of traffic ahead of you and behind you. Notice any traffic signals, signs, and road markings.

Time Be aware of the speed limit on the roadway and how fast the vehicles in the lane into which you want to move and the lanes next to it are moving. Will you have enough time to move into your lane? Will vehicles behind you have to slow down or stop when you merge into traffic?

Space Check the space in front of and behind your vehicle. Decide whether or not you have room to pull out of your parked position in one smooth move or whether you will have to maneuver back and forth to clear a vehicle parked in front of you. Make sure you have room to enter the roadway and still keep a safe distance between your vehicle and the one in front of you.

◆ *Once you have prepared in advance, you are ready to move into the traffic flow.*

Making the Move from the Right Curb

Once you've made your plan to leave the curb, follow these steps for making the move.

1. Using both your sideview and rearview mirrors, check the traffic around you.
2. When you have decided it is safe to move into traffic, signal your intention to leave the curb.
3. Turn to your left and look over your shoulder to check traffic in your blind spot.
4. Steer away from the curb and directly into the nearest lane of traffic, accelerating moderately. If traffic is heavy, you may want to use an arm signal. (See Chapter 11 for instructions on how and when to use arm signals.)

What Is the Procedure for Steering to the Curb?

Steering your car out of traffic and toward a curb also requires advance planning before you actually make the move.

TIPS   **FOR NEW DRIVERS**

Parking Beyond an Intersection

Be especially careful if you have decided to park in a space or make a turn just beyond an intersection. Follow these steps.

1. Do not signal right or left as you approach the intersection. Other drivers may think you're going to turn at the intersection.
2. If other vehicles are near the intersection, move carefully into the correct lane and slow down.
3. Use your signals only after you have entered the intersection.

Advance Planning

You need to make plans in advance whenever you move your vehicle out of traffic.

As with moving away from a curb, visibility, time, and space are key factors in your plan to move *toward* the curb.

Visibility Pick out the spot where you want to stop. Scan the traffic scene in front of you, and use your mirrors to check traffic behind you and to your sides.

Time Note the speed of the traffic you're in. Consider how much you'll have to slow down to make the move.

Space Notice the amount of room available to you to move into another lane, if you need to do so to get to the curb. Is there space to move your vehicle directly into the parking place, or will you need to maneuver to parallel park?

Making the Move

After you have planned your move and decided it is safe to move toward the curb, follow these steps.

1. Signal your intent to move.
2. Tap your brakes lightly, signaling to drivers behind you that you are going to stop.
3. Apply gradual pressure on the brakes to reduce speed.
4. Steer out of the traffic lane to where you want to go, using your brakes as needed to stop the vehicle.

Lesson 1 Review

1. What are some factors to consider when moving your vehicle away from a curb and into the flow of traffic?
2. How can your wish to park near an intersection affect the way you exit from the flow of traffic?

WHAT WOULD YOU DO?

You hear an emergency vehicle approaching as you are about to pull away from the curb. What steps would you take?

Managing Power and Speed on Hills and Mountains

OBJECTIVES
1. Describe how to drive up-hill and downhill.
2. Describe safe procedures for driving on mountain roadways.

Whenever you drive, you always have an invisible passenger with you. That passenger is the force of gravity. Gravity works both inside and outside your vehicle at the same time.

If you drive uphill, gravity works against your vehicle, so you need to use more power. If you drive downhill, gravity is working with you, so you need to use less power, and you may have to use your brakes. For more information about how gravity affects your vehicle, see Chapter 15.

How Do You Drive Uphill and Downhill?

Driving on hills takes special effort, regardless of whether your vehicle has an automatic transmission or a manual transmission.

Driving Uphill

As you drive uphill, your vehicle needs more power in order to keep moving at the same speed. How you provide that power depends on whether your vehicle has an automatic or a manual transmission.

◆ *Whether you are driving up-hill or downhill, the force of gravity is pulling on your car.*

Automatic transmission Before your vehicle begins to lose speed by moving uphill, slowly increase the amount of pressure you are putting on the gas pedal. Notice your speedometer. When you've reached the speed you want to maintain, keep your foot at that point until you near the crest of the hill or need to slow down for any reason.

Manual transmission Before your vehicle begins to lose power and speed, downshift to a lower gear in order to increase the engine's pulling power. (For more information on downshifting, see Chapter 8.)

Driving Downhill

As you drive downhill, your car will gain speed, so you need to decrease the engine power.

Automatic transmission Ease the pressure you are applying to the gas pedal. Your vehicle will begin to coast. If it begins to pick up too much speed, press the brake pedal lightly to slow down. If you're going to go down a long, steep hill, it is best to move the selector lever to a lower gear before starting down the hill. Doing so gives you better control of your speed and steering and saves on braking. If you need to use the brake, use periodic light pressure. Do not ride the brake pedal.

Manual transmission If you're going to go down a long, steep hill, it is best to downshift to a lower gear before you start down the hill. Doing so gives you more control over the speed of your vehicle by allowing you to use the engine to help slow the vehicle. If you wait to shift until you are moving downhill and picking up speed, you will need to apply the brakes lightly while shifting to the next lower gear. If the hill is steep, your engine's braking power may not be enough to slow the vehicle unless you continue to apply the brakes. If this is the case, quickly downshift again. Use the brakes to slow down even more if you need to.

SAFETY TIPS

Be especially alert when you are driving through a falling rock zone. Be prepared to brake suddenly or to take other evasive maneuvers.

◆ *Shift to a lower gear to control speed when driving down a long, steep hill.*

How Do You Drive in the Mountains?

Driving up or down mountains presents special problems. The roads are curved and the grades may be steep. You need to use extra care to be able to control your vehicle under these conditions.

Special Roadway and Traffic Problems

Sharp curves, steep grades, and other vehicles limit how much of the road ahead you can see at one time. When you come to a curve where it is difficult to see oncoming traffic, slow down. If necessary, tap your horn and flash your lights to warn approaching drivers.

If you are behind a truck or vehicle with a trailer, increase your following distance. Pay attention to signs and pavement markings.

Effects of Weather and Altitude

Rain, snow, haze, and fog are especially dangerous when you are driving in the mountains. Try to find out about the weather conditions in the area before you begin a mountain drive.

In high altitudes, the air contains less oxygen. Lack of oxygen can cause you to feel short of breath and sleepy. Your heart may beat faster, and you may get a headache. If any of these symptoms occur, change drivers, stop driving, or find a route at a lesser altitude, if possible.

Mountain air also affects your vehicle's engine. It, too, gets less oxygen and loses power. It heats up faster, and gas may vaporize in the fuel line, causing the engine to sputter and stall. Keep an eye on the temperature gauge. If it shows red or hot, stop and allow the engine to cool.

Driving up a Mountain

If your vehicle has an automatic transmission, use the same procedure to drive up a mountain as you would use if you were driving up a hill. The transmission will downshift automatically. If you have a manual transmission, you may need to downshift often to go up steep inclines.

Driving down a Mountain

If you are driving with an automatic transmission, downshift manually for better control when going down a mountain. Do not ride the brake pedal. Use periodic light pressure on the brakes to slow down gradually. If you are driving with a manual shift, downshift as often as necessary to reduce speed, maintain control, and save on braking.

Lesson **2** Review

1. How are procedures for driving uphill different from those for driving downhill?
2. How can high altitude affect you and your vehicle if you are driving in the mountains?

WHAT WOULD YOU DO?

Your vehicle has an automatic transmission, and you've been using the Drive gear. Describe your procedure as you are about to head up a hill.

OBJECTIVES

1. Describe several factors involved in planning a lane change correctly.
2. Understand the steps involved in making a lane change.

Managing Visibility, Time, and Space When Changing Lanes

You have probably seen drivers who are constantly changing lanes, swooping between other vehicles on the highway. Chances are they're exceeding the speed limit and endangering lives. Of course, there are times when you and other drivers need to change lanes. You can minimize risk by learning the right way to do it.

TIPS FOR NEW DRIVERS

Communicating with Other Drivers

Your safety, the safety of your passengers, and the safety of other roadway users depend to a large extent on how well you communicate with other drivers and with pedestrians. Good roadway communication involves giving clear signals and warnings, paying attention to signals and warnings given by other drivers, and noticing where pedestrians are and what they are doing.

Drivers exchange four basic kinds of communication.

Intentions
plan to turn left or right; slowing down; plan to pass (please move over); plan to back up

Warnings
trouble ahead in my lane; need to stop suddenly; danger in your lane; headlights are blinding

Presence
parked vehicle; disabled vehicle

Feedback
recognizing another driver's signal; recognizing the presence of a pedestrian; thanks to a driver for allowing you to pass

Here is how to communicate.

Electronic signals
turn-signal lights, brake lights, backup lights, emergency hazard flashers; horn (short, sharp, or steady blasts); headlights (flash on and off, switch from high to low beams)

Body gestures
hand signals; nodding up and down; shaking head sideways; smiling; puzzled or confused look; raised eyebrows

What Is the Safest Way to Change Lanes?

As with other safe driving procedures, changing lanes involves two major phases: advance planning and making the change.

Advance Planning

You may have any of a number of reasons for changing lanes. You may need to change lanes to make a turn, pass another vehicle, avoid an obstacle in your lane, park, or exit a road. Whatever the reason for changing lanes, you need to plan ahead in order to make the move safely. Planning includes knowing where you are now, where you want to go, and what the road and traffic conditions are between the two. Check these items as you plan your move.

Visibility What is the path of travel like in the lane you are in? Note if there are vehicles in the path ahead and what they are doing. Use your mirrors to check for vehicles behind you. What is the path of travel like in the lane you want to enter? Search ahead 20 to 30 seconds and to the sides and rear.

Are other vehicles signaling to move into the lane you want to move to? If they are, wait until the other vehicles have changed lanes. Then check again.

Time How fast will you be going? You may need to increase or decrease speed to change lanes.

Space Do you have room to make the move safely? Make sure there is a 4-second gap between vehicles that you can move into.

◆ *You should take road conditions into account before you decide to change lanes.*

Making the Change

After you have checked out your plan to change lanes and are ready to make the move, follow these steps.

1. Check your mirrors again.
2. Signal your intent to move right or left.
3. Check over your shoulder on the side next to the lane you want to enter for vehicles in your blind spot.
4. Adjust your speed as necessary.
5. Move only when you have the time and space to do so.
6. Steer smoothly into the next lane. Push-pull-feed steering is best. After you have steered into the next lane, turn off your signal.

Lesson **3** Review

1. What factors are involved in planning a lane change?
2. What steps would you follow to make a lane change?

WHAT WOULD YOU DO?

You want to move into the right-hand lane. How will you manage visibility, time, and space?

OBJECTIVES

1. Name conditions you should be aware of when you want to pass another vehicle.
2. Describe the procedure for passing another vehicle.
3. Describe what to do when another vehicle passes you.

Passing Another Vehicle and Being Passed

Passing another vehicle on a two-lane, two-way roadway can be one of the most dangerous movements in driving.

What Conditions Will Help You Decide Whether You Should or Should Not Pass?

Before you pass another vehicle on a road with one lane of traffic in each direction, you need to know whether or not passing is legal. If passing is legal, you then need to decide whether it makes sense to pass under existing traffic, weather, and road conditions. Finally, you need to decide whether your speed, the speed of the vehicle ahead of you, and the speed limit make it possible for you to pass safely.

Road Signs and Pavement Markings

Warning signs and roadway markings will tell you whether passing is allowed in the area in which you are driving. (See Chapter 5.)

Atmospheric Conditions

Bright sunlight, rain, snow, sleet, hail, and fog add to the danger of passing. If you're driving under these conditions, it is wiser to slow down, proceed with caution, and perhaps avoid passing even if road signs and markings indicate that passing is allowed.

Nighttime visibility and the condition of the road surface can also add to the danger of passing. If you cannot see ahead to the place where you will reenter the lane after passing, do not attempt to pass. If the road surface seems rough or in poor condition, avoid passing.

Your Speed and the Other Vehicle's Speed

As you approach a vehicle in front of you, note your speed. You may have to slow down to keep a margin of safety between your vehicle and the one ahead. Estimate how fast the other vehicle is moving. If it is going 5 to 10 miles per hour more slowly than you were before you began to slow down, you might decide to pass.

FYI

If you're driving a vehicle at 50 miles per hour, it will take you about 16 seconds to pass another vehicle traveling at 40 miles per hour. Longer vehicles, such as trucks and campers, take even more time to pass.

You must also be aware of the speed limit on the roadway. You will typically need to accelerate to 10 to 15 miles per hour faster than the vehicle in front of you in order to pass it. However, you cannot legally exceed the speed limit to pass another vehicle.

How Do You Pass Another Vehicle?

Once you know it is legal to pass and it makes sense to pass in the situation, follow this procedure.

1. Check the path ahead, the off-road areas, behind you, and the lane you want to enter. Make sure no other vehicles are signaling to move into the lane. If you are on a two-lane, two-way road, check that there are no oncoming vehicles. If there are, make sure that they are far enough away to allow you to complete the passing safely. If you have any doubt, do not pass.

2. If the way is clear, signal your intent to pass. Flash your headlights. Use your left turn signal.

3. Check over your left shoulder for vehicles in your blind spot. Adjust your speed upward as necessary, and steer smoothly into the passing lane. Use very slight controlled movement of the wheel—usually not more than one-eighth of a turn.

4. Accelerate firmly. If you are on a road with a single lane in each direction, keep watching for oncoming traffic.

5. Check your rearview mirror quickly. When you see both headlights of the vehicle you've passed in the rearview mirror, signal your intent to return to the right lane and steer gradually in that direction. Turn off your signal, and maintain an appropriate speed.

◆ *Before you pass, check your path ahead and to the sides and rear. Signal, pass, and signal again before returning to your lane. Keep in mind that if you're traveling 40 mph, you will need 10 to 13 seconds to pass a vehicle traveling 30 mph. However, if you're traveling 60 mph and the other vehicle is traveling 50 mph, the passing time increases to 16 to 19 seconds.*

Barry Caruso
Coordinator, Traffic Safety Education, Wayne County Public Schools, Ohio

Basic on-road procedures—such as moving to and from the curb, driving on grades, changing lanes, and passing—never change. The better you perform these procedures, the more predictable you are. A good driver is very predictable. A predictable driver communicates every move. Once you have perfected basic on-road procedures, you need to tell other drivers what you are doing.

Remember, as the driver you are responsible for the action of your vehicle. Be as good a driver as you can, and THINK!

What Should You Do If You Are Being Passed?

Drivers of vehicles that are passing you assume the responsibility for their safety and yours, but you can often protect yourself and be of help to the passing driver.

By regularly checking your sideview and rearview mirrors, you can remain aware of the movement of vehicles behind you and alongside of you. When you see that you're being passed, stay to the right in your lane.

Do not speed up: It is illegal to do so when you're being passed.

Remain aware of the traffic situation around you. Sometimes a passing vehicle will decide to drop back rather than complete the pass. Do not accelerate unless it is necessary to give the vehicle more room to get back behind you.

WHAT WOULD YOU DO?

Does it make sense for the driver of the car behind the van to try to pass the van?

Lesson 4 Review

1. What should you consider before deciding to pass another vehicle?
2. How are visibility, time, and space important when passing another vehicle?
3. How can you help another driver who is passing you?

Using Prefixes and Combining Forms

The vocabulary describing vehicles and roadways is full of interesting words. Several of these words are formed by using a prefix and a root word.

A prefix is a word part that has a meaning of its own but cannot stand alone as a word. Here are some examples of prefixes and their meanings:

anti—not, against
de—removed, reversed
dis—apart, away from
inter—between, among
re—again
trans—across, beyond, or through
un—not

The vocabulary of driving also includes words that begin with a combining form. This is a word part that can act like a prefix, but it can also join another combining form to make a word, such as *photo + graphy*. Two common combining forms are *auto,* meaning "self," and *semi,* meaning "half" or "partly."

Knowing the meanings and uses of prefixes and combining forms can help you figure out the meanings of new words.

Try It Yourself

Choose a prefix or combining form from those above in order to complete each word or term below. Define the words and terms, using what you already know and what you've learned about prefixes and combining forms. If you don't know what a word or term means, ask someone or look it up.

1. ___celeration
2. ___preciation
3. ___national symbols
4. ___action time
5. ___abled
6. ___protected left turn
7. ___change
8. ___section
9. ___alignment
10. ___lock brakes
11. ___freeze
12. ___fogger
13. ___theft device
14. ___tread
15. ___mission

KEY POINTS

Lesson One

1. To move your vehicle away from a curb and into the flow of traffic, check traffic in front and in back of you, the speed of vehicles already on the roadway, and the space available to you for moving away from the curb.

2. To move your vehicle out of traffic and toward the curb, prepare the move well in advance. Check traffic behind you, signal your intention, steer toward the curb, and brake as needed.

Lesson Two

1. To drive up or down hills, downshift and accelerate or brake as necessary.

2. Use your horn and lights to signal your presence when you cannot see around a sharp curve ahead. Increase your following distance, and be aware of the effects of low oxygen on your body and your vehicle.

Lesson Three

1. To change lanes correctly, plan your move in advance. Check your visibility, the time you will need to change lanes, and if you have room to make the move safely.

2. Communicate your intent to other drivers, check your blind spot, and begin and complete the move. Adjust your speed to meet the situation.

Lesson Four

1. Before you pass another vehicle, note whether passing is legal. Consider the effects of weather and road conditions on your ability to manage visibility, time, and space.

2. To pass another vehicle, make sure you have a clear path of travel, signal your intent, check your blind spot, and begin the pass. Accelerate and return to the lane when you see both headlights of the vehicle you've passed in your rearview mirror.

3. If you are being passed, pay particular attention to the movement of the passing vehicle. You can help a driver who is passing you by giving his or her vehicle enough time and space, remaining aware of the movement of other vehicles, and not speeding up.

PROJECTS

1. Take a ride as a passenger, and record the different forms of communication you notice between drivers. Include communication by mechanical or electronic signals and by body signals. What kinds of information do drivers communicate by each method?

2. Can you tell from reading your state's driver's manual whether your state is one that has many mountain roads? How much space does the manual devote to mountain driving?

inter NET CONNECTION

Explore the Web for more information on how to pass a vehicle safely. Find and study illustrations on correct and incorrect ways to pass a vehicle. **www.glencoe.com/sec/driver.ed**

CHAPTER TEST

Write the letter of the answer that best completes each sentence.

1. When passing another vehicle, you must
   a. drive 5 mph above the speed limit.
   b. typically accelerate to at least 10 mph faster than the other vehicle.
   c. briefly flash your emergency lights.

2. To complete a pass safely, you should
   a. see the other vehicle's headlights in your rearview mirror.
   b. have at least 5 seconds total passing time.
   c. tap your horn lightly.

3. When you see a parking space you want across an intersection, you should
   a. enter the intersection, signal, and park.
   b. signal, cross the intersection, and park.
   c. cross the intersection, park, and signal.

4. When driving downhill in a vehicle with a manual transmission, you should
   a. downshift to gain more control.
   b. upshift to decrease engine power.
   c. ride the clutch to maintain an even speed.

5. Driving on mountain roads can cause you to
   a. become short of breath and feel sleepy.
   b. lose control of the gears.
   c. lose the effects of gravity.

6. When changing lanes,
   a. turn off the radio.
   b. make sure you are not on a one-way street.
   c. use push-pull-feed steering.

7. Drivers exchange information about
   a. intentions. b. communications.
   c. markings.

8. You can help another driver pass you on a two-way, two-lane road by
   a. moving to the right.
   b. speeding up.
   c. putting on your high beams.

9. In moving from a curb, you must
   a. quickly accelerate and join the flow of traffic.
   b. avoid using hand signals.
   c. make judgments about visibility, time, and space.

10. When you come to a curve where you cannot see oncoming traffic, you should
    a. tap your horn and flash your lights.
    b. change lanes.
    c. use both your sideview and rearview mirrors.

Write the word or phrase that best completes each sentence.

communicate   altitudes
advance planning   gravity
atmospheric conditions

11. You should avoid passing other vehicles in rain, snow, or other dangerous _____.

12. Driving at high _____ can affect the performance of your vehicle.

13. You can _____ with other drivers with electric signals or body gestures.

14. _____ causes a vehicle to speed up when it is traveling downhill.

15. Checking mirrors, the roadway, your path of travel, and traffic behind you are all part of _____.

DRIVER'S LOG

In this chapter, you have learned about some basic driving skills, such as moving to and from a curb, changing lanes, and passing and being passed. Which do you think will be hardest for you? Write two paragraphs explaining why and what you will do to gain confidence in your ability to execute the maneuver.

This review tests your knowledge of the material in Chapters 1–9. Use the review to help you study for your state driving test. Choose the answer that best completes each statement.

1. A driver gathers the most information through
   a. hearing.
   b. vision.
   c. touch.
   d. memory.

2. Administrative laws require
   a. vehicle owners and drivers to be financially responsible.
   b. manufacturers to buy insurance.
   c. the governor to make traffic laws.
   d. the federal government to set vehicle prices.

3. When you are being passed on the left,
   a. speed up slightly.
   b. stay in the right side of the lane.
   c. stay in the left side of the lane.
   d. change lanes.

4. If you are involved in a collision,
   a. stop immediately.
   b. go home and call the police.
   c. find witnesses.
   d. sign documents at the scene.

5. Traffic control signals are typically located
   a. on expressways.
   b. at intersections.
   c. at interchanges.
   d. on the dashboard.

6. An extremely dangerous drug that changes the way you see, think, and act is a
   a. stimulant.
   b. hallucinogen.
   c. depressant.
   d. prescription.

7. Strong emotions can
   a. improve your driving ability.
   b. cause you to be inattentive.
   c. help you stay alert.
   d. improve your judgment.

8. A vehicle with a manual transmission has a
   a. clutch pedal.
   b. choke pedal.
   c. gear selector lever.
   d. Smith System.

9. When a license is taken away permanently,
   a. it is revoked.
   b. it is suspended.
   c. it is intoxicated.
   d. it is inhibited.

10. Traffic moving in opposite directions is separated by
    a. white lines.
    b. yellow lines.
    c. regulatory signs.
    d. shock absorbers.

11. Alcohol is absorbed into the bloodstream
    a. through the skin.
    b. through the stomach wall.
    c. through the adrenal gland.
    d. through the tongue.

12. The basic speed rule states that you should
    a. adjust your vehicle's speed to weather and road conditions.
    b. drive at one-half the posted speed limit.
    c. drive at the posted speed limit.
    d. check your vehicle's speedometer every few seconds.

13. The direction of a vehicle's front wheels is controlled by the
    a. accelerator.
    b. steering wheel.
    c. clutch.
    d. alternator.

14. Roadway warning signs are usually
    a. yellow or orange.
    b. blue and white.
    c. green or blue.
    d. black and white.

15. HOV lanes are for
    a. cyclists.
    b. pedestrians.
    c. vehicles carrying two or more occupants.
    d. emergency vehicles.

16. To start a vehicle with an automatic transmission, the gear selector lever should be in
    a. Park.
    b. choke.
    c. Neutral.
    d. First gear.

17. Using headlights during daylight
    a. can increase your visibility to others.
    b. is a waste of energy.
    c. is illegal in some states.
    d. can increase your risk of a collision.

18. You can prove ownership of a vehicle with a
    a. birth certificate.
    b. certificate of title.
    c. certificate of registration.
    d. driver's license.

19. A vehicle's engine will run more efficiently at high speeds when in
    a. Reverse gear.
    b. Low gear.
    c. First gear.
    d. Overdrive gear.

20. When driving down a mountain,
    a. shift to a lower gear.
    b. shift into Reverse.
    c. lock the brakes.
    d. exceed the speed limit.

21. A driver can usually sense a clutch's friction point best in
    a. First gear.
    b. Third gear.
    c. Reverse gear.
    d. Neutral gear.

22. To keep a parked vehicle from rolling, use
    a. cruise control.
    b. the accelerator.
    c. the parking, or emergency, brake.
    d. the SIPDE process.

23. Roadway regulatory signs
    a. control the flow of traffic.
    b. warn of changes in roadway conditions.
    c. are usually spaced 100 feet apart.
    d. are usually green or brown.

24. To prevent locking a vehicle's wheels, use
    a. the Smith System.
    b. threshold braking.
    c. the ignition switch.
    d. motor oil.

25. Recreational area signs on roadways are
    a. brown.
    b. blue.
    c. green.
    d. red.

26. To warn others that your vehicle is stopped on the side of the road, use
    a. the dome light.
    b. a dipstick.
    c. an emergency brake warning light.
    d. emergency flashers.

27. Large trucks
    a. gain speed slowly.
    b. gain speed quickly.
    c. frequently roll over.
    d. usually have 4-cylinder engines.

UNIT 3

Moving onto the Road

Once you are behind the wheel, you need to perform many complicated maneuvers. This unit will help you understand these maneuvers in order to become a responsible driver.

CHAPTER 10

Turning and Parking

The ability to execute turns and parking maneuvers properly requires practice, good judgment, and knowledge of traffic laws. It is important that you learn the techniques that will enable you to perform these maneuvers safely.

LESSON ONE
How to Prepare for and Execute a Right Turn

LESSON TWO
How to Prepare for and Execute a Left Turn

LESSON THREE
Planning and Executing a Reverse in Direction

LESSON FOUR
How to Prepare for and Execute a Parking Maneuver

OBJECTIVES

1. List the procedures to follow when preparing to turn right at an intersection.
2. Describe the steps needed to execute a right turn.

How to Prepare for and Execute a Right Turn

Suppose that you are driving and want to turn right. What should you do? To answer that question, you need to learn the basics of control and visual search and make good use of time and space.

How Do You Prepare to Make a Right Turn?

Before you make a right turn, check the roadway, choose the correct lane, communicate your intentions, and position the vehicle correctly. Prepare for the turn 8 to 12 seconds in advance of reaching the intersection. This equals a distance of about 500 feet or 1 city block.

Check

Check for signs and markings that control your movement. Is a traffic signal, a yield sign, or a stop sign present? Are turns allowed? If so, are they restricted to certain times of day or to certain types of vehicles? Are there special turning lanes?

Choose

Choose the correct lane. Move into the lane if necessary, after you make sure that it is clear, and reduce your speed.

Communicate

Check your mirrors again, and signal early to let other drivers know that you intend to turn. Tap the brake pedal to flash your brake lights. Use your turn signal 3 to 4 seconds, or at least 150 feet, in advance of the turn in the city, and up to a quarter of a mile on a highway in the country.

Manage risk. Be aware that more than one-third of all collisions occur at intersections.

◆ *Make right turns from the lane closest to the right curb unless they are allowed from other lanes. Turn into the lane corresponding to the one you just left.*

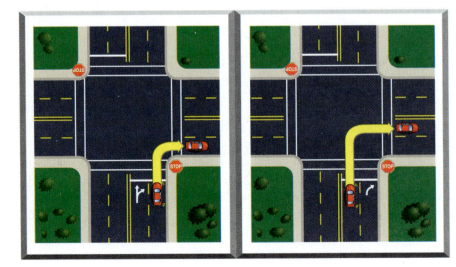

Position the Vehicle

Position your vehicle to the right side of the right lane, 3 to 5 feet from the curb or shoulder. Check other traffic in, at, and approaching the intersection. Make sure there are no cyclists to your right. If you are at a stop sign or red signal, stop before the cross-walk. Then slowly move up to a point where you can see cross traffic. Be prepared to yield to pedestrians.

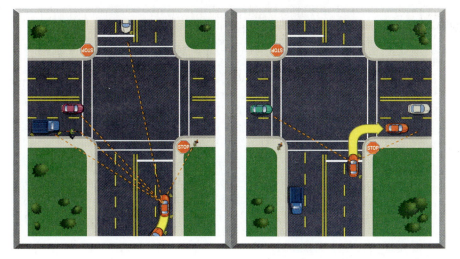

◆ *Move to the right lane in advance of a right turn. Check for pedestrians and other vehicles, including those across the intersection, before turning.*

How Do You Execute a Right Turn?

The steps for executing a right turn are the same whether you are turning onto a one-way or a two-way street. After you have positioned yourself correctly and signaled your intentions, check again for cross traffic. Then follow these steps.

1. Find a 6- to 8-second gap in traffic to your left. Just before turning, search the intersection again to the left.
2. When your front wheels are opposite the point where the curb begins to curve, look through the turn along your intended path of travel. Begin the turn.
3. Follow the general curve of the curb as you turn. Stay in the right lane by looking through the turn along the intended driving path.
4. Complete the turn by reversing your steering as you accelerate. Make sure the turn signal is off.

Lesson 1 Review

1. What should you do before you turn right at an intersection?
2. How do you make a right turn?

WHAT WOULD YOU DO?

You want to turn right at the intersection. How will you proceed?

OBJECTIVES

1. Describe how to prepare for a left turn.
2. State how to make a left turn from a one-way street and from a two-way street.

How to Prepare for and Execute a Left Turn

When you make a left turn, you follow many of the same procedures you use to make right turns. However, be aware that a driver turning left *must* yield the right-of-way to any cross traffic and to vehicles approaching from the opposite direction. Drivers should also be alert for pedestrians and be prepared to yield to anyone in the crosswalks.

How Do You Prepare for a Left Turn?

To prepare for a left turn, check the roadway, choose the correct lane, communicate your intentions by signaling, and position your vehicle correctly. Remember to reduce speed before making your turn.

Check

Look through the turn on your intended path of travel. Check for traffic signs and signals and for traffic ahead and to the left and right. Be sure no one is about to pass you on your left side.

◆ *Position your car in advance of a left turn. Check for pedestrians and other vehicles in and across the intersection.*

Choose the Correct Lane

Signal and move into the correct lane. Stop behind the stop line if there is one. Keep your wheels straight.

Communicate Your Intentions

Signal your turn 3 to 4 seconds, or at least 150 feet, in advance. Flash your brake lights by tapping the brake pedal before slowing. Use your turn signal.

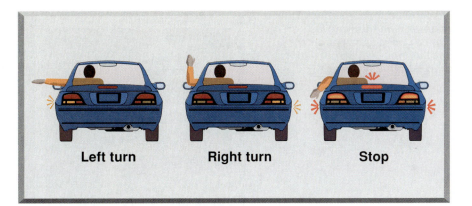

Left turn **Right turn** **Stop**

◆ *Use an arm (or hand) signal to communicate better with drivers behind you.*

Position the Vehicle

Position your vehicle just to the right of the center line or, on a one-way street, the left curb.

How Can You Execute a Left Turn?

The steps for executing a left turn depend on the type of street you are on and the type of street you are turning onto.

Turning Left from a Two-Way Street onto a Two-Way Street

1. Check that there are no vehicles, pedestrians, or other obstacles in your intended path of travel.
2. Find a 9-second gap to your right and a 7-second gap to your left.
3. Proceed into the intersection until you are about one lane width away from its center. Yield to any approaching traffic and pedestrians in the intersection. Keep your wheels straight.
4. Look through the turn along your intended path of travel. Begin the turn.
5. Follow the path of travel so that you arrive in the lane just to the right of the center line. Complete the turn by reversing your steering as you accelerate. Be sure the turn signal is off.

Turning Left from a Two-Way Street onto a One-Way Street

Turning onto a one-way street is like turning onto a two-way street except that you enter the lane of traffic closest to you.

SAFETY TIPS

When you are turning either right or left at an intersection, be very careful not to signal too early if there are other places to turn before the intersection. A driver on another roadway who believes you intend to turn somewhere else could pull out in front of you.

◆ *You need to learn which lane to enter when turning left from a one-way street onto another one-way street and onto a two-way street.*

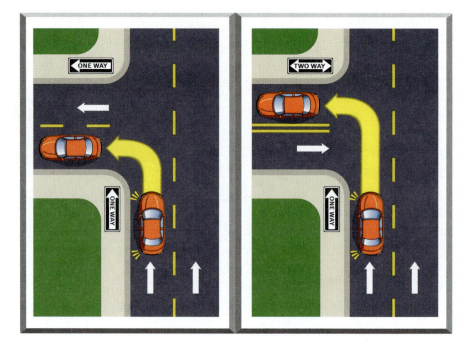

Turning Left from a One-Way Street onto a One-Way Street

Making a left turn from one one-way street onto another is similar to making other left turns. However, you will not have to cross a lane of traffic coming toward you.

You want to turn left. How will you prepare for the turn? To whom will you yield the right-of-way?

Turning Left from a One-Way Street onto a Two-Way Street

If you are turning left from a one-way street onto a two-way street, position your vehicle in the far left-hand lane. Turn into the first lane of traffic going in your direction.

Lesson 2 Review

1. What should you do *before* you make a left turn?
2. How would you make a left turn from a two-way street onto another two-way street?

Planning and Executing a Reverse in Direction

OBJECTIVES
1. Describe how to prepare to make a turnabout.
2. Describe four ways to make a turnabout.

KEY TERMS
turnabout
two-point turn
three-point turn
U-turn

No matter how skillful a driver you are, you may sometimes miss a street or building you are looking for. If so, you may have no choice but to turn around, or make a **turnabout.**

How Should You Prepare to Make a Turnabout?

As in all maneuvers you make with your vehicle, careful preparation is a key to managing risk. Before you make a turnabout, consider the following.

- Are there signs that prohibit the turnabout?
- Are there specific laws that prohibit the turnabout when there are no signs?
- Is there at least 500 feet of visibility in each direction?
- Are you near hills, curves, or within 200 feet of an intersection?
- Is there heavy traffic?
- Do you have enough space to complete the maneuver?
- Are there traffic and pedestrians in your path?

How Can You Make a Turnabout?

You can make a turnabout in one of four ways. Use the method that best suits traffic conditions, the street, and local traffic laws.

Two-Point Turns

The **two-point turn** is one method to use when making a turnabout. Either head into or back into a driveway to reverse direction.

Backing into a driveway Back into a driveway when there is no traffic close behind you in your lane and there is a clear driveway on your right.

1. Signal early. Flash your brake lights to alert following drivers. Check for objects or children in or near the driveway as you drive past.
2. Stop about 3 feet from the curb, with your rear bumper just beyond the driveway you will enter. With your foot on the brake, shift into Reverse. Check again for obstacles in your intended path.

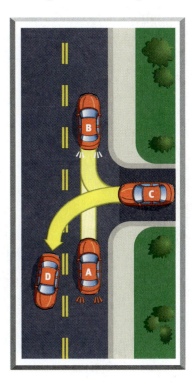

◆ *If you can't go around the block, make a turnabout by backing into a driveway.*

3. When it is clear, look over your right shoulder. Back up slowly, turning the wheel rapidly all the way to the right. As the rear of the vehicle enters the driveway, turn the wheel to the left, centering the vehicle in the driveway. Stop when the front of the vehicle is clear of the curb.

4. Shift to Drive or First gear, signal, check traffic, and leave the driveway when it is safe to do so.

Heading into a driveway on the left When you head into a driveway, you will have to back into the street. Select a driveway on the left that affords good visibility. Make sure there are no hedges or other objects along the driveway that will obscure your view of the road.

1. Signal a left turn. Check for traffic, flash your brake lights, and stop if necessary. When the driveway is clear, turn into it as close to the right side as you can. This allows more room for the front of the vehicle to swing left as you back out to the right.

2. When the rear bumper clears the edge of the roadway, stop with your front wheels straight. With your foot on the brake, shift into Reverse gear.

3. Look in all directions for pedestrians and over your right shoulder for traffic in your planned path. Back up slowly, rechecking traffic, and stop before crossing the curb.

SAFETY TIPS

By backing into a driveway rather than heading in, you can see in both directions to better assess risk when you prepare to reenter traffic.

◆ *You can make a turnabout by heading into a driveway on the left (below) or on the right (below right).*

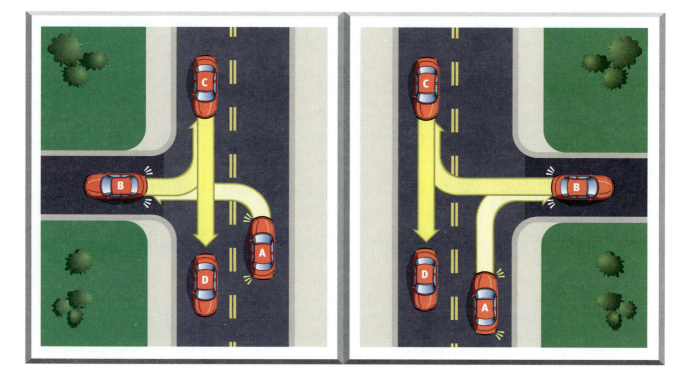

4. While slowly moving the vehicle back, turn the wheel quickly all the way to the right. Keep your vehicle in the first lane of traffic. Halfway through the turn, start to straighten the steering wheel.

5. Stop when the front wheels are straight. Check mirrors and over your shoulder, signal, shift to Drive or First gear, and accelerate to traffic speed.

Heading into a driveway on the right Heading into a driveway on the right in order to make a turnabout is very dangerous because a driver must back across at least two lanes of traffic before moving forward. You should make this maneuver only in low-speed, low-traffic residential areas. Follow the steps for heading into a driveway on the left, but reverse the directions in Steps 1, 3, and 4.

◆ *You need to have a good sense of speed and steering control to make a three-point turn.*

Three-Point Turns

One of the hardest turnabouts for the new driver is the **three-point turn.** To minimize risk, make a three-point turn only when the street is narrow, there are no driveways to turn into, you have very good visibility, traffic is very light, and you cannot drive around the block. To make a three-point turn, follow these steps.

1. Stop as close to the right edge of the curb as possible. Check for traffic in both directions. Wait until you have a 20- to 30-second gap to complete the turn.

2. Signal a left turn. Look over your left shoulder for any vehicles in your blind spot. Then move the vehicle slowly while turning the steering wheel rapidly to the left to bring the vehicle into the opposite lane. Hold this position.

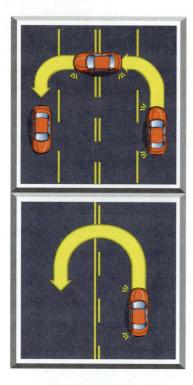

◆ **To make a U-turn, move your car slowly, but turn the steering wheel rapidly.**

3. When the front wheels are almost to the curb (about 4 feet away), turn the steering wheel rapidly to the right. Then, stop the vehicle just short of the curb.
4. Check traffic to your left, then over your right shoulder. Shift into Reverse, and while backing slowly, turn the wheel to the extreme right position. About 4 feet before stopping, turn the wheel quickly to the left. Keep looking back until you have stopped the vehicle.
5. Shift into Drive or First gear. Check traffic. Signal, move into the proper lane, and accelerate to normal speed.

U-Turns

To make a **U-turn,** you do not back up, and therefore you need a wide street in which to make the turn. Be aware that U-turns are illegal in some places.

Here is how to make a U-turn on a two-lane road after first making sure the turn is legal.

1. Stop your vehicle close to the right edge of the curb. Check for traffic in both directions. Signal a left turn. Check over your left shoulder again before starting the turn. Do not start the turn if you will interfere with traffic.
2. Turn the steering wheel rapidly all the way to the left, moving the vehicle slowly until it is facing in the opposite direction.
3. When the turn is almost completed, straighten the wheels, and proceed in the proper lane at normal speed.

Around the Block

The fourth way to reverse direction is to drive around the block. This method is often the easiest and safest to use.

Lesson 3 Review

1. What should you consider before making a turnabout?
2. How can you reverse your vehicle's direction?

WHAT WOULD YOU DO?

You are driving north and need to turn around. How will you make the turnabout? Why?

How to Prepare for and Execute a Parking Maneuver

Parking can be one of the most exasperating experiences of driving. Sometimes you feel the only way you can get into a space is by bumping nearby vehicles out of the way. So how can you park easily?

Parking is an art. To park quickly, easily, and safely, you need good control of your vehicle, accurate judgment of space, a good understanding of steering, and continuous practice.

To park safely, you need to understand the different ways to park. They are angle parking, perpendicular parking, and parallel parking.

How Do You Angle Park and Perpendicular Park?

When you park at an angle, you have little room to maneuver and cannot see very well. You must therefore be very careful when entering and leaving angled and perpendicular parking spaces.

Right- or Left-Angle Parking

You may have seen angled parking spaces in parking lots or along the streets of towns and smaller cities. These spaces are set at an angle from 30 degrees to 90 degrees to the curb or line.

To execute **angle parking** on the right, follow these steps.

1. Stay 5 or 6 feet from parked vehicles to give yourself room to see and maneuver. Observe traffic in all directions and be alert for vehicles about to leave nearby spaces. Signal for a right turn.
2. Proceed until you can see along the left side of the vehicle to the right of the space you will enter. Steer sharply right. Creep ahead at 3 to 5 mph into the space midway between the lines. Check the left front and right rear of your vehicle to make sure you have clearance.
3. As you straighten the wheels, move forward until the front of your vehicle is aligned with those on both sides.

◆ *You need to position your car carefully before you enter an angled parking space.*

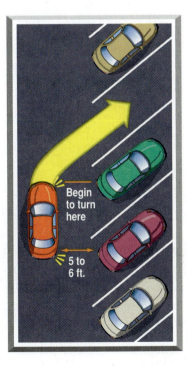

Begin to turn here

5 to 6 ft.

◆ *Check that your left front fender doesn't scrape the car on the left when you exit an angled space.*

◆ *Whether entering or leaving a perpendicular space, keep your car positioned 7 to 8 feet from the row of parked cars.*

Angle parking on the left is similar to that on the right. In this case, start turning the steering wheel to the left when you can see along the right side of the vehicle parked to the left of your chosen space. Now you must keep track of the right front bumper and the left rear fender.

Perpendicular Parking

Many parking lots have parking spaces that are marked at a 90-degree angle to the curb or line. These are perpendicular parking spaces. **Perpendicular parking** is risky because it is hard to see at that angle and there is very little room for maneuvering. If possible select a perpendicular parking spot that allows you to drive forward rather than backing in order to exit.

To enter a perpendicular parking space on the right, follow these steps.

1. Stay 7 to 8 feet from parked cars for best visibility. Observe all traffic conditions, and check for vehicles about to back out of other spaces. Signal for a right turn.
2. Slow to 3 to 5 mph. Start turning right when you can look down the right side of the vehicle parked to the right of your chosen space. Steer sharply right. Proceed slowly, checking for clearance of your left front bumper. Check your right rear fender to see that it does not scrape the rear of the vehicle on your right.
3. As you straighten the wheels and center in your space, move forward slowly and stop just short of the curb or in line with the vehicles parked beside you.

Entering a perpendicular parking space on the left is similar to entering one on the right. In this case, you turn the steering wheel in the opposite direction and keep track of the right front bumper and the left rear fender.

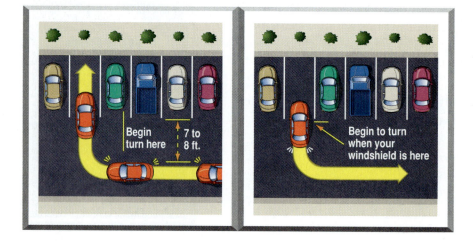

Exiting an Angled or a Perpendicular Parking Space

To leave an angled or a perpendicular space, follow these rules.

1. Turn on your turn signal to alert drivers of your intentions. With your foot on the brake, shift into Reverse. Check all traffic

around you. Back very slowly with your wheels straight, looking to your left and over your right shoulder. Keep checking the back and sides for obstacles. Yield to any oncoming traffic.

2. To exit an angled space on the right, backing to the right, turn the steering wheel sharply right when your front bumper will clear the rear of the vehicle on your left.

3. When you exit from a perpendicular space, turn the steering wheel slightly right or left when your windshield lines up with the rear bumpers of the vehicles on both sides. Make sure your front fender clears the rear of the vehicle opposite to the direction in which you are turning.

4. As your vehicle enters the traffic lane, quickly turn the steering wheel in the opposite direction to straighten the front wheels. Keep looking out the rear window until the vehicle stops.

5. Shift into Drive or First gear, accelerate, and move into traffic.

◆ *It takes a great deal of practice to be able to parallel park efficiently.*

How Do You Parallel Park?

You parallel park most often along the side of a street. **Parallel parking** may seem hard at first, and you'll have to practice to become expert at it. To parallel park, you need a space at least 5 feet longer than the length of your vehicle.

Parallel Parking

Here is how to parallel park.

1. Approach the parking space in the proper lane. Check traffic behind you. Signal in the direction of the curb and flash your brake lights to alert following drivers of your intention to stop.

2. Move parallel to the vehicle in front of the space, leaving about 3 feet between vehicles. Stop when the center door posts, or the backs of the front seats of the vehicles are even. Keep your foot on the brake, and shift into Reverse.

3. Back up, steering sharply to the right. Align the back of the front seat with the rear bumper of the vehicle in front. Continue backing slowly, straightening your front wheels, until your front bumper lines up with the rear bumper of the vehicle in front.

4. Back up, steering rapidly to the left. Stop before making contact with the bumper of the vehicle behind the space.

5. With your foot on the brake, shift into Drive or First gear. Move forward slowly, centering your vehicle in the parking space. Stop and set the parking brake.

To exit a parallel parking space on the right, follow these steps.

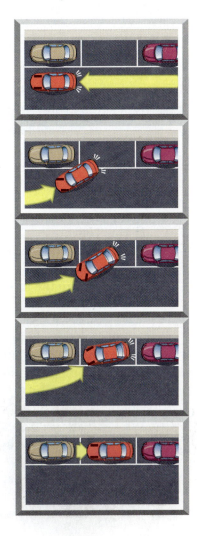

1. Shift into Reverse. Back slowly, with your wheels straight. When your vehicle is about 1 foot from the vehicle behind you, turn the steering wheel rapidly to the left and stop.
2. With your foot on the brake, shift into Drive or First gear. Check your mirrors. Signal a left turn. Move forward slowly, steering rapidly the rest of the way to the left.
3. Check your blind spots. Yield to approaching traffic. Then move forward slowly. When your center door post is even with the rear bumper of the vehicle in front of you, turn the steering wheel right until the front wheels point straight ahead.
4. Check the position of the vehicle to your right, being careful not to scrape it. When your rear bumper is opposite its rear bumper, accelerate gently and steer right as necessary into traffic.

How Would You Park in Other Areas?

Parking lots and city streets are not the only areas where you park. You might have to park in a driveway or a garage or on a steep hill.

Parking in a Driveway

At times, you may have to park in a driveway. Driveways may have trees and shrubbery or fences and buildings on either side. Centering your vehicle is especially important in a narrow driveway. Furthermore, because many driveways are often sloped downward, you should make sure to set your parking brake.

Parking in a Garage

Parking in a garage is also similar to perpendicular parking. You must make sure to center your vehicle, either between the walls of the garage or between the sides of the garage door opening. Good positioning and the ability to judge space to your sides are important in parking in a garage. Remember to check both fenders for clearance as you back slowly out of the garage.

Parking on a Hill

Parking on a hill is similar to parking on a flat surface. However, you must make sure your vehicle will not roll into traffic after you leave it. The procedures described here are for parking on the right side of the street. To park on the left side, make appropriate right-left adjustments.

Parking downhill with a curb To make sure your vehicle does not roll, take these precautions.

1. Bring the vehicle to its normal parallel-parked position. Turn the steering wheel sharply right and move slowly forward.
2. Stop the vehicle when the front right wheel touches the curb. Set the parking brake. If your vehicle has a manual transmission, shift into Reverse.

Parking downhill without a curb You may need to park facing downhill on a roadway that has no curb. Follow the same procedure for parking downhill with a curb, but move as close to the inner edge of the shoulder as possible.

Parking uphill with a curb Follow these guidelines to park facing uphill when there is a curb at the edge of the roadway.

1. Bring the vehicle to a normal parallel-parked position.
2. Move forward slowly, turning the wheels sharply left as far as they will go. Move about 2 feet and stop.
3. In Neutral, with your foot covering the brake, allow the vehicle to roll back slowly with the wheels cramped left until the rear of the right front tire touches the curb. Set the parking brake. If your vehicle has a manual transmission, shift to First gear.

Parking uphill without a curb To park uphill on a road without a curb, follow the procedure for uphill parking with a curb. However, center the vehicle in the space with the front wheels turned to the right so that if the vehicle begins to roll, it will move off the roadway.

Restrictions on Parking

Every state has its own parking restrictions. Before you decide to park your vehicle anywhere, make sure that you will be parked legally. Parking laws may differ from state to state. However, in most states it is illegal to park in these areas:

- at a bus stop
- in a loading zone

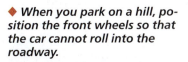

◆ *When you park on a hill, position the front wheels so that the car cannot roll into the roadway.*

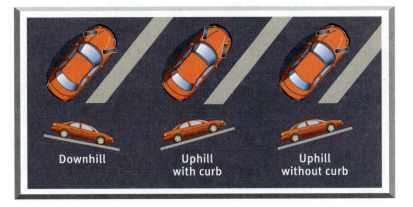

Downhill   Uphill with curb   Uphill without curb

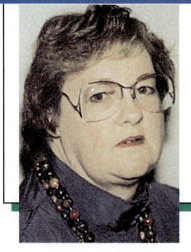

Carolyne Wilmoth
Classroom Driver Education Instructor, AAA Colorado

You use the same techniques to park, make turnabouts, and turn at intersections. The maneuvers you can make are not always the same. So, you need to understand signs, signals, and pavement markings. You must also practice proper techniques for visual search, steering, speed-control, and space management.

While low-speed and close-quarter maneuvers are rarely associated with serious injuries or deaths, it is still worthwhile always to use the correct procedures.

WHAT WOULD YOU DO?

What procedures will you follow in order to park on the hill?

- in the traffic lane beside another vehicle (double parking)
- on a sidewalk
- half in, half out of a driveway
- across someone else's driveway
- within a given distance of a fire hydrant
- in the fire zone in front of schools and in front of other public and private buildings
- in a no-stopping or no-standing zone

Lesson 4 Review

1. What should you do when entering an angled parking space?
2. How would you parallel park?
3. What should you do when parking on a hill or in a driveway or in a garage?

Using Junctions and Interchanges

Roadways that are numbered routes meet, or intersect, at junctions. On a map, junctions may be marked by a ○, in the same way that towns are. On an expressway, junctions are interchanges, shown by a ◇ on the map. You need to know about junctions and interchanges to get from one roadway to another.

Suppose you are in Oswego and want to travel to Rome. You might drive south on Routes 81 and 481 until you reach the junction of Routes 481 and 90, at an interchange. Then you would drive east on Route 90 to the interchange that is the junction of Routes 90 and 365. You would drive north on Route 365 to Rome.

Try It Yourself

1. Is there a junction of Routes 20 and 90?
2. How would you drive from Chittenango to Eaton?
3. How would you drive from Florence to Parish, stopping in Williamstown? How many junctions are there? Where are they?
4. Describe the fastest and safest route from Hannibal to Syracuse. How many junctions are there? How many interchanges?

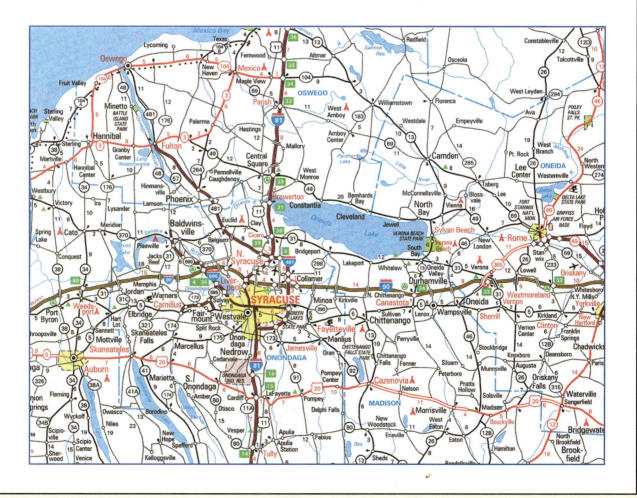

KEY POINTS

Lesson One

1. To prepare for a right turn, check the roadway, choose the correct lane, and communicate by signaling well in advance of the turn. Position your vehicle to the right side of the right lane.

2. To execute a right turn, find a gap in traffic to your left, look along your intended path of travel, and turn the vehicle, following the curve of the curb.

Lesson Two

1. To prepare for a left turn at an intersection, check the roadway, choose the correct lane, and communicate your intentions. Position your vehicle just to the right of the center line or, on a one-way street, the left curb.

2. When turning left, check for other vehicles and pedestrians across the intersection. Look for a 9-second gap to your right and a 7-second gap to your left. Look through the turn along your intended path of travel, and turn your vehicle.

Lesson Three

1. To prepare to make a turnabout, consider its legality in the situation, the amount of visibility, the amount and position of traffic, and the space available.

2. To turn your vehicle around, you can make a two-point turn by heading into or backing into a driveway, make a three-point turn, make a U-turn, or drive around the block. The method you use depends on its legality and on traffic and roadway conditions.

Lesson Four

1. To perform a perpendicular or angle parking maneuver, position your car correctly for best visibility; check for traffic and obstructions and signal; turn into the space when you have clearance on all sides.

2. To parallel park, move parallel to the vehicle in front of the space; back slowly into the space; and center your vehicle in the space.

3. Be aware of objects on either side when you park in a driveway or garage. Centering your vehicle is especially important. To park uphill or downhill, position the front wheels in such a way that your vehicle cannot roll onto the roadway.

PROJECTS

1. Observe a spot where turnabouts are permitted on a well-traveled road. Prepare a chart showing the kinds of turnabouts you observed drivers making and the frequency of each type of turnabout. Note any problems the drivers had in making the turnabouts. Discuss your observations with your class.

2. Observe several vehicles parked uphill and downhill. Record how each vehicle's front wheels are positioned. Make a diagram showing how each vehicle would move if it started to roll. Determine which vehicles had their wheels positioned correctly.

*inter*NET
CONNECTION

To learn more about reducing risk when making turns or parking, visit Glencoe's driver education Web site.
www.glencoe.com/sec/driver.ed

CHAPTER TEST

Write the letter of the answer that best completes each sentence.

1. When you park uphill against a curb on the right, your vehicle's front wheels should be
   a. turned to the right.
   b. turned to the left.
   c. positioned straight ahead.

2. The safest way to reverse direction is to
   a. make a U-turn.
   b. drive around the block.
   c. make a three-point turn.

3. You should signal for a right or left turn
   a. 200 to 300 feet in advance.
   b. 7 to 8 feet in advance.
   c. at least 150 feet in advance.

4. To parallel park, move your vehicle parallel to the vehicle in front of the space, at a distance of
   a. 1 to 2 feet.
   b. about 3 feet.
   c. about 5 feet.

5. The steps for making a right turn
   a. are the same whether turning onto a one- or two-way street.
   b. depend on the kind of street you turn into.
   c. depend on the presence of traffic in the cross street.

6. Before you turn left, the traffic gap should be
   a. 7 to 8 seconds in both directions.
   b. 9 seconds to the right and 7 seconds to the left.
   c. 200 to 300 feet in either direction.

7. To make a two-point turn, you
   a. drive around the block.
   b. head into or back into a driveway.
   c. shift to Neutral.

8. To exit from an angled parking space, first
   a. turn the steering wheel sharply right.
   b. shift into Reverse.
   c. move parallel to the vehicle in front.

9. If you park downhill in a vehicle with a manual transmission,
   a. shift into Reverse.
   b. shift into Neutral.
   c. shift into First gear.

10. Your vehicle should be positioned next to the center line before you
    a. make a right turn from a one-way street.
    b. make a left turn from a two-way street.
    c. move straight across an intersection.

Write the word or phrase that best completes each sentence.

| three-point turn | turnabout | right turn |
| perpendicular | roundabout | travel path |

11. A _____ parking space is set at an angle of 90 degrees to the curb.

12. To make a _____, position your car to the right side of the right lane.

13. One example of a _____ is the U-turn.

14. Make a _____ only when the street is narrow, you have good visibility, and traffic is light.

15. When turning at an intersection, look through the turn along your intended _____.

DRIVER'S LOG

In this chapter, you have learned about preparing for and executing maneuvers such as making right and left turns and turnabouts and parking. Which of these maneuvers do you think will be hardest? What will you do to help you overcome the difficulty? Write two paragraphs to explain your ideas. You may draw a diagram to help you.

CHAPTER 11

Driving Environments

Whether you drive on a quiet country road or a busy four-lane highway, you must be alert to an increase in the level of risk. Learning how to manage visibility, time, and space in different environments will help you minimize risk.

OBJECTIVES

1. Describe how to manage visibility as a driver.
2. Describe ways that you can manage time as a driver.
3. Describe how to manage space as a driver.

KEY TERMS

visibility
braking distance
total stopping distance
tailgate

Managing Visibility, Time, and Space

Whenever you drive, the risk of collision is always present. However, you can minimize that risk by learning to manage visibility, time, and space.

As you read about visibility, time, and space, keep in mind that they are closely related. To become a safe driver, you must understand how visibility, time, and space work together in all driving situations.

How Can You Manage Visibility?

Visibility refers to your ability to see and to be seen by other roadway users. You can take specific actions to maximize visibility both before you begin driving and once you are on the road.

Advance Preparations

Take these steps to manage visibility before you begin driving.

- Clear and clean the inside and outside of your vehicle windows.
- Make sure all vehicle lights are clean and in good working order.
- Make sure your defroster and windshield wipers and washer work properly.
- Adjust rearview and sideview mirrors for maximum visibility. Also adjust the driver's seat properly.
- Obtain and keep handy any items you might need to improve visibility, such as sunglasses, a flashlight, and a windshield scraper.
- Remove obstructions inside the vehicle, such as ornaments that hang from the rearview mirror or packages that block your view.

Behind-the-Wheel Actions

The first step in making your vehicle more visible while you are driving is to turn on your headlights whenever you drive, day or night. Driving with your low beams on in daylight makes your vehicle visible to drivers and pedestrians more than 2,200 feet sooner than it would be with no headlights.

Maximize your visibility to other roadway users by signaling your intentions well in advance. Also avoid driving in another driver's blind spot.

To help ensure your ability to see the roadway, always wear glasses or contact lenses if you need them. To shield your eyes from glare, put on sunglasses or use your sun visors.

◆ *To reduce risk and manage visibility, clean your headlights regularly.*

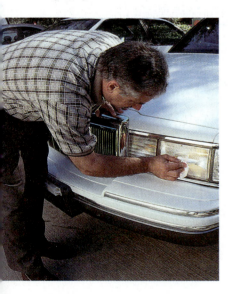

How Can You Manage Time?

By managing time wisely, you increase your control over driving situations and help reduce risk. Decreasing or increasing your vehicle's speed, for instance, can enable you to avoid colliding with other vehicles or a pedestrian.

To manage time effectively while driving, always keep in mind that time, speed, and distance are closely linked. For example, the amount of time and distance you need to stop your vehicle increases with your speed. Similarly, the time and distance required to pass depends on how fast your vehicle and the other vehicle are traveling.

Initial driver reaction time to a roadway problem, once the problem is spotted, is generally one-half to three-fourths of a second. During that time, your vehicle continues to move forward. The **braking distance** is the distance your vehicle travels until it stops, after you apply your brakes. **Total stopping distance** includes the distance traveled from the moment you recognize and respond to a problem plus the braking distance.

◆ *Drive with your low-beams on, even in the daytime, to enable other drivers to see you better.*

◆ *Stopping distance depends on many factors, including the size of your car, the condition of the road, and the car's speed.*

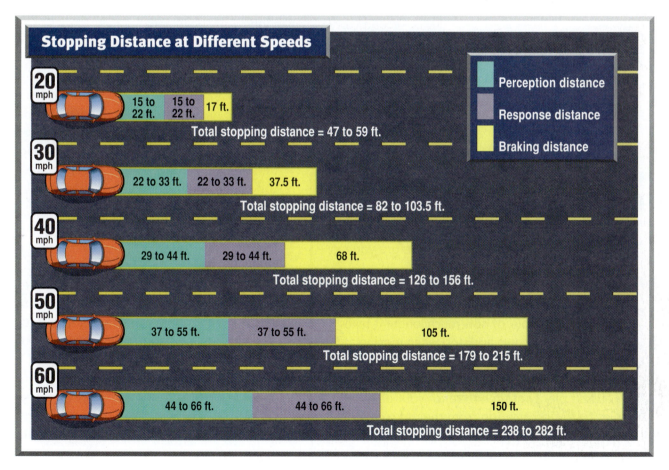

Stopping Distance at Different Speeds

Legend:
- Perception distance
- Response distance
- Braking distance

20 mph
15 to 22 ft. | 15 to 22 ft. | 17 ft.
Total stopping distance = 47 to 59 ft.

30 mph
22 to 33 ft. | 22 to 33 ft. | 37.5 ft.
Total stopping distance = 82 to 103.5 ft.

40 mph
29 to 44 ft. | 29 to 44 ft. | 68 ft.
Total stopping distance = 126 to 156 ft.

50 mph
37 to 55 ft. | 37 to 55 ft. | 105 ft.
Total stopping distance = 179 to 215 ft.

60 mph
44 to 66 ft. | 44 to 66 ft. | 150 ft.
Total stopping distance = 238 to 282 ft.

In Chapter 1 you learned how you can use the SIPDE process to reduce risk. By helping you identify threatening objects or conditions as early as possible, the SIPDE process maximizes the amount of time available for you to take whatever evasive action may be required.

Here are some guidelines for managing time. Note how managing time and space, and distance are the same.

Search ahead 20 to 30 seconds as you drive for information that can help you select a safe path of travel. Twenty to 30 seconds equals about 1½ to 2 blocks at 25 to 30 mph in the city, and about ½ mile at 50 to 65 mph on the highway.

Identify objects or conditions within 12 to 15 seconds ahead that could increase the level of risk. Objects or conditions 12 to 15 seconds ahead are at a distance equal to about 1 city block or ¼ mile when you're on the highway.

Keep a minimum 3-second following distance between your vehicle and the vehicle ahead. You need at least 3 seconds to steer evasively. To figure the distance between your vehicle and the vehicle ahead, notice when the rear of the vehicle ahead passes a fixed point, such as a sign or tree. Count "one-second-one, two-seconds-two, three-seconds-three." If the front of your vehicle passes the point before you finish counting "three-seconds-three," you're following too closely.

How Can You Manage Space?

Managing space when you drive means managing the distance between your vehicle and the vehicles ahead, behind, and to the sides. Your goal is to allow yourself enough space to maneuver safely at all times. By managing space wisely, you also increase your ability to see and be seen.

Consider Time, Distance, and Speed

In learning to manage time, you have already learned a great deal about managing space. For example, by maintaining a minimum following distance of 3 seconds, you are managing both time *and* space.

The close link between managing time and space is also clear in terms of your vehicle's speed. The faster you're traveling, the more time *and* distance you need to brake to a stop.

In fact, if you double your speed, you need *four* times the distance to brake to a stop. Moving at 30 mph on a dry road after you apply the brakes, for instance, you need about 37.5 feet to stop. At 60 mph, however, you need at least 150 feet (4 × 37.5). In mathematical terms, the braking distance increase (in feet) equals the square of the increase in speed.

Assess and Adjust the Space Around Your Vehicle

Having ample space around your vehicle gives you time to observe, think, decide, and act or react. By adjusting your vehicle's position to maintain a safe margin of space, you can generally avoid the need to brake, accelerate, or swerve suddenly. A cushion of space also gives you room to steer in case of emergency.

Here are some guidelines for managing space.

Adjust your following distance as needed. Leave at least 3 seconds distance between your vehicle and the one ahead. Leave 4 to 5 seconds at speeds of 40 mph or more plus another 5 to 6 seconds if the road is slippery or you're behind a vehicle that blocks your view.

Try to keep a 3-second distance behind your vehicle. Distance behind your vehicle is the hardest to maintain because other vehicles may **tailgate,** or follow too closely. If you are being tailgated, *increase*—do *not* decrease—the space between you and the vehicle ahead to make up for the lack of space behind you. If possible, let the tailgater pass.

Whenever possible, try to keep as much as 8 feet on either side of you. At the very least, keep a vehicle's width to one side of you. The more room you have around your vehicle, the more space you have to react to threatening situations.

If there is insufficient space ahead, behind, or to the side of your vehicle, take prompt action to increase the space. For example, if you're boxed in by vehicles, adjust your speed to move away from the pack.

Lesson 1 Review

1. In what ways can you manage visibility while driving?
2. How can you manage time while driving?
3. What actions can you take to manage space when you drive?

WHAT WOULD YOU DO?

What are some ways that you can manage visibility, time, and space before driving this vehicle? What steps will you take while driving?

Visibility, Time, and Space on Urban Streets

The hustle and bustle of city streets can make driving a real challenge, especially for new drivers. By understanding the factors that affect driving in the city and by managing visibility, time, and space effectively, you can meet the demands of urban driving.

What Special Factors Affect City Driving?

Cities can be hectic places. Pedestrians fill the sidewalks and cross the street at any time, while cars, buses, and other vehicles crowd the streets. Double-parked vehicles often block visibility, and potholes may interrupt traffic flow.

Traffic Density

In city traffic, you will generally be driving among many more vehicles than you will in suburban or highway driving. The traffic is dense and often slow moving, and threatening situations can occur more frequently. Maintaining a margin of space around your vehicle can be difficult.

Number of Pedestrians

At times, large cities seem to overflow with people: workers, shoppers, children, and others. Expect to encounter pedestrians anywhere and everywhere. Never assume that pedestrians will see you or that they will obey traffic rules or signals.

Intersections

Cities are filled with intersections. In the city, intersections are frequently jammed with both vehicles and pedestrians moving in all directions. When approaching or crossing any intersection, you need to use maximum care.

◆ *City streets, crowded with vehicles and pedestrians, demand an extra degree of driver alertness.*

Slow or Irregular Traffic Flow

On congested city streets, vehicles often move in packs or lines. The movement may be in a steady stream or with frequent starts and stops.

Vehicles stopping to park or parked vehicles pulling away from the curb may interrupt the flow of traffic. Roadwork or construction can also slow traffic. While you may move more slowly than you'd like to when you drive in a city, it is usually dangerous to try to move any faster.

◆ *Congested city streets severely limit your ability to search ahead and manage time and space.*

Lower Speed Limits

City speed limits are lower than suburban or highway speed limits. In addition, they may change in different parts of a city.

Sight Obstructions

Several factors tend to limit visibility in city driving. Double-parked vehicles as well as parked vehicles can partially block your view, as can buses, trucks, and vans.

Potholes and Other Road Defects

In cities with heavy traffic, streets take a lot of wear and tear. Potholes and rough surfaces may develop. They slow traffic and pose a potential danger to drivers, pedestrians, and cyclists.

How Can You Manage Visibility, Time, and Space in City Driving?

By knowing the special factors to be alert for when driving in the city, you can manage visibility, time, and space to minimize risk.

Guidelines for Managing Visibility in the City

Here is how you can manage visibility on urban streets.
- Search 1 to 2 blocks, or 20 to 30 seconds, ahead and from one side of the street to the other. Do not focus on any one object in your path.
- Keep your low-beam headlights on at all times.
- Check your rearview and sideview mirrors to monitor traffic every time you approach an intersection or when you intend to slow or stop.
- Signal your intention to turn or pull over well ahead of time.

Energy Tips

Avoid "jackrabbit" starts when traffic signals first turn green. Search the intersection before proceeding on a fresh green light. Accelerating gradually saves fuel—and is safer.

◆ *In the city, search carefully for pedestrians, cyclists, and other cars at intersections. Before entering an intersection, make sure nothing is blocking your intended path of travel.*

- Keep alert to the movement of vehicles four or five vehicles ahead of you so that you can anticipate when other drivers are braking or planning to turn. However, always be prepared for unexpected stops or turns.
- Be alert for pedestrians darting out from between parked vehicles or crossing streets illegally.
- Be on the lookout for warning signs and signals. Also be alert for the sirens and flashing lights of police vehicles, ambulances, fire engines, and other emergency vehicles.
- Be aware of entrances and exits for apartment buildings, parking lots, and the like. Often they are not visible until the last moment.

Guidelines for Managing Time in the City

Follow these guidelines for managing time while driving in the city.

- Drive at a moderate speed. Use the SIPDE process to help you identify objects or conditions that could increase the level of risk, particularly as you approach intersections.
- Dense traffic makes some drivers tense and impatient—and sometimes reckless. Always be ready to stop or steer to avoid a collision.
- Often braking is the only response you can make in city traffic to avoid a collision. When you spot a possible threatening condition but are not sure if you'll have to stop, take your

---

TIPS

FOR NEW DRIVERS

Problem Behavior

When you search the roadway, observe the behavior of other drivers for clues to potential problems. Watch for drivers:

- taking their eyes off the road while talking with others.
- using cellular phones.
- smoking, eating, reading, or looking at a map.
- with unusual postures at the wheel, which may indicate intoxication.
- signaling late or not at all.
- moving too slowly or too rapidly or following too closely (tailgating).
- drifting from side to side in their lane.
- whose view may be obstructed by packages, other objects, or tall passengers.
- with out-of-state license plates, who may be searching for an address or unaccustomed to driving in your area.

---

foot off the accelerator and place it just over the brake pedal without pushing down. By "covering the brake" in this manner, you reduce reaction time if you need to slow or stop.

- To give drivers and pedestrians maximum time to see and react to you, drive with your low-beam headlights on, and always signal your intentions well in advance.

- Give yourself extra time for driving in city traffic, particularly during rush hours and other busy periods. Know what route you'll be traveling, and listen to the radio for traffic information before setting out.

Guidelines for Managing Space in the City

Use these guidelines to manage space in city traffic.

- Do not follow other vehicles too closely, even in bumper-to-bumper traffic. Never follow less than 2 seconds behind.

- When stopping behind a vehicle, stop well back—20 to 30 feet—and watch the rearview mirror until two or three vehicles have stopped behind you. Then you can move up slightly. Always leave extra space in front in case the vehicle ahead stops suddenly or you have to steer out of your lane to avoid being struck from the rear. Wait for the vehicle ahead to move before you start moving forward.

- Keep as wide a margin of space as possible between your vehicle and parked vehicles. Watch for people leaving parked vehicles and for vehicles pulling out suddenly.

- Avoid driving in the blind spot of other vehicles on multiple-lane streets. Either move ahead of the other vehicles or drop back.

- Keep as much space as you can between your vehicle and vehicles in the oncoming lanes.

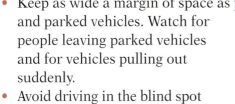

Lesson 2 Review

1. What are some special factors that affect city driving?
2. What actions can you take to manage visibility, time, and space when you are driving in the city?

SAFETY TIPS

Rear-end crashes are more common than any other kind. Leave enough following distance. Too often drivers follow more closely than they should and are unable to stop in time. The increased chance of being struck in the rear while driving in the city makes it all the more important to monitor your mirrors effectively.

WHAT WOULD YOU DO?

You are driving through the city during rush hour. What steps will you take to manage visibility, time, and space?

OBJECTIVES
1. Describe the special factors that affect driving on rural roads.
2. List ways to manage visibility, time, and space when driving on rural roads.

Visibility, Time, and Space on Rural Roads

Country driving often seems easier than city driving. Traffic is generally lighter, and there are fewer pedestrians and not as many distractions. However, driving in rural areas poses a special challenge. A majority of occupant fatalities occur on country roads.

What Special Factors Affect Driving on Rural Roads?

When driving on rural roads, be especially alert for off-road conditions that limit your ability to see or maneuver.

Road Conditions

Many rural roads are two-lane, two-way roadways. Curves may be sharper and hills may be steeper than on many city streets. Roads may have concrete, asphalt, gravel, or dirt surfaces, with or without a shoulder. Many rural roads may even have drainage ditches close to both sides. At night, most rural roads are poorly lit—or not lit at all. Drivers must exercise special care, for example, when passing other vehicles and when driving on loose, low-traction road surfaces.

◆ *Snow on the road and a ditch alongside make maneuvering on this roadway difficult.*

Higher Speed, Fewer Controls

Sound judgment is more important than ever when driving in rural areas. Country roads typically have higher speed limits than city streets. You'll encounter fewer traffic lights and stop signs. At railroad crossings, there may be no signs, signals, or gates. Drivers must remain alert for traffic crossing the roadway.

Slow-Moving Vehicles

Tractors and other farm vehicles travel at much slower speeds than other vehicles. As a result, drivers on rural roads often have to pass such slow-moving vehicles. Some farm vehicles, such as harvesters, are very wide, limiting the visibility of following drivers and making passing extremely difficult, if not impossible.

Sight Obstructions

Trees, bushes, and tall crops growing close by the road all limit visibility for drivers on country roads. These obstructions can make driving even more challenging on narrow, winding, or sharply curving roads.

Hills, too, can reduce visibility. As you near the top of a hill, your view of the road ahead will be limited. The steeper the grade, the less you can see.

Animals and Objects on the Road

Deer, raccoons, cows, and other animals, both wild and domestic, frequently cross rural roads. To learn more about the very real dangers posed by animals on the roadway, see Chapter 13. Other possible threatening conditions on rural roads include fallen rocks, tree branches, and wet leaves.

◆ *You may encounter slow-moving vehicles more frequently in rural areas.*

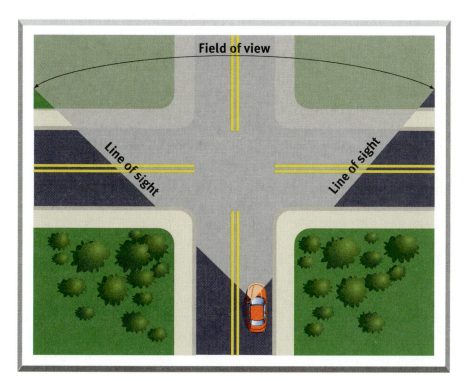

◆ *Trees close to the road limit visibility. To have a wider field of view, the driver must move closer to the intersection.*

SAFETY TIPS

Search the roadway and off-road area ahead. If you see a rider on horseback, reduce your speed and pass slowly, giving horse and rider as much leeway as possible. Never sound your horn to warn of your approach.

◆ *When driving on low-traction roadways, lower your speed to manage risk.*

How Can You Manage Visibility, Time, and Space in Rural Driving?

Because of less traffic, many drivers are less attentive when driving on rural roads than on city streets. You must remain fully attentive at all times. Just as you would while driving on city streets, use the SIPDE process, and be ready to deal with the unexpected. More than 50 percent of occupant fatalities on rural roads and highways involve only one vehicle. The driver drifts or steers off the road and loses control.

Guidelines for Managing Visibility in Rural Areas

Here are some guidelines to help you manage visibility on country roads.

- During the day, always drive with low-beam headlights on. Use high beams at night on very dark roads when there are no other vehicles around.
- Search ahead 20 to 30 seconds, looking for vehicles, pedestrians, animals, and objects on or near the roadway. If road or weather conditions limit your ability to see, reduce your speed.
- Identify objects or conditions within 12 to 15 seconds ahead that may pose a danger. If you cannot see that far, slow down until your visual path clears.
- Drive at a speed that will let you respond safely to threatening conditions that may be just over a hill or around a curve.
- Follow at least 200 feet behind large vehicles so that they do not block your view of potential dangers.
- Always signal your intention to turn, to pull over, to pass, and to get back into your lane.

Guidelines for Managing Time in Rural Areas

Use these guidelines to help you manage time on rural roads.

- Watch for slow-moving vehicles. Adjust your speed as needed.
- Reduce your speed as you approach intersections, particularly those without traffic control devices. Be prepared to slow down further or even stop.

SAFETY TIPS

Do not underestimate the risks of rural driving. In the city, there is a greater danger of colliding with another vehicle. In the country, there is a greater chance of your vehicle going out of control and colliding with a fixed object or overturning. Drive cautiously at all times. Use low-beam headlights during daylight hours to make it easier for other vehicles to see you when trees and brush block visibility.

- Allow extra time for driving on unfamiliar roads. Plan your route in advance.
- Reduce your speed when driving on gravel, dirt, or other low-traction road surfaces.
- When approaching or passing an animal on or near the road, drive slowly in case the animal bolts across your path.

Guidelines for Managing Space in Rural Areas

Follow these guidelines for managing space on rural roads.

- Adjust following distance for speed, traffic, roadway, and off-road conditions that affect your ability to see. Identify an escape path to which you can steer.
- If a vehicle is tailgating you, give it as much space as possible to pass and pull in front of you. If there is a vehicle ahead of you, increase your following distance.
- On two-lane roads, keep as much space as possible between your vehicle and oncoming traffic.
- Never pass on curves or hills when you do not have a clear path ahead in which to complete the pass.
- As you search the road for vehicles, animals, or objects that could threaten your safety, weigh the consequences of acting to avoid the threat against the danger of collision.

Lesson 3 Review

1. What are some special factors that affect rural driving?
2. What actions can you take to manage visibility, time, and space when you drive on rural roads?

WHAT WOULD YOU DO?

You are traveling on a two-way hilly road that has many sharp curves. What special factors affect visibility? What are some ways to manage time and space?

Visibility, Time, and Space on Multiple-Lane Highways

Traveling on multiple-lane highways and expressways is usually faster than traveling on local roads. Driving at higher speeds is demanding, however. You need to concentrate fully in order to manage visibility, time, and space.

This section focuses on expressways and other multiple-lane and limited-access highways, including freeways, interstate highways, parkways, and turnpikes and other toll roads. **Limited-access** or controlled-access **highways** allow vehicles to enter and exit only at specific places.

What Special Factors Affect Driving on Multiple-Lane Highways?

Driving on an expressway or other high-speed roadway is quite different from driving on urban streets or rural roads. There are usually two or more lanes of traffic moving in the same direction. Cars, trucks, buses and other vehicles pass you at high speeds. The scenery seems to whiz by—along with route markers and other road signs containing all sorts of information.

Higher Speed Limits

Expressway speed limits are always higher than those on city streets and most rural roads. Higher speeds mean that drivers must manage time and space with particular care when following and passing vehicles, changing lanes, and reducing speed. High-speed collisions result in more damage and serious injuries than those occurring at lower speeds.

◆ *Traveling on multiple-lane, high-speed highways poses special challenges for the driver.*

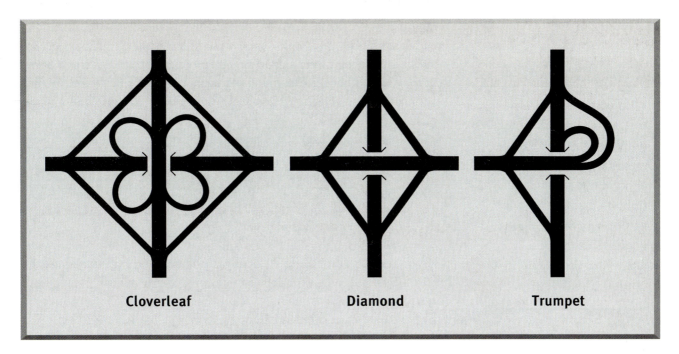

| Cloverleaf | Diamond | Trumpet |

Limited Entrances and Exits

Entrance and exit ramps on limited-access highways may be many miles apart. Entrances and exits are usually made from the extreme right-hand lane. However, there are entrance and exit ramps located in the extreme left-hand lane.

Signs posted along the highway tell drivers when they are approaching an exit or interchange. **Interchanges** are points where you can enter or leave the expressway or connect with a highway going in another direction.

Interchanges are made up of through lanes, ramps, and speed-change lanes. Ramps are short, one-way roads connecting two highways. Speed limits on ramps typically range from 25 to 45 mph. Speed-change lanes are short lanes next to the main travel lanes of a highway. A deceleration lane allows vehicles to reduce speed to exit; an acceleration lane lets vehicles increase speed to merge with traffic.

Frequent Passing

Passing other vehicles and having other vehicles pass you is an integral part of driving on multiple-lane highways. Depending on the roadway and on your lane position and speed, you may find yourself being passed on your left, on your right, or on both sides simultaneously.

Trucks and Other Large Vehicles

Trucks, tractor-trailers, buses, and other large vehicles add additional challenges to driving on multiple-lane highways because they hamper

◆ *Three common interchange designs are the cloverleaf, the diamond, and the trumpet.*

SAFETY TIPS

Sometimes the same lane is used for both entering and exiting a highway. It may be less risky to let the vehicle getting on the highway go first, but be prepared to yield whether you are the one who is exiting or the one who is entering.

visibility. Large vehicles can also buffet smaller vehicles with wind gusts as they pass.

Because of their larger size, you need more time to pass a truck or bus than to pass another vehicle. If you're traveling at 60 mph, it takes you 5 to 7 seconds longer to pass a tractor-trailer traveling at 50 mph than it would to pass a car.

How Can You Manage Visibility, Time, and Space on Multiple-Lane Highways?

Safe and responsible driving on multiple-lane highways and expressways requires careful decision making on the part of every driver. You should focus on managing visibility, time, and space to reduce the risk of a collision or other mishap.

Guidelines for Managing Visibility on Highways

Here are some guidelines for managing visibility on multiple-lane and limited-access highways.

- Search 20 to 30 seconds ahead for vehicles, objects, animals, and even pedestrians on or near the roadway.
- Be alert for the dangers of entrances and exits. Drivers may merge too slowly or without looking or cut across lanes at the last moment.
- Check your rearview and sideview mirrors frequently to monitor the position of traffic around you, especially before changing lanes or exiting a highway.
- Always signal your intention to change lanes, merge, or exit well in advance of the move.
- Drive with your low beams on at all times. Use your high beams on very dark highways, but only when there are no other vehicles around.

◆ *Always signal while still in the acceleration lane and before merging into highway traffic.*

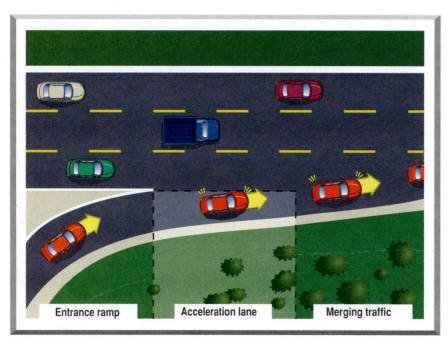

Entrance ramp   Acceleration lane   Merging traffic

- Check the movement of vehicles several vehicles ahead to know when other drivers are slowing down or planning to pass or change lanes.
- Position your vehicle so that large vehicles do not block your view of the roadway ahead or to the sides.
- Look for road signs to learn what the speed limit is and to know when your exit is approaching and which side it is on.

Guidelines for Managing Time on Highways

Use these guidelines to help you manage time on highways.
- Use the SIPDE process to help you identify threatening conditions within 12 to 15 seconds ahead.
- Always adjust your speed and following distance so that you have at least 4 to 5 seconds to stop or steer evasively in case of an emergency.
- When you merge into traffic, try to enter the stream of vehicles at the speed they are traveling.
- When exiting an expressway, move over toward the exit lane as soon as you can. Wait until you're actually in the exit lane before reducing your speed.
- Adjust your speed to avoid traveling in packs of vehicles.
- Watch for vehicles that may have trouble keeping up with the speed of traffic. Adjust your speed or position in advance.
- Plan your route ahead of time. Know which highways you'll be traveling on and where to exit.
- Avoid driving on congested highways during peak traffic periods or in bad weather. Listen to the radio for roadway information before starting out. Allow extra time if you must drive.

Guidelines for Managing Space on Highways

Follow these guidelines to manage space on multiple-lane and limited-access roadways.
- Adjust your vehicle's position for the speed that you and other drivers are traveling and for road and weather conditions. Allow yourself a margin of space to accelerate, brake, and steer.
- Allow yourself a gap of at least 4 seconds when merging with other traffic, changing lanes, or entering an expressway from an entrance lane.
- To change lanes, turn the steering wheel slightly. Oversteering, or steering too sharply into another lane, can lead to loss of control at higher speeds.
- If you must cross several lanes, move over one lane at a time, signaling each time.

SAFETY TIPS

There may be more lanes at toll plazas than on the highway itself. Choose a lane with a green signal well in advance and stay in that lane. Be especially alert to drivers ahead of you who switch lanes suddenly.

SAFETY TIPS

At highway speeds of 40 to 65 mph, you'll need at least 4 to 5 seconds to react to a threatening situation and brake your vehicle to a stop. Therefore, you must be able to see ahead at all times an absolute minimum of 4 to 5 seconds. Furthermore, if a vehicle is tailgating you or a large vehicle is behind you, you should identify an escape path for evasive steering. Too often such vehicles cannot stop in time to avoid rear-ending the smaller vehicle in front of them.

Bill Wen
Manager, Driver Training and Professional Development, AAA

Ask yourself three questions while driving: (1) What can I do to reduce the probability of a dangerous event? (2) How can I increase my opportunity to manage a dangerous event should one occur? (3) If a collision is unavoidable, how can I reduce its consequences?

Regardless of the driving environment, the first objective is to prevent a high-risk situation from developing by improving your visibility to others and by giving yourself enough time and space.

- Make room for vehicles entering expressways. If there are no vehicles in the lane next to you, move over a lane as you approach an entrance ramp.
- If a vehicle is tailgating you, change lanes—when it is safe—to let the vehicle pass. In the meantime, increase your following distance behind vehicles ahead.

- Never cut in too soon in front of a vehicle you are passing.
- When passing a large truck or other wide vehicle, keep in mind that you have less space to the side between your vehicle and the large vehicle than you do when passing a car.
- Be alert for places where highways may narrow—when approaching tunnels or bridges, for example. Reduce your speed and proceed cautiously.
- When crossing bridges or driving in hills and mountains, be alert for strong crosswinds that can buffet your vehicle.

WHAT WOULD YOU DO?

You are in the left lane of a crowded multiple-lane highway. Suddenly you realize you are approaching your exit, which is all the way over on the right. How will you handle this?

Lesson 4 Review

1. What factors affect driving on multiple-lane and limited-access highways?
2. What actions can a driver take to manage visibility, time, and space on an expressway?

Names and Meanings of Roadways

A route in a rural area is generally described as a road. A roadway within an urban area is usually called a street. Streets are usually paved and have more traffic, while rural routes are usually less traveled.

The roadways that connect cities and towns have many names, which vary somewhat in meaning. A highway is a main public roadway, especially one that runs between cities. An expressway is a high-speed divided highway with limited access that has more than one lane running in each direction. A freeway, sometimes called a superhighway, is generally a synonym for expressway, but usually refers to a highway that has no tolls.

A turnpike is a road, usually an expressway, that requires drivers to pay a toll. The word "turnpike" comes from early days when travelers on a road stopped at gates made of logs or pikes. When a toll was paid, the pike was opened or turned, allowing the travelers to pass through. A toll road may also be called a tollway.

A beltway is a highway that goes around an urban area. A parkway is a wide, landscaped highway that may be limited to non-commercial vehicles. Except for occasional rest stops, there may be few or no commercial establishments such as stores or office buildings on a parkway.

What Do You Think Now?

What do names and meanings of roadways tell you about the road systems in the United States?

KEY POINTS

Lesson One

1. In addition to making advance preparations, you can manage visibility by keeping your low beams on (even in daylight), signaling intentions well in advance, and avoiding driving in another driver's blind spots.
2. You can manage time by being aware of the link among time, speed, and distance and by using the SIPDE process.
3. You can manage space by allowing enough distance between your vehicle and other vehicles to the front, rear, and sides.

Lesson Two

1. Special factors that affect city driving are traffic density, number of pedestrians, number of intersections, slow or irregular traffic flow, lower speed limits, sight obstructions, and potholes and other road defects.
2. Some ways to manage visibility, time, and space on city streets are to search 1 to 2 blocks ahead, use your mirrors to monitor traffic, signal early, be ready for pedestrians and hidden exits, always be prepared to steer or stop, use the SIPDE process, and keep a margin of space around your vehicle.

Lesson Three

1. Factors that affect driving on rural roads are road conditions, higher speeds, fewer traffic controls, slow-moving vehicles, sight obstructions, and animals and objects on the road.
2. Among the ways to manage visibility, time, and space on rural roads are to identify dangerous objects 12 to 15 seconds ahead, drive slowly if an animal is nearby, avoid passing if your view is not clear, and use the SIPDE process.

Lesson Four

1. Special factors that affect visibility, time, and space on multiple-lane and limited-access highways are higher speed limits, limited entrances and exits, frequent passing, and the presence of trucks and other large vehicles.
2. Some ways to manage visibility, time, and space on multiple-lane and limited-access highways are to use the SIPDE process, signal when changing lanes, position your vehicle so that you can see and be seen, adjust your speed to avoid traveling in packs, and plan your route ahead of time.

PROJECTS

1. Use a road map to plan a trip from one city to another. List the highways you would travel on, and the numbers of the exits you would use. Take the trip as a driver or passenger, and compare the accuracy of your plan to what you actually experience on the trip.
2. Compare city driving and driving on a rural road. Observe differences in road surfaces, traffic signs and signals, density of traffic, and visibility.

interNET CONNECTION

Use the Web to learn more about stopping distances at different speeds. Investigate how time is related to these total stopping distances.
www.glencoe.com/sec/driver.ed

CHAPTER TEST

Write the letter of the answer that best completes each sentence.

1. A limited-access highway
   a. allows vehicles to enter or exit only at certain places.
   b. does not permit trucks or buses.
   c. has no shoulders.

2. When you spot a threatening traffic condition in city traffic, you should
   a. shut your windows.
   b. cover the brake.
   c. use the total stopping method.

3. One way to manage time and space is to
   a. drive parallel to other vehicles.
   b. ride a bicycle.
   c. maintain a margin of space around your vehicle.

4. Speed limits on country roads are typically
   a. lower than those on urban roads.
   b. higher than those on urban roads.
   c. between 15 and 30 miles per hour.

5. Managing space while you drive means
   a. managing the distance between your vehicle and vehicles around you.
   b. reaching your destination safely.
   c. successfully passing other vehicles on multiple-lane highways.

6. As you near the top of a hill,
   a. your view of the road ahead is limited.
   b. your view of the road behind you is limited.
   c. you should accelerate.

7. When driving on a dirt road, you should
   a. pull over to the right side.
   b. increase your speed.
   c. reduce your speed.

8. The first step in managing visibility while driving is to
   a. stay away from large obstructions.
   b. turn on your low-beam headlights.
   c. look in your blind spots.

9. During urban driving, you should
   a. look at least 1 block ahead.
   b. look at least 5 blocks ahead.
   c. use your high-beam headlights.

10. On multiple-lane highways, passing other vehicles
    a. should be avoided.
    b. is an integral part of driving.
    c. is a method of staying alert.

Write the word or phrase that best completes each sentence.

distance   interchange   expressway
lead time   margin of space   rural road

11. The faster you travel, the more time and _____ you need to come to a stop.

12. Always keep a(n) _____ around your vehicle.

13. A(n) _____ may have drainage ditches alongside of it.

14. A freeway is one example of a(n) _____.

15. A(n) _____ is made up of through lanes, ramps, and speed-change lanes.

DRIVER'S LOG

In this chapter, you have learned about managing visibility, time, and space in different driving environments. Write two paragraphs in response to these questions:

In which driving environment do you think you will have the most difficulty managing visibility, time, and space? What steps will you take to overcome this difficulty?

CHAPTER 12

Light and Weather Conditions

Good drivers are prepared for any kind of light or weather conditions. It is important for you to understand how to manage visibility, time, and space in order to minimize the risk caused by poor light or inclement weather.

LESSON ONE
Driving Safely in Low Light and at Night

LESSON TWO
Visibility, Bright Light, and Glare

LESSON THREE
Minimizing Risk in Rain and Snow

LESSON FOUR
Other Hazardous Weather Conditions

OBJECTIVES

1. Describe how visibility is affected by low light conditions.
2. Explain how to drive safely in low light and at night.

KEY TERM

overdriving your headlights

Driving Safely in Low Light and at Night

Your ability to see is decreased at night and just before sunrise or after sunset. As visibility decreases, your risk of being in a collision increases. To lessen risk, you must understand how reduced light limits visibility and how to better manage the driving task in low light conditions.

How Do Low Light Conditions Affect Visibility?

Your ability to see and to be seen diminishes when the amount of available light is lessened.

Reduced sunlight during dusk and dawn hours makes it difficult to see the roadway and vehicles traveling on it. Other drivers as well as pedestrians have difficulty seeing your vehicle, particularly if you don't have your headlights on.

Night driving presents special challenges. At night, darkness limits your view of the road ahead and the surrounding area. Even with your headlights on, your ability to see ahead when turning or driving around a curve is severely reduced. In addition, the glare of other vehicles' headlights can be distracting—or blinding.

How Can You Drive Safely When the Amount of Light Is Low?

To drive safely in low light conditions, you must maximize visibility and manage time and space wisely.

When your view of the road is limited, slow down. Maximize your ability to see

TIPS | **FOR NEW DRIVERS**

More Suggestions for Dealing with Visibility Problems at Night

Slow down. Remember that your visibility is limited. Avoid looking directly into the headlights of oncoming vehicles. When necessary to maintain your bearings, glance down at the right edge of your traffic lane beyond oncoming vehicles.

To remind an approaching driver that his or her high beams are on, quickly switch your own headlights from low to high and back again.

If you can, adjust your rearview mirror for night driving to cut glare from the headlights of vehicles behind you.

If you must stop along the road, use your emergency flashers to enable other drivers to see you.

Watch for animals, joggers, bicyclists, and obstacles in the road.

Always remove sunglasses once the sun sets.

and maneuver. Drive with your headlights on whenever you drive, day and night. Your headlights and taillights help illuminate your vehicle, making it easier for others to see you in all kinds of light.

During Dusk and Dawn Hours

All states require that you use your headlights either from sunset to sunrise or between a half hour after sunset and a half hour before sunrise. Using your headlights makes it easier to see and be seen in the dim light of dusk and dawn. Do *not* use your parking lights. They are not designed to light the road ahead but to indicate your position when you are parked safely off the roadway.

At dawn or dusk, increase the distance between your vehicle and the one ahead, and use your turn signals well in advance.

At Night

Night driving requires extra concentration and a greater level of awareness. With darkness limiting visibility, it is wise to drive more slowly at night than you do during the day and to leave more distance between your vehicle and the vehicle ahead.

Use low beams and high beams correctly. On very dark roads with no other vehicles around, use your high beams to increase visibility. Be sure to switch back to low beams as soon as you spot the headlights or taillights of a vehicle ahead of you. The glare of your high beams can momentarily blind another driver.

Do not overdrive your headlights. At night, drive at a speed that will allow you to stop within the range of your lights—that is, within the distance you can see. Driving faster than that is called **overdriving your headlights** and makes you vulnerable to unseen hazards.

Use the 3- or 4-second rules you have learned to help you judge a safe following distance.

Look beyond your headlights. Get into the habit of looking for objects just beyond your headlight beams to see possible threatening conditions. Looking beyond your headlights is essential when making turns or rounding curves.

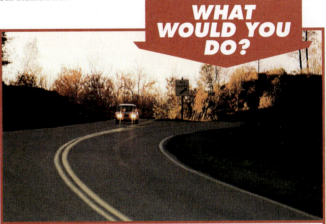

WHAT WOULD YOU DO?

What kinds of visibility problems do you face in this situation? How can you manage time and space to reduce the risk of collision?

Lesson **1** Review

1. Describe how visibility is affected by low light conditions.
2. What can you do to minimize risk when driving at night?

OBJECTIVES
1. Describe the conditions that create glare from the sun.
2. Explain how you can drive safely in the glare of the sun.

Visibility, Bright Light, and Glare

Think of a bright summer morning. The sky is cloudless and everything is bathed in sunlight. That's a pretty picture for a day at the beach, but it's not always so pretty when you're behind the wheel of a vehicle. The glow of that sunlight can turn to dangerous glare.

What Conditions Create Glare from the Sun?

Sunlight increases visibility, but the glare caused when the sun hits your windshield can act in the opposite way—it can reduce your ability to see. The sun's glare is most dangerous at certain times.

In the morning or late afternoon, for example, when the sun is low on the horizon, glare can make it hard to see the road ahead. Glare can also reduce your ability to see the brake lights of other vehicles, especially if you're driving toward the sun and its rays shine directly in your eyes.

◆ *Glare decreases visibility and causes you to become more easily fatigued.*

How Can You Drive Safely in the Glare of the Sun?

As in all driving situations, advance preparation can help you minimize the risk of glare. As part of your predriving check, you should always make sure that your vehicle's windshield is clean. As part of your overall vehicle maintenance, you should replace the windshield if it is badly scratched or pitted. Glare is worse through a dirty or scratched windshield.

Have sunglasses handy. As soon as you begin to squint, slip them on to shield your eyes. Reduce speed, increase your following distance, and adjust your sun visor to block out the sun. However, be careful that the visor does not hinder your view of overhead signs and signals.

Use the SIPDE process to help you manage risk in glare situations. Give yourself an extra margin of safety by leaving more distance between your vehicle and other vehicles. Check carefully for pedestrians—remember, they are having trouble seeing too. Even if you have your sunglasses on and can see road signs and signals, keep in mind that others on the roadway may not be able to see as clearly. Always be alert for the sudden, careless, or unsafe actions of other drivers and pedestrians.

◆ *The reflection of sunlight off snow and ice causes wide areas of glare.*

Keep in mind that if you are having trouble seeing, so are the drivers around you. The sun shining on the back of your vehicle may make it very difficult for the driver behind you to see your brake lights or directional signals. For this reason, it's wise to tap the brake pedal to flash your taillights, to use your turn signals well in advance, *and* to use hand or arm signals as well to communicate your intentions.

Keep in mind, too, that when the sun is behind you, oncoming drivers have the sun's glare in *their* eyes and may have trouble seeing you. Drive with your low-beam headlights on to make your vehicle more visible, and signal well in advance your intention to turn or change lanes.

Lesson 2 Review

1. Describe the circumstances in which the sun's light can create dangerous glare.
2. What steps would you take to minimize overall risk in a glare situation?

WHAT WOULD YOU DO?

The sun is shining behind you. What can you do to minimize risk for both yourself and the drivers behind and ahead of you?

OBJECTIVES

1. Explain how to manage visibility, time, and space in rain and snow.
2. Explain how to minimize risk in snow and rain.

KEY TERM

hydroplaning

Minimizing Risk in Rain and Snow

It might be pleasant if you could just stay indoors when it is raining or snowing outside. However, if you have to drive somewhere in rainy or snowy weather, you must understand and manage the risk that driving in such weather presents.

TIPS FOR NEW DRIVERS

Stuck in the Snow?

If you get stuck in snow, you may be able to free your vehicle by "rocking" it. Follow the steps below.

1. Keep your front wheels pointed straight ahead, if possible. The vehicle will move more easily in a straight line.
2. Shift back and forth between Drive (or First gear) and Reverse. Accelerate forward slowly and steadily. When the vehicle will move forward no farther, press firmly on the brake to stop and hold the vehicle while you quickly shift to Reverse.
3. Release the brake and accelerate with gentle pressure as far back as the vehicle will go until the wheels start to spin. Step on the brake again and hold it while shifting to Drive or First gear.
4. Repeat as necessary. Do *not* spin your wheels: You'll only dig yourself in more deeply.

Repeat these shifts as quickly and smoothly as possible, but be sure to use the brake to hold the vehicle at a stop while shifting gears. Each forward-and-backward movement should take the vehicle a little farther in one direction or the other.

When rocking a vehicle, proceed cautiously. If the tires do suddenly grip, the vehicle may lurch forward, backward, or sideways. Warn bystanders to keep their distance, and take care not to strike nearby vehicles or objects.

How Can You Manage Visibility, Time, and Space in Rain and Snow?

Rain and snow decrease your ability to see ahead, to the sides, and to the rear. Decreased visibility, in turn, makes it more difficult than usual for you to judge distances and to manage time and space well. Bad weather conditions also make it much harder for other drivers and pedestrians to see your vehicle.

Heavy rain or snow can limit your view so much that you can't see very far ahead or even the edges of the roadway. Snow and sleet collecting on your windshield can produce blind areas that your windshield wipers can't reach. Snowy or rainy weather can also make the roadway slick, reducing the ability of your tires to grip the road and increasing your risk of collision. Here are some steps you can take to control the level of risk.

Prepare in advance. Start by cleaning your vehicle's windows and lights. Check the tread and pressure of your tires. Check the headlights, windshield wipers, defroster, and other equipment to make sure they are in good working condition.

Allow an extra margin of safety. Drive more slowly and leave extra space between your vehicle and other vehicles.

On a wet pavement, drive in the tracks of the vehicle ahead of you. Those tracks are drier than the surrounding surface and offer better traction.

Give other drivers plenty of advance notice. When you intend to slow down or turn, communicate your intentions early so that other drivers have time to react accordingly.

Be alert. Be on the watch for pedestrians dashing for shelter, or with umbrellas restricting their view of traffic.

Keep your low-beam headlights on. Increase the distance you can see, and make your car more visible to other drivers and pedestrians.

Ease your way into turns and curves. Avoid sudden acceleration, starts, or stops.

If rain becomes so heavy that even your windshield wipers' highest speed cannot keep up with the downpour, signal, then pull well off the road in a protected area and wait for the storm to lessen in intensity. Remember to switch on your emergency flashers so that other drivers can see your vehicle.

You may also need to pull over if, in snow or sleet, your windshield wipers become crusted with ice or if accumulating snow or sleet creates blind areas on your windshield. Use a scraper and brush to remove all of the buildup, and run your defroster before you resume driving.

How Can You Minimize Risk in Snow and Rain?

If you've ever gone sledding, skiing, or ice-skating, you know just how slippery a snow- or ice-covered surface can be. Imagine trying to maneuver a heavy, fast-moving vehicle on such a surface. One way to reduce the level of risk is to postpone driving until the weather clears. Whenever possible, wait until the roads are plowed and sanded or salted before venturing out on them.

Sometimes you cannot postpone a trip. If you do have to drive under snowy or icy conditions, be aware that there is a great danger of skidding. Drive slowly and extremely cautiously. Allow yourself an extra large margin of safety. When you do want to slow down, stop, or turn, maneuver the vehicle gently and gradually.

Keep on hand cold-weather items such as a windshield scraper and brush, a shovel, jumper cables, emergency flares, and gloves.

Energy Tips

Even though snow tires may be necessary during winter months, they reduce fuel economy. Remove them as soon as winter is over.

SAFETY TIPS

If you are approaching a large vehicle on a slush-covered roadway, turn on your windshield washers and wipers about 2 to 3 seconds before you meet. This gets the glass wet and will help clean the glass quickly after you pass.

Anticipate and Prevent Skids

If you change speed or direction gradually and smoothly rather than abruptly, you will minimize the chance of skidding. In Chapter 14 you will learn what to do if your vehicle starts to skid.

Anticipate situations in which skids are likely, and take steps to maintain control of your vehicle. For example, when driving on a wet road when the temperature is near freezing, allow yourself extra time and space to brake and steer. If you're approaching a sharp curve or steep hill, slow down well in advance and keep a firm grip on the steering wheel. When you have to turn the wheel, do so slowly and only as much as necessary.

When you know that you'll have to stop for a stop sign or red signal light on an ice- or snow-packed roadway, shift to Neutral and press the brake pedal down gently. Shifting to Neutral helps you brake and prevent skidding by eliminating the thrust effect of the wheels.

Anticipate and Prevent Hydroplaning

During the first 10 to 15 minutes of a rainfall, the roads are at their slickest. This occurs because the rain's moisture mixes with surface dirt and oil to form a slippery film. This film greatly reduces the ability of your tires to grip the road.

Additionally, at speeds as low as 35 mph, the tires of a vehicle can begin to skim along the wet surface of the road, much like a water-skier zipping across the surface of a lake. The vehicle's tires may completely lose contact with the road and be moving on a thin film of water. This is called **hydroplaning.** Hydroplaning is very dangerous because it severely limits your ability to control your vehicle. To reduce the chance of hydroplaning, reduce speed by about one-third when driving on wet roadways. Be sure your tires have plenty of tread and are properly inflated.

WHAT WOULD YOU DO?

How would you get your vehicle out of the snowdrift?

Lesson 3 Review

1. What strategies can you use to manage visibility, time, and space in rainy or snowy weather?
2. What risks can you anticipate when driving in rain or snow? What steps can you take to minimize them?

Other Hazardous Weather Conditions

OBJECTIVES

1. Describe five hazardous weather conditions other than snow and rain.
2. Understand the risks involved in driving under each condition.

Fog, industrial smog, or a sudden dust storm or sandstorm can diminish the light of a bright, clear day. Strong gusts of wind can blow your vehicle off the road. You can minimize risk under these conditions.

How Can You Minimize Risk in Other Hazardous Weather Conditions?

Just as you must understand and learn how to manage risk when driving in rain and snow, you must also understand and learn how to manage risk posed by other weather hazards.

Fog or Smog

Dense fog poses hazards. Scattered patches of fog may suddenly occur, cutting your field of vision without warning. If humidity is too high, moisture can form on both inside and outside the windshield, further reducing visibility. Turn on the windshield wipers and defogger as necessary.

Low-beam headlights are essential when driving in fog. You may also want to switch on your emergency flashers to further increase the ability of other highway users to see you. Resist the temptation to put on your high beams. The small droplets of water in fog reflect light back into your eyes, making visibility worse with high beams than with low beams.

To better manage time and space when driving in fog, reduce speed, increase your following distance, and remain alert for sudden movements.

If fog is very dense, the wisest thing to do is to signal, pull off the road, and wait for conditions to improve. Do *not* stop on the road. Stop outside a guardrail if possible, and turn off all lights.

In some areas, industrial smoke and other kinds of air pollution create smog that decreases drivers' visibility as much as does fog. Methods described for driving in fog are equally useful for smog conditions.

Sand and Dust

In some parts of the country, sand and dust cause serious visibility problems. In desert areas, for example, these storms can cause a severe decrease in visibility that greatly increases the risk of a collision.

Gary Guzouskas
Administrator, New Hampshire Department of Education

As you drive you may encounter various conditions that affect your ability to see and operate your car safely. To reduce risk, use your headlights every time you drive and keep them clean and aligned. Be alert to changing environmental and roadway conditions. When buying a car, consider one whose design limits blind spots and whose color enhances its ability to be seen.

Whenever visibility becomes limited, adjust your speed and position to provide more space between your car and other highway users.

If you're caught in such a storm, signal, pull off the road, turn on your flashers, and wait for the storm to pass. If you must drive, use your low-beam headlights, and proceed slowly and very cautiously.

Wind

Depending on the size and weight of the vehicle you're driving, high winds can be a nuisance—or dangerous. Wind can buffet vehicles traveling on a highway like boats tossed in stormy seas. A strong enough gust of wind can actually push a lightweight vehicle right out of its lane!

Under windy conditions, reduce speed and grip the steering wheel firmly to maintain control of your vehicle. Leave extra space between your vehicle and nearby vehicles, especially those that are likely to be affected by the wind, such as vans, recreational vehicles, and vehicles pulling trailers.

Nature is not the only source of wind. When a bus, truck, or tractor-trailer speeds by you—in either direction—you'll feel a powerful blast as it passes. Always allow as much distance as possible to the side between your vehicle and a passing large vehicle. In this way, you can minimize the force of the resulting wind gust.

WHAT WOULD YOU DO?

Explain how you would manage risk in this situation.

Lesson 4 Review

1. What weather conditions other than snow and rain pose dangers for drivers?
2. What risks would you anticipate in these conditions?

Using a Triptik

A *Triptik* is a continuous series of strip maps in booklet form put out by AAA. A Triptik provides detailed routing from one place to another. All you have to do is flip the strips.

The front page of each strip map shows a section of a through, cross-country route and all necessary highway details (Map A). The centerfold contains an area map (Map B). It shows the area surrounding the major route so that you can deviate from the marked route if you choose. The back page ordinarily shows detailed maps of cities along the marked route (Map C).

Try It Yourself

1. On which map would you find the route highlighted for best travel through Baltimore? What route is this? What else does the map tell you about this route?

2. You are at the corner of Bentwood Avenue, heading west on Chase Street. Describe how you would get to the Baltimore Arena. Which map would you use?

3. Suppose you are north of Baltimore, traveling south on Route 83. You want to take Route 45 into the city. Which map would you use? How would you get to Route 45?

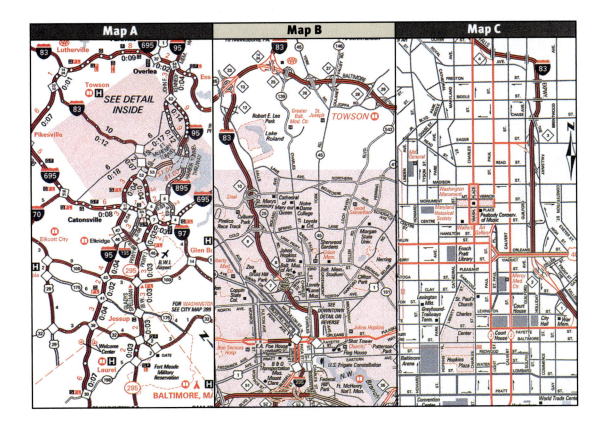

KEY POINTS

Lesson One

1. Reduced light during dusk and dawn and at night makes it harder for you to see and harder for others to see you. At night, your view of the roadway is limited, and you have to cope with glare from the lights of oncoming vehicles.
2. When driving in low light, reduce speed, increase following distance, signal turns well in advance, and use your low or high beams as appropriate.

Lesson Two

1. When the sun is low on the horizon, glare makes it hard to see the road and the brake lights of other vehicles.
2. To minimize the risk from sun glare, wear sunglasses and use your sun visor. Reduce speed and increase your following distance.

Lesson Three

1. Steps you can take to manage visibility, time, and space in rain or snow are to prepare in advance, leave an extra margin of safety, drive in the tracks of the vehicle ahead of you, signal other drivers early, keep your low-beam headlights on, ease your way into turns and curves, and slow down gradually for stops.
2. To minimize risk in rain or snow, maneuver the vehicle gently and gradually to prevent skids, allow extra time for braking and steering, and drive slowly to avoid hydroplaning.

Lesson Four

1. Five hazardous weather conditions other than snow and rain are smog, fog, sandstorms, dust storms, and wind.
2. Fog and smog decrease visibility. Keep on low-beam headlights, reduce speed, and increase following distance. If the fog or smog is very dense, pull off the road and wait for driving conditions to improve.

   In a sandstorm or dust storm, pull off the road. Use emergency flashers to alert others of your presence. If you must drive, use low-beam headlights and proceed with caution.

   In heavy winds, reduce speed and grip the steering wheel firmly; increase the distance between your vehicle and other vehicles. When being passed by a large vehicle, allow as much distance as possible to minimize the force of the resulting wind gust.

PROJECTS

1. Laws governing the use of headlights and parking lights vary from state to state. Find out what the rules are in your state. Take an informal survey of drivers you know. How many are aware of your state's regulations?
2. Stores sell products designed to help drivers cope with winter driving. Visit a store and evaluate several such products. Which would you buy? Which would you avoid? Why? Discuss your findings with the class.

inter NET CONNECTION

Look forward to becoming an experienced driver! Use the Internet to learn more about minimizing risk while driving in poor light and weather.
www.glencoe.com/sec/driver.ed

CHAPTER TEST

Write the letter of the answer that best completes each sentence.

1. You can lessen the risk of sun glare by
   a. opening your sunroof.
   b. using your high beams.
   c. wearing sunglasses.

2. You should keep your low-beam headlights on
   a. at all times, day or night.
   b. from dusk until dawn.
   c. only when you cannot see.

3. As visibility decreases,
   a. your risk of being involved in a collision decreases.
   b. your risk of being involved in a collision increases.
   c. the barometer rises.

4. Using your high beams in fog can
   a. increase visibility by as much as 250 feet.
   b. decrease your ability to see.
   c. warn other drivers of your approach.

5. A dirty or scratched windshield
   a. can cause you to skid in bad weather.
   b. can worsen the effects of glare.
   c. has no effect on glare.

6. During dusk and dawn hours, it is
   a. more difficult for other drivers and pedestrians to see you.
   b. easier to hydroplane.
   c. easier to see the roadway.

7. To brake safely on a snow-packed road,
   a. quickly press the brake all the way to the floor.
   b. shift to Neutral and press the brake gradually.
   c. shift to Overdrive and press the brake.

8. Dense fog can
   a. permanently affect the surface of your windshield.
   b. cause moisture to accumulate on the inside of your windshield.
   c. cause elevated roadways to freeze.

9. If you are caught in a sandstorm, you should
   a. use your windshield wipers.
   b. pull off the road and put on your emergency flashers.
   c. use your high beams.

10. A car traveling on a wet road at 35 mph can
    a. get increased gas mileage.
    b. lose contact with the road entirely.
    c. develop engine trouble.

Write the word or phrase that best completes each sentence.

| sun visor | temperature | smog |
| hydroplane | windshield | taillights |

11. When you _____, your car skims along the surface of water on the roadway.

12. Your headlights and _____ help illuminate your car.

13. One way to avoid glare is to use your _____.

14. Air pollution and smoke can create _____, which decreases drivers' visibility as much as fog does.

15. Glare caused when the sun hits your _____ can diminish visibility.

DRIVER'S LOG

In this chapter, you have learned how different light and weather conditions affect the driving task. Imagine that the temperature is between 25°F and 35°F and that it is beginning to rain. Write a weather advisory for drivers that gives hints on driving safely in these conditions and what conditions drivers might expect later in the day.

CHAPTER 13

Sharing the Roadway

The society of roadway users includes motorists, pedestrians, and cyclists. It is important to learn how to interact safely with others on the roadways. Good drivers do this by communicating with and anticipating the actions of others.

OBJECTIVES

1. Describe problems that pedestrians can pose.
2. Explain how to avoid collisions with pedestrians.
3. Describe pedestrian responsibilities.
4. Identify ways drivers can avoid collisions with animals.

KEY TERMS

jaywalking
ground viewing

Sharing the Roadway with Pedestrians and Animals

Drivers must be alert to all roadway users, not just other motorists. Other roadway users such as pedestrians and animals can present special problems. Anticipating these problems can help you protect yourself and others.

What Problems Do Pedestrians Pose to Drivers?

In 1997, some 5,300 pedestrians were killed and about 77,000 injured in the United States.

Intersections are the most common scene of collisions with pedestrians. Drivers concentrating on traffic, signs, and signals, as well as other roadway users, often fail to see pedestrians until it is too late.

Moreover, pedestrians may be distracted and cross streets without looking. They often run across streets either against a red light or just as a light is turning red.

◆ *Be on the lookout for pedestrians who cross the street illegally or who may need extra time to cross the street.*

Jaywalking, crossing without regard for traffic rules or signals, is a common pedestrian error, as is walking into the street from between parked vehicles.

When traffic is light, pedestrians sometimes cross at places other than intersections because they assume no vehicles are coming. In areas without sidewalks, pedestrians walk in the street or roadway, posing an additional risk to drivers.

Children

Children are at a disadvantage as pedestrians because they're smaller and less visible than adults to drivers. They are also less capable than adults

of judging when it's safe to cross a street and less likely to understand fully the consequences of their misjudgment.

In many urban and suburban areas, children use the street as their playground. When playing on sidewalks, children tend to forget about traffic and dart into the street, often between parked vehicles.

Children on skateboards, sleds, roller skates, or bicycles sometimes lose control and shoot over the edge of a sidewalk into the street.

Adults

Adults should know better than children, but they don't always act that way. Adults commonly jaywalk, particularly when rushing to get somewhere or to escape harsh weather. Adults often assume not only that drivers will see them but that the drivers will always grant them the right-of-way. Making these two assumptions can prove fatal.

◆ *Be on the alert for children on bicycles in suburban areas.*

How Can You Avoid Collisions with Pedestrians?

The SIPDE procedure—particularly the first step, Search—is essential to drivers in avoiding and preventing collisions with pedestrians.

Search the roadway and sides of the road continuously as you drive. Watch for children on or near the roadway. Also look for clues that children may be present. Playground and school-crossing signs, toys in a front yard, or a tricycle in a driveway all indicate that children may be nearby.

In residential areas, reduce speed and drive as far away from the curb or parked vehicles as you safely can. Use **ground viewing,** which means searching beneath parked vehicles, for any sign of movement.

Exercise special care at intersections, particularly when you're making a turn. Be alert for people crossing against the light, stepping off a curb prematurely, or rushing to beat a changing light. Watch, too, for pedestrians who need more time to cross a street than the "Walk" signal allows them. Although not exactly a pedestrian, someone riding a skateboard or on roller skates should deserve your attention, especially near intersections.

More than 120 people are killed each year in the United States in collisions with deer and other animals. An equal number are killed when drivers try to avoid striking an animal and instead crash into another vehicle or an object or cause their own vehicle to roll over.

Be alert for adults and children near bus stops, train stations, in school zones, near parks, and in shopping areas.

When backing up, never rely on your rearview mirror alone. Before backing, make certain there is no one behind or next to your vehicle. This is particularly important with regard to children, who may be too small for you to see them when you are behind the wheel.

Never assume a pedestrian can see your vehicle. A pedestrian who is preoccupied, or who has been drinking, may not notice your approach. You should always be ready to take evasive action. To warn a pedestrian that you are approaching, tap your horn. Blasting a horn loudly could frighten a pedestrian into doing something dangerous. You should always yield to pedestrians. They have the right-of-way, even if they are crossing the road illegally.

◆ *Because of their size, buses can block your view of pedestrians who are about to cross the street.*

What Responsibilities Do Pedestrians Have?

Like drivers, pedestrians, too, must pay attention to rules, signals, and signs. Pedestrians must learn to judge gaps in traffic and then cross streets only when and where it is safe—and legal—to do so.

- Never assume that a driver will see you and stop.
- Cross only at intersections.
- Cross only when the light is green or when a pedestrian signal shows a "walk" symbol.
- Do not step off the curb while waiting for the light to change.
- Pause before crossing to look and listen for approaching traffic.
- When walking on or near a roadway, walk facing traffic.
- When walking or jogging on or near a roadway, wear reflective clothing, especially when visibility is reduced. In addition, do not wear headphones.
- When walking with young children, always take them by the hand when crossing streets.

Most pedestrians who are hit at intersections are struck just as they step onto the street. Many walk into the side of a moving vehicle that they fail to see.

How Can Drivers Avoid Collisions with Animals?

The dangers posed by animals on the roadway should not be taken lightly. Smashing into a 150-pound deer at 50 miles per hour, for example, will not only kill the animal but will also wreck the vehicle and may well kill the passengers.

The problem of animals on the roadway is particularly severe during the hours between sunset and sunrise, when light conditions limit visibility. Fog can also contribute to vehicle–animal collisions.

Small Animals

Whether it's a cat darting across a city street or a raccoon crossing a highway, small animals cause a surprising number of collisions. In trying to avoid the animal, the driver might swerve and strike another vehicle or a fixed object along the road. Or the driver might slam on the brakes— and be struck in the rear by the vehicle behind. Violent evasive action is not advisable.

Large Animals

Hitting a large animal can prove fatal for both the animal and the vehicle's occupants. Deer are the large animals most often struck, but drivers also have collisions with horses, cows, and other farm animals.

Using SIPDE to Avoid Collisions with Animals

Whether you're driving on city streets or along country roads, using the SIPDE procedure will help you avoid having a collision with an animal.

Be especially cautious when driving through farmland or any wooded areas where you are more likely to encounter deer or other animals alongside or in the road. Search for movement along the sides of the road. At night, search for sudden, unusual spots of light that may be identified as the reflection of your headlights off animals' eyes.

As you're driving, think about what you could do if an animal suddenly darted onto the road and into the path of your car.

FYI

Each year, motor vehicles kill hundreds of thousands of deer, antelope, and other large wild animals.

TIPS **FOR NEW DRIVERS**

Pedestrians to Watch For

Certain pedestrians require drivers to pay special attention.

- Elderly pedestrians may have impaired eyesight or hearing. They may move and react slowly and require extra time to cross streets.
- The physically challenged, such as people who are blind and people in wheelchairs, may need extra time to cross streets.
- Pedestrians with strollers or carriages may need extra time to move onto or off a sidewalk.
- Joggers running with their backs to traffic can pose a hazard. Many do not wear reflective clothing, which makes them difficult to see when visibility is low.
- People on the job, such as mail carriers, delivery people, or roadway maintenance workers, may be distracted by their work and step out into the roadway without checking traffic.
- Umbrellas and hooded parkas may impair pedestrians' ability to notice traffic.

SAFETY TIPS

While hitchhiking may be legal in some areas, it is not a safe practice. The hitchhiker has no idea what kind of person the driver is, and there is no guarantee that the hitchhiker will not be robbed or assaulted by the driver, or the driver by the hitchhiker.

What you can do, if you encounter an animal, will depend on the kind of road you're on, traffic conditions, and other factors. As a general rule, try to position yourself so that you have extra room to manuever. If you're driving on a two-lane road, drive with your headlights on, and when there is no oncoming traffic, move toward the center line to improve visibility. That way, you'll have more room to spot an animal on the side of the road without having to swerve immediately to avoid it. However, always avoid swerving to the left into the path of oncoming vehicles.

Be especially careful when driving at night and in fog. At dusk and dawn, deer move around to feed, and these are also the times during the day when visibility is reduced. If you do spot an animal near or on the road, slow down and be prepared to adjust speed or position as necessary. Leave as wide a safety margin as you can when driving around or past an animal. If you spot one animal, assume that others are nearby.

If it appears impossible to avoid striking a large animal, brake firmly and steer to strike it at an angle. Let up on the brake pedal just before hitting the animal. This will cause the front of the car to rise and reduce the chance that the animal will come through the windshield.

If you see signs that say "Cattle Crossing" or "Open Range" or signs that warn of horseback riders, keep a lookout for animals on or near the roadway. Reduce speed as soon as you see an animal.

Always drive past any animal slowly and cautiously; a frightened animal may bolt in any direction.

Finally, keep in mind that in certain situations your best choice is to strike an animal rather than try to evade it. For example, if a small animal darts in front of your vehicle, and swerving or hard braking might cause a collision with a pedestrian or other vehicle, you must choose the less serious of the collisions.

WHAT WOULD YOU DO?

What possible unseen hazards may be present in this situation? How can you manage risk?

Lesson 1 Review

1. What are some pedestrian behaviors that lead to collisions with vehicles?
2. What precautions can drivers take to avoid collisions with children?
3. What are some of the basic safety rules pedestrians should follow?
4. If you can't avoid hitting a large animal, what steps should you take to minimize the damage to your vehicle?

Sharing the Roadway with Motorcycles and Bicycles

OBJECTIVES

1. Identify situations involving cyclists, and explain actions that drivers can take to reduce the risk of collision with them.
2. Describe the responsibilities of motorcyclists on the roadway.

KEY TERM

moped

In 1997, 813 bicyclists and more than 2,100 motorcyclists were killed in collisions in the United States. As the number of people riding bikes and motorcycles increases, the number of collisions with cars and other large vehicles may increase too.

As a driver, you should recognize the potential risk of collisions posed by cyclists and take precautions to minimize the risk.

How Can You Recognize and Reduce the Risk of Problems Caused by Cyclists?

Both motorcycles and bicycles are smaller, less stable, and less visible than other vehicles. Two wheels provide less stability than four, making motorcycles and bicycles harder to steer and handle than many people realize. As a driver, you need to be aware of cyclists and of how the roadway problems they face are different from yours.

◆ *Cyclists should be especially careful to stay out of a driver's blind spots.*

Watching Out for Cyclists

Two-wheeled vehicles are much more difficult than other vehicles for drivers to spot, especially when they approach from behind or from the side. A **moped** is a low-powered, two-wheeled vehicle that shares some of the same visibility problems as a bicycle or motorcycle and is most commonly driven on city streets. On highways, a motorcycle does not take up an entire lane and may not be seen. In addition, drivers tend not to look for cyclists.

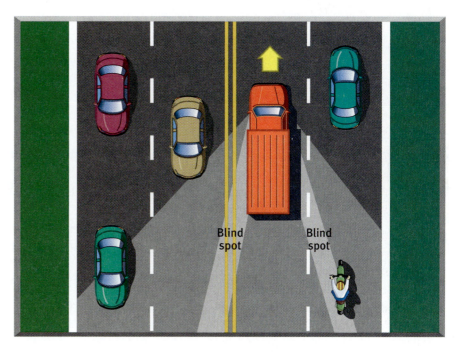

Blind spot   Blind spot

Motorcycles and bicycles also are easily hidden from drivers' sight by larger vehicles sharing the roadway. The small handlebar mirrors on both motorcycles and bicycles offer their drivers only a limited view to the rear. In addition, some motorcycles have no windscreen or windshield wipers to aid visibility in case of a sudden shower.

Always make cyclists aware of your intentions and position. Drive with your headlights on, and signal well in advance when turning, changing lanes, or stopping. Tap your horn early to warn a cyclist of your approach.

Dangerous Roadway Conditions

Drivers must be aware of the problems that cyclists face in order to anticipate situations in which a cyclist might veer or skid into the path of a vehicle, or might suddenly slow down, steer widely left or right, or stop suddenly.

Cyclists must make a much more major adjustment in speed or position than a driver in situations such as these:

- encountering a storm drain, a gravel surface, or a pothole
- driving on a rain-slicked road or through a large puddle
- getting caught in an unexpected rain or snow shower
- being blown by a sudden strong gust of wind

To minimize risk, search the roadway ahead for problems that may cause a cyclist to change speed or direction, skid, or make a sudden stop. Anticipate potential risk by allowing cyclists as much maneuvering space as possible. When driving behind a cyclist, increase your following distance. *Never* try to pass a cyclist in a tight space.

If a cyclist is carrying a passenger, be especially careful. A passenger leaning the wrong way can throw a motorcycle or bicycle off balance.

Use your mirrors to check for cyclists approaching from the rear. They often squeeze between vehicles traveling in parallel lanes. Always check your blind spots, too, before changing lanes. Be on the lookout for cyclists approaching intersections and coming around curves.

Lack of Protection

Unlike drivers, who have the protection of their vehicle's shell, cyclists are unprotected. In the event of a mishap—collision, skid, blowout—the risk of serious or fatal injury is high to the cyclist. Keep this in mind when dealing with cyclists.

When driving through residential areas, watch for bicycles and motorcycles entering the roadway from driveways and side streets.

Failure to Obey Traffic Laws

Human error or ignorance accounts for countless collisions involving cyclists. Although motorcycles are subject to the same laws that other

FYI

Motorcycles have a shorter stopping distance than other motor vehicles. This means you need to increase your following distance when there is a motorcycle in front of you.

motor vehicles are, some cyclists seem to break every rule. They ride between lanes, weave in and out of traffic, ride in drivers' blind spots, and fail to signal their intentions.

Some bicyclists show an equal disregard for safety. They shoot through stop signs and red lights, and cut in front of vehicles. Children on bikes may ride the wrong way on one-way streets or sail through intersections with barely a glance to either side.

Such careless riding poses a danger not just to the cyclist but to all roadway users. You should be alert to the possibility that cyclists may not follow traffic laws, and you should always be prepared to take evasive action if necessary.

On the other hand, you should follow all traffic laws so that you do not endanger cyclists and other users of the roadway.

Irresponsible Drivers

Many collisions involving cyclists occur because drivers have difficulty seeing motorcycles and bicycles. However, some cyclists become the victims of careless or inconsiderate drivers. These drivers may tailgate cyclists, cut them off, or pass too close for safety. Such reckless actions put both driver and cyclist at risk.

What Special Responsibilities Do Motorcyclists Have?

Motorcyclists have the same rights on the roadways as any other drivers. They also have the responsibility of driving safely and watching out for drivers of other vehicles.

Motorcyclists should not take advantage of the smaller size of their vehicles to weave in and out of lanes of traffic at high speeds. This behavior is highly dangerous to the cyclist. Motorcyclists should take care to stay out of other drivers' blind spots. Other drivers might not be as aware as they should be about looking in their mirrors for motorcycles to begin with, so it is important that a motorcyclist never be in a spot that is not visible to nearby vehicles.

Lesson 2 Review

1. Describe problems that cyclists can cause for a driver. Explain how you would manage risk in each circumstance.
2. What should motorcyclists do to avoid risks on the roadway?

WHAT WOULD YOU DO?

Motorcyclists are approaching you. What can you do to minimize the risk?

OBJECTIVES

1. Describe ways to share the roadway with vehicles other than cars and cycles.
2. Describe at least three precautions you should take around slow-moving vehicles.

Sharing the Roadway with Other Vehicles

When driving on any street or highway, you'll share the road with vehicles that range in size from 2-wheel, 30-pound bicycles to 18-wheel, 80,000-pound tractor-trailers. You've already explored some problems you might encounter with bicycles and motorcycles. To manage time and space near larger vehicles, you need to understand their characteristics and limitations.

Energy Tips

Save fuel by using public transportation, such as buses, or riding a bicycle whenever possible.

How Can You Safely Share the Roadway with Other Vehicles?

Keep in mind that differences in the size, shape, and weight of vehicles affect handling ability as well as the amount of visibility a driver has.

Trucks and Tractor-Trailers

Trucks on the road today can be up to 120 feet long and weigh up to 60 tons. That's about 8 times as long as the average car and 40 to 60 times

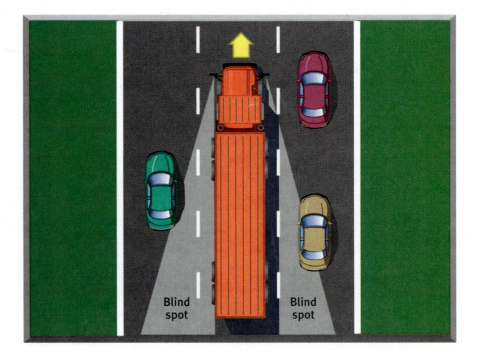

◆ *Tractor-trailer mirrors are mounted high, so the driver loses sight of your car if you travel alongside the trailer.*

heavier. Put yourself in the truck driver's place. Being aware of problems he or she faces will help you better manage risk.

Visibility Truck drivers sit high above the roadway and have excellent visibility ahead. However, it is hard for them to see to the side and behind the truck. Despite the use of sideview mirrors, some vehicles may be all but invisible to a truck driver.

Trucks create visibility problems for other drivers. With a truck blocking your view, you can't see other traffic or the roadway ahead.

Time Handling a truck is more difficult than handling a car. Weighed down with cargo, a truck accelerates slowly and tends to lose speed when climbing an uphill road. Going downhill, however, a truck's momentum causes it to pick up speed. See Chapter 14 for more on momentum.

When you're passing a truck, allow much more time than you'd need in order to pass a car. Not only is the truck longer, but its bulk creates a wind factor that you'll also have to be aware of as you steer around the vehicle.

Space Trucks, of course, take up much more room on the roadway than do cars. As a result, it's much harder to see around one when you're following it. Increase your following distance when you're behind a truck. Remember that a truck requires a wide turning space and more time and space to stop than cars do. When you approach a truck in an oncoming lane, leave as much space as possible between the truck and your vehicle.

Buses

The same visibility and handling factors that pertain to trucks also apply to buses. Allow buses an equal amount of "elbow room," and follow the same 4-second distance rule when following a bus. Remember that local buses stop frequently to pick up and discharge passengers, often disrupting traffic flow in the process.

TIPS | **FOR NEW DRIVERS**

How to Safely Share the Roadway with a Truck

Always allow at least a 4-second following distance to make yourself visible to a truck driver and to allow you to see more of the roadway.

When stopping behind a truck stopped at a sign or signal, allow extra distance in case the truck rolls back when starting off.

Allow yourself extra time and space when passing. When a large truck is about to pass you, steer to adjust to the gust of air caused by the truck.

If a truck is bearing down on you as you drive downhill, move into another lane or pull over to let the truck pass.

Try not to drive on the right side of a truck, especially just below the right-front passenger side. This is a blind spot for the truck driver.

Never try to drive by the right side of a truck at an intersection if the truck's right-hand signal is on, even if the truck is in the left lane. Large trucks make very wide right-hand turns.

Never pass a truck on the right side on the roadway.

After passing a truck, do not pull right in front of it after you clear it. Leave plenty of room in case you have to apply your brakes.

You should be especially careful when you approach or pass a stopped bus. Reduce speed and keep alert for pedestrians rushing to catch the bus and discharged passengers hurrying across streets in front of the bus. Always be ready to stop.

Remember, drivers traveling in either direction on a nondivided roadway must stop for a school bus that has flashing red lights to indicate it is picking up or dropping off children.

Small Cars

There are more small cars on the road today than ever before. While these vehicles may cost less to buy and operate than larger vehicles, they have some drawbacks.

Small cars may have less power than larger vehicles. As a result, a small car may take a lot longer to pass other vehicles. Small cars may also lose speed when climbing a steep hill. In many small cars, the driver also sits lower and therefore has reduced sight distance.

When driving a small car, allow yourself extra space and time to pass another vehicle. If a small car is passing you, give the driver ample space and time to maneuver.

Also give small cars extra room when roads are slippery or there are strong winds. Lightweight cars tend to skid more easily than heavier vehicles on slick roadways.

CONNECTIONS

History

CULTURAL CROSSROADS

In Japan in the year 1635, a law was passed that caused Japanese lords and thousands of their household staff to take to the roadways of that island nation. The law required that the nation's lords, known as *daimyo,* or "great names," build mansions in the capital city of Edo, now known as Tokyo. The lords were to keep their families in Edo and spend every other year at the court of the ruler, or *shogun.*

Because of this law, the daimyo had to travel once a year to or from their country estates and Edo. Moreover, the daimyo were told how many of their household staff must travel with them, what equipment to take, and what route to follow. The wealthiest daimyo had to take 1,000 or more of their household staff both to and from Edo.

Since there were more than 250 daimyo to which the law applied, there would be many great processions criss-crossing Japanese roads in all seasons. These groups, known as *Daimyo Gyoretsu* or "Processions of the Lords," were on the roadways for several weeks. Each night they would stop at one of a huge network of inns established along the national roadways to accommodate the travelers in these processions. In no other country of the world was there such an extensive and elaborate system of overnight accommodations at the time.

Other Kinds of Vehicles

You may encounter other kinds of vehicles on the roadway.

Emergency vehicles When you meet ambulances, police vehicles, and fire trucks with lights flashing or sirens blaring, you should yield the right-of-way. Pull to the right and stop, or otherwise provide a clear path for the emergency vehicle.

Snowmobiles Snowmobiles are allowed on certain roads in some states. They can come onto the roadway in unexpected places. They are often hard to see and can be difficult for their drivers to handle and to stop. Allow extra time and space to adjust to any maneuver that a snowmobile makes.

Sport utility vehicles Sport utility vehicles (SUVs) are taller than the average passenger car. This gives the driver a better view of the traffic ahead. It also means that a driver following an SUV will have an obstructed view of the traffic ahead. Keeping an extra distance behind an SUV may help you to see around the vehicle. Also remember that sport utility vehicles need extra stopping distance.

Ice-cream trucks Approach ice-cream trucks cautiously. Watch for children darting into the street and emerging from between parked vehicles. In some states, drivers must stop for an ice-cream truck equipped with flashing red lights and must yield the right-of-way to pedestrians going to and from the truck. Check your state driver's manual.

Maintenance vehicles Roadwork involves vehicles of many sizes and shapes with the potential to disrupt traffic. Drivers need to be alert to such vehicles and to adjust speed and position to accommodate sudden changes in traffic flow.

How Do You Deal with Slow-Moving Vehicles?

Slow-moving vehicles, such as farm tractors, horse-drawn wagons, and various special-purpose vehicles, move at a much slower speed than other traffic.

Try to spot a slow-moving vehicle as early as possible, because your vehicle will approach it

◆ *You may encounter slow-moving maintenance vehicles in city traffic.*

◆ *Allow a wide vehicle more room to maneuver, especially on turns.*

more rapidly than a vehicle traveling at a normal rate of speed. Slow-moving vehicles often, but not always, display special signs identifying them as slow-moving. If a vehicle is especially wide, it may carry a "wide load" sign on the rear. Once you identify such a vehicle, reduce speed immediately and follow at a safe distance.

Before passing, consider the driver's likely actions. For example, the driver of a construction vehicle may drive on the roadway for only a short distance before turning off. A road maintenance or utility truck may stop or pull over to the side.

If you decide to pass, do so safely and only where it is legal to pass. Be especially careful on narrow, single-lane country roads, where you're more likely to encounter a slow-moving vehicle. Visibility and space are limited on such roads, and if the vehicle you're following is large, you'll have added difficulty seeing past it.

If you see a slow-moving vehicle traveling in the opposite direction, be alert for oncoming vehicles moving into your path as they pass the vehicle.

WHAT WOULD YOU DO?

You are passing this truck. What should you do?

Lesson 3 Review

1. Name three types of motor vehicles with which you might share the roadway. Explain how you can reduce risk when interacting with these vehicles.

2. When you are sharing the roadway with a slow-moving vehicle, what are three precautions you should take?

Safe Driving Procedures at Railroad Crossings

OBJECTIVES
1. Explain how to drive safely through a railroad crossing.
2. Describe what to do if your vehicle stalls on railroad tracks.

Despite warning signs, crossing gates, and signals, many collisions occur at railroad crossings each year. Among the causes of these crashes are driver impatience, driver inattention, and poor judgment.

How Can You Drive Through a Railroad Crossing Safely?

Too many drivers forget, or ignore, safe-driving procedures at railroad crossings, often with fatal consequences. This lesson describes those procedures.

Determine When It Is Safe to Cross

Slow down as you approach a railroad crossing. Look for warning lights or signals or lowered crossing gates.

Stop no closer than 15 feet from a railroad crossing if a train is approaching. *Never* attempt to cross a track if warning lights are flashing.

Even if warning lights are not flashing, look both ways and listen to make sure no train is coming before you cross a track. Never rely solely on mechanical warning equipment—it could be broken.

If there are no lights or crossing gates present at a railroad crossing, proceed with extra caution. If there is any question about safety, stop, look, and listen for approaching trains before moving ahead.

After a train has passed, check in both directions to see that no other trains are coming, especially before you start across multiple sets of tracks.

Always wait for the vehicle ahead of you to clear the tracks before you start across. Never stop on the railroad tracks.

◆ *Be patient and very cautious at railroad crossings. Never think you can beat the train to the crossing.*

Bruce J. Oliver
Manager of Driver Training, AAA Mid-Atlantic

Remain alert to share the roadway safely:
- *Bicyclists are expected to obey all traffic laws and regulations. Bicyclists have the same rights, privileges, and responsibilities as drivers.*
- *Think ahead. Drivers can often anticipate dangers involving pedestrians.*
- *Even if you obey all traffic laws, unexpected events can and do occur. Managing time and space effectively will help minimize risk should an emergency occur.*
- *Maintain respect for all roadway users to aid in the safe, smooth flow of traffic.*

Stay Alert

Drivers who travel the same route day after day tend to pay less attention to their surroundings. Such inattention can have tragic consequences at a railroad crossing.

Don't take familiar crossings for granted. Never assume that the track is clear: be alert, look, and listen for trains.

Do Not Panic If Your Vehicle Stalls

Never stop your vehicle on railroad tracks for any reason whatsoever. In the rare event that your vehicle stalls on the tracks, don't panic.

Immediately check in both directions for approaching trains. If a train is coming, leave your vehicle at once, walk in the direction the train is coming from, but move away from the tracks. If no train is approaching and you have a clear view of the tracks in both directions, try to restart your engine. Continue to check for trains.

If you can't start your vehicle and you're sure no trains are coming, try to push your vehicle off—and well away from—the tracks.

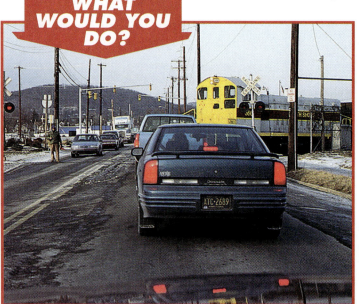

WHAT WOULD YOU DO?

The train has just about passed. Describe your procedure as you get ready to resume movement.

Lesson 4 Review

1. What must you do to negotiate a railroad crossing safely?
2. What would you do if your vehicle stalled on railroad tracks?

Figuring Travel Time

Travel involves rate of speed, distance, and time. To find how long it will take you to get somewhere when you know your distance and speed, divide the distance by the speed. (To get an exact answer, you may have to change miles per hour to miles per minute by dividing mph by 60.)

$$T = D \div S, \text{ where } T = \text{time,}$$
$$D = \text{distance, and } S = \text{speed.}$$

For example, suppose you will drive 270 miles at an average speed of 45 mph. How long will the trip take?

$$T = 270 \div 45$$
$$T = 6$$

The trip will take 6 hours.

Figure the time for each distance and speed below.

TIME	DISTANCE	SPEED
(a)	20 miles	30 mph
(b)	40 miles	35 mph
(c)	115 miles	50 mph

To estimate distance when you know speed and time, multiply the speed and the time.

$$D = S \times T$$

How far can you travel in 5 hours at an average speed of 35 mph?

$$D = 35 \times 5$$
$$D = 175$$

You can travel about 175 miles.

Figure the distance for each speed and time below. Round your answer to the nearest whole mile.

DISTANCE	SPEED	TIME
(d)	25 mph	30 minutes
(e)	45 mph	2¼ hours
(f)	30 mph	1 hour 20 minutes

Now look back at each problem. If you wanted an estimate instead of an exact answer, what shortcuts could you take?

Try It Yourself

1. Traveling at local speeds, about how many miles away is someplace 20 minutes from your home?
2. Use a map to plan a trip from one city to another. Estimate the amount of time it will take to travel the distance between the two cities.
3. Use a map to figure out which cities or towns are about 3 hours away from your home.

KEY POINTS

Lesson One

1. Pedestrian problems may be caused by people who cross a roadway without regard for rules or signals, children who run into or play in the street, people who need extra time to cross, and joggers.
2. To prevent collisions with pedestrians, use the SIPDE process to develop effective visual search habits.
3. Pedestrians should obey all rules, signals, and signs; walk facing traffic if walking on the road; wear reflective clothing when jogging; hold children by the hand; cross streets only when and where it is safe and legal to do so.
4. To avoid collisions with animals, be careful when driving through wooded areas, especially when visibility is reduced.

Lesson Two

1. Motorcycles and bicycles have less stability and protection than other vehicles. To reduce the risk of collision with cyclists, anticipate problems they may have, and adjust your speed or position. Always make cyclists aware of your position and intentions.
2. Cyclists should not weave in and out of traffic and should make themselves visible to drivers.

Lesson Three

1. Trucks and tractor-trailers: when passing allow extra time; when you approach a truck or tractor-trailer in an oncoming lane, leave plenty of space between it and your vehicle. Buses: react as you would to a truck, but remember that approaching and passing requires special care because buses may be picking up or discharging passengers. Small cars: allow extra room on slippery roads or windy days.
2. Try to spot a slow-moving vehicle early. Reduce your speed, and follow at a safe distance. Pass only where it is legal and safe to do so.

Lesson Four

1. Slow down as you approach a railroad crossing. Look for warning lights or signals or lowered gates. Before you cross, stop, look, and listen for trains. Never assume the track is clear.
2. If your vehicle stalls on a railroad track and a train is approaching, leave the vehicle and walk in the direction the train is coming from, but away from the track. If no train is coming, try to restart the engine or push the vehicle off the track.

PROJECTS

1. Observe the interaction between pedestrians and traffic at a busy intersection for about 15 minutes. Make note of unsafe actions taken by both pedestrians and drivers. Discuss your observations with the class.
2. Visit a bicycle shop or sporting goods store. What products does the store sell to help make cyclists, joggers, and others more visible in dim light?

*inter*NET CONNECTION

To learn more about safety on the road, visit Glencoe's driver education Web site for the most current Traffic Safety Facts from the U.S. Department of Transportation.
www.glencoe.com/sec/driver.ed

CHAPTER TEST

Write the letter of the answer that best completes each sentence.

1. When driving behind a tractor-trailer,
   a. allow at least a 4-second following distance.
   b. attempt to pass.
   c. tap your horn lightly.

2. Collisions with pedestrians occur most often
   a. at intersections.
   b. on highways.
   c. on weekends.

3. Drivers who travel the same route every day
   a. have fewer collisions than other drivers.
   b. pay less attention to their surroundings.
   c. fall asleep at the wheel more often.

4. As the use of cycles increases,
   a. collisions with other vehicles will decrease.
   b. air pollution will decrease.
   c. the number of collisions with other vehicles might also increase.

5. Drivers use ground viewing to
   a. search the road for animals.
   b. search beneath parked vehicles for signs of movement.
   c. avoid large puddles.

6. Because truck drivers sit high above the surface of the roadway, they
   a. don't have any blind spots.
   b. have great visibility of the road ahead.
   c. are able to see above fog.

7. If it appears impossible to avoid striking a large animal, you should
   a. accelerate and move forward.
   b. turn off your vehicle's engine.
   c. steer to strike it at an angle.

8. When driving behind a cyclist, you should
   a. increase your following distance.
   b. pass at the first opportunity.
   c. turn on your high beams.

9. Most small cars have
   a. more power than larger cars.
   b. the ability to pass easily.
   c. less power than larger cars.

10. If you approach a railroad crossing when a train is coming, you should
    a. stop at least 15 feet from the crossing.
    b. stop directly in front of the crossing signal.
    c. try to cross the tracks if the gate is open.

Write the word or phrase that best completes each sentence.

| traffic flow | parallel | hazard |
| stability | stalls | jaywalking |

11. Crossing a street without regard for traffic rules or signals is called _____.

12. Motorcycles are harder to steer than many people realize because two wheels provide less _____ than four.

13. If your vehicle _____ on railroad tracks while a train is coming, you should leave the vehicle at once.

14. Cyclists often squeeze between vehicles traveling in _____ lanes.

15. Local buses stop frequently to pick up and discharge passengers, often disrupting _____ in the process.

DRIVER'S LOG

In this chapter, you have learned about the responsibilities and risks of sharing the roadway with motorists, pedestrians, cyclists, and animals. Write what you think are the five most important responsibilities a driver has when sharing the roadway.

CHAPTER 14

Natural Laws and Driving

Natural laws, which include the laws of inertia, gravity, and momentum, affect a driver's ability to perform the driving task. It is important to understand natural laws so that you can use your knowledge of them to help you manage risk in different driving situations.

OBJECTIVES

1. Describe the natural laws of inertia, friction, momentum, kinetic energy, and gravity.
2. Explain the relationship of these natural laws to driving.

KEY TERMS

inertia
friction
traction
adhesion
momentum
kinetic energy
gravity
center of gravity

Natural Laws and the Movement of Your Vehicle

Does this sound familiar? You're in a vehicle and the driver applies the brakes. The vehicle stops, but your books on the backseat of the vehicle continue moving forward onto the floor. Why did this happen? A natural law is the culprit.

What Are Natural Laws?

Natural laws are always at work. Some of these laws are inertia, friction, momentum, kinetic energy, and gravity.

Inertia

Inertia caused your books on the backseat to continue moving forward even after the driver braked. Two properties govern inertia. One is that objects at rest do not move unless some force acts on them. The other is that moving objects continue to move in a straight line unless some force acts on them.

All things have inertia. As the vehicle was moving, so were your books. When the driver braked, a force was exerted to make the vehicle stop, but unrestrained, your books kept moving forward in a straight line. Then they fell to the floor.

You have to understand inertia when you drive because you and your passengers have inertia. If you brake a vehicle hard, everyone in it will tend to keep moving forward. Drivers must manage risk by anticipating how to reduce inertia's effects.

One way to do this is to wear safety belts. These belts provide a force that acts against inertia. If you brake hard and are not wearing a safety belt, you may be thrown forward against the windshield or dashboard.

Another way to manage risk is to be sure to secure all loose objects, such as your books, luggage, or boxes.

TIPS **FOR NEW DRIVERS**

Drying the Brakes

Wet brakes do not work as efficiently as dry brakes. After you have driven through heavy rain or deep puddles, always check for wet brakes. If you apply the brakes lightly and the vehicle pulls to one side or does not slow as quickly as normal, your brakes are probably wet. Dry the brakes by driving slowly and applying light pressure on the brake pedal with your left foot. The friction created will generate heat, which will dry the brakes.

Friction

Press your foot down hard on a carpeted floor. Keep it pressed down as hard as you can and try to move across the carpet. Does it feel as if some kind of force is trying to stop your foot from moving, almost as if your foot and the carpet are sticking together?

The force that seems to try to make the surface of your shoe "stick" to the surface of the carpet is friction. **Friction** is a force between two surfaces that resists the movement of one surface across the other. You can make your foot move across the carpet by applying more force than friction can resist or overcome.

Just as friction tries to make your foot stick to the carpet, it tries to make the surface of your tires "stick" to the surface of the road. Your vehicle has to overcome friction in order to move. Your vehicle stays on the road, however, because a certain amount of friction is always present.

Friction between the road and your tires is called **traction,** or **adhesion,** which means "sticking together." Adhesion, or traction, holds your vehicle on the road. Here are some factors affecting traction.

Tire pressure Tires are made with grooved surface treads that are designed to grip the road in a wide variety of conditions. For best traction, inflate tires to the maximum pressure recommended by the manufacturer. Properly inflated tires grip the road evenly. Under- or overinflation reduces traction. If you underinflate your tires, only the outer edges grip the road. If you overinflate them, only the centers tend to make contact with the road.

Tire condition Would you try to walk on slippery packed snow or ice with rubber boots worn smooth? Of course not! You would slide all over. The same concept applies to tires. Bald tires— tires with very little or no tread—provide almost no traction on wet, icy, or snow-covered roads. Even on dry roads, bald tires reduce directional control, particularly if there is sand or debris on the road, and are more apt than treaded tires to get punctured.

Rain When the road is wet, water gets between the surface of the road and the tires. At 55 mph, tires can lose contact with the road surface if the water is as shallow as $\frac{1}{12}$ inch. Water provides a smooth, nearly frictionless, surface for the tires to move across, and it does not provide good traction. If tires are properly inflated and have good tread, much of the water will go into the grooves between

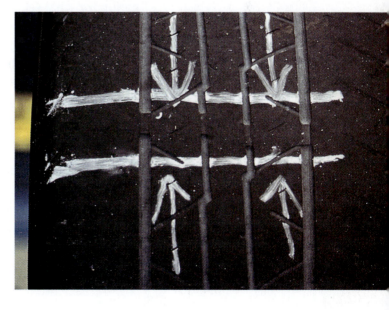

◆ *The minimum legal—though not necessarily safe—tread depth for your tires is $\frac{1}{16}$ inch. To check your tire's tread depth, examine the tread-wear bars that are built into the tire. When the tread-wear bars are even with the surface of the tread at more than two spots around the tire, the tire is no longer legal or safe to use.*

the treads. This means that the treads themselves will maintain contact with the road surface.

Ice and snow Ice and snow can reduce traction more than rain. Traction is poorest near 32°F, when snow and ice start to become a slippery, watery slush. Any road is dangerous when covered with ice or snow, so adjust your driving habits accordingly.

Snow tires help increase traction in snow but not necessarily on ice. Chains are helpful in increasing traction on ice, but they provide poor traction on pavement. In states where studded tires are allowed, they can help on ice but are not as effective as chains. All-weather tires are a good choice for most drivers.

◆ *Snow and ice make a roadway slick, reducing friction between your car and the road's surface.*

Road condition Road condition also affects traction. Rough roads and potholes make your vehicle's tires bounce up and down, reducing traction. Wet leaves on the road also reduce friction, causing the tires to lose traction and slide.

Momentum

If a 12-pound bowling ball and a 16-pound bowling ball were rolling toward an object at the same speed, which ball would cause more damage? Because it is heavier, the 16-pound bowling ball would.

Momentum is the product of weight and speed. It provides an explanation for what seems obvious in the bowling ball example. All objects in motion have momentum. The greater the momentum of the vehicles, the greater the damage in a collision will be.

A vehicle's momentum depends on its weight and its speed. If either the weight or the speed doubles, so does the vehicle's momentum. If the weight or the speed triples, so does the momentum.

In short, as speed increases, so does the likelihood of damage in case of a collision. Lighter vehicles may cause less damage because of reduced momentum. However, the lighter your vehicle, the greater the likelihood that it will be damaged when in a collision.

Kinetic Energy

All objects in motion have kinetic energy as well as momentum. **Kinetic energy** is the energy of motion. The faster a vehicle moves, the more energy of motion it has.

What does this mean to you as a driver? You need to know that the more energy of motion a vehicle has, the more time and distance it will take to stop.

The faster a vehicle moves, the more energy of motion it has. If a vehicle's speed doubles, its stopping distance increases by an amount equal to the square of the difference in speed.

Here is what kinetic energy and momentum can mean when you are accelerating or braking.

Acceleration Suppose that you drive a van or sport utility vehicle (SUV) and usually carry one or two passengers and light packages. You are aware of how your vehicle accelerates when you enter an expressway. Now suppose that you are going on a trip with four other people, and the back of the van or SUV is fully packed. You have increased the weight of your vehicle. It will not accelerate as quickly. Thus, you will not be able to enter an expressway as quickly as you usually do. You may need to manage time and space differently. You might want to press down more on the accelerator to compensate for the extra weight and wait for a larger gap in traffic before entering the roadway.

Braking Once you are moving on the expressway, the van or SUV's momentum and kinetic energy have increased because its weight and speed have been increased. Its stopping distance has also increased. Reduce risk by leaving a greater distance between your vehicle and the one in front of you.

Gravity

If you toss a ball into the air, it comes down. The ball falls because of gravity. **Gravity** is a force that pulls all objects toward the center of the Earth. Because gravity affects all objects, it can make a vehicle speed up or slow down.

CONNECTIONS
Math

It's a mathematical fact that the faster you drive, the more braking distance you will need to have.

Use the following formula to demonstrate this. If S is the speed, the formula is:

$(S \times \frac{1}{10} S) \div 2.4$ = braking distance in feet

Braking distance at a speed of 50 miles per hour can be calculated as follows:

$(50 \times \frac{1}{10} \times 50) \div 2.4$

$(50 \times 5) \div 2.4$

$250 \div 2.4 = 104$ feet

You don't have to do the calculations as you drive to realize that the faster you are traveling, the more space you have to leave in front of you in case you have to brake suddenly.

◆ *Overpacking can make a vehicle less stable by changing its center of gravity.*

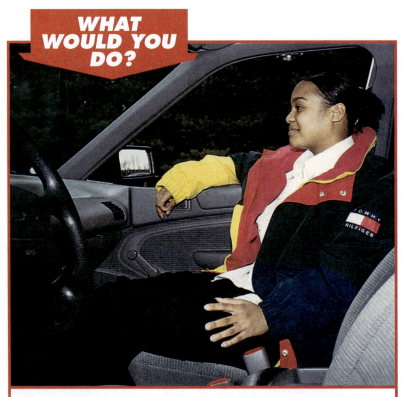

WHAT WOULD YOU DO?

What would you say to the passengers about wearing safety belts?

When you drive uphill, gravity acts to slow your vehicle. To maintain speed, accelerate just before the vehicle begins to climb the hill. When you drive downhill, gravity acts with your vehicle, so your speed increases. To keep the vehicle from moving too fast, ease up on the accelerator. You may also have to use your brakes or downshift.

Center of Gravity

Gravity gives objects their weight. The weight of an object, such as your vehicle, is distributed evenly about a point. This point is called the object's **center of gravity.**

The lower an object's center of gravity, the more stable the object. Most vehicles are designed to have a low center of gravity in order to handle well in turns and during quick maneuvers. Changes in a vehicle's center of gravity affect how well the vehicle handles. A roof carrier loaded with heavy objects raises the vehicle's center of gravity, making it less stable and difficult to control on turns and curves and during sudden changes in braking, acceleration, and direction. Vehicles that have a high center of gravity, such as sport utility vehicles, some types of vans, and pickup trucks, also have these problems.

Lesson 1 Review

1. What affects traction? How?
2. How would changes in a vehicle's center of gravity affect its stability?

Natural Laws and Steering and Braking

OBJECTIVES

1. Explain how natural laws affect a vehicle's stopping distance.
2. Identify the factors that affect steering.
3. Name the ways that natural laws affect steering around a curve.
4. Describe how gravity and the contour of the road affect steering.

KEY TERMS

total stopping distance
perception distance
reaction distance
braking distance
directional control
centrifugal force
banked curve
crowned road

Natural laws affect stopping distance, braking, and steering. Understanding the relationships between natural laws and driving can help you to be a better and a safer driver.

How Do Natural Laws Influence Braking Distance?

The distance your vehicle takes to stop is its **total stopping distance.** Perception distance, reaction distance, and braking distance make up total stopping distance. For estimating stopping distance use the 3- or 5-second rule. See Chapter 10 for more information.

In order to stop, you must (1) identify a need to stop (this is your **perception distance**), (2) react by braking (your **reaction distance**), and (3) slow your vehicle to a stop (your **braking distance**).

Natural Laws and Braking

Braking is a result of friction between the brake linings and the wheel drums or wheel discs and pads. This friction slows the rotation of the wheels and tires. The adhesion between the tires and the road increases. As you brake, you decrease your vehicle's momentum and kinetic energy.

Factors Affecting Braking Distance

The following factors can increase braking distance.

Speed The greater the speed, the longer the braking distance.

Condition of the vehicle Worn brakes, tires, or shock absorbers reduce traction. Reduced traction increases braking distance.

Condition of the roadway Braking distance is greater when roadway friction is reduced, such as during bad weather or if the road is unpaved.

Hills and mountains Gravity affects the time and space needed to stop a vehicle going downhill. Because a vehicle going downhill has the added force of gravity contributing to its inertia, the braking distance increases.

Telephone poles usually are 100 feet apart. Use this measure to help you estimate distance while you are driving.

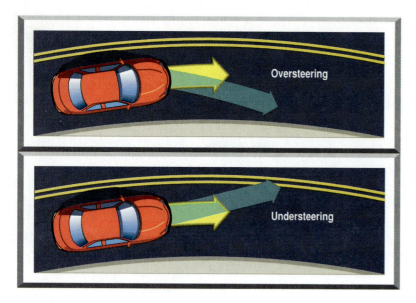

Oversteering

Understeering

◆ *Monitor your speed as you enter a curve so that you neither oversteer nor understeer.*

What Factors and Natural Laws Affect Steering?

Your ability to steer a vehicle depends on many factors. The steering mechanism, tires, and suspension are three mechanical factors. Wheel alignment and road conditions are also important in steering, as is the way you load the vehicle.

Friction helps to keep your vehicle on the road. When a driver turns the steering wheel, the front tires provide the friction, or traction, to turn the vehicle.

Because of inertia, a moving vehicle will tend to go in a straight line. The vehicle, however, may wander, and regular steering corrections will be necessary. **Directional control** is a vehicle's ability to hold a straight line. You will have an easy time keeping the vehicle moving in the direction in which you steer it.

Hand position is another factor that affects vehicle control. Hold the steering wheel firmly, but with your fingers rather than the palms of your hands. Keep your thumbs along the face of the steering wheel, not wrapped around it. This gives you better control.

◆ *A car handles differently on (1) banked roads, (2) crowned roads, and (3) flat roads.*

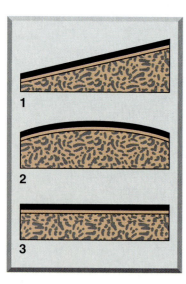

1

2

3

How Do Natural Laws Affect Steering Around a Curve?

Inertia tends to keep a vehicle moving in a straight path. As you enter a curve or turn, you must overcome the effects of inertia by turning the steering wheel. You are moving the vehicle out of its straight path. At the same time, you feel as if you are being pulled toward the door into the curve. What you feel is **centrifugal force** pushing you in the direction opposite to the way you are turning.

As you slow down and enter the curve or turn, you turn the wheel. Friction between the tires and the road acts against centrifugal force and allows the vehicle to follow a curved path. As long as there is enough friction to overcome centrifugal force, you can make the turn. As you turn the wheel, the front tires provide the traction needed to turn the vehicle.

Slow your vehicle as you approach a curve or turn. The faster you go, the more difficult it is for traction to overcome inertia.

How Do Gravity and the Contour of the Road Affect Steering?

Gravity in relation to the contour of the road affects how well a vehicle will take a curve.

Banked Roads

Have you ever seen the Indy 500 auto race? The track is banked, or higher on the outside of curves than on the inside. On a properly **banked curve,** the roadway tilts down toward the inside of the curve. Although a vehicle tends to move toward the outside of a curve, the downward tilt of a banked curve improves steering control by working with the force of gravity. If the banking or downward tilt were toward the outside of the curve, gravity and inertia would tend to pull the vehicle off the road, making steering more difficult.

Crowned Roads

Crowned roads are higher in the center than at either of the edges to facilitate drainage. When driving in the right lane on a two-way crowned road, gravity will tend to pull your vehicle to the right, off the roadway. You must counteract the effect of gravitational pull by exerting more force on the steering wheel to keep the vehicle on the road. Slowing down will give you more control on this type of roadway.

◆ *Turning the steering wheel enables friction to overcome centrifugal force.*

Lesson 2 Review

1. How do speed, traction, and gravity affect braking distance?
2. Describe how steering is affected by traction and inertia.
3. What role do friction and centrifugal force play in steering around a curve?
4. How does gravity affect steering on a banked or crowned road? How should you respond?

WHAT WOULD YOU DO?

You are driving at 30 mph. Explain what you will do before you enter the curve.

OBJECTIVES

1. List factors that can cause your vehicle to skid.
2. Name and describe the kinds of skids there are.
3. Describe how to manage risk in responding to a skid.

KEY TERMS

skid
braking skid
power skid
cornering skid
blowout skid

Using Natural Laws to Manage Skids

Understanding the natural laws that affect the control of your vehicle can help you regain that control when you lose it through skidding. When you **skid,** you lose control of the direction and speed of your vehicle's movement because of reduced traction. If you skid, you are not helpless. Once you understand what causes a skid, you're already on your way to dealing with one.

What Can Make Your Vehicle Skid?

Whenever you skid, one of three things has happened: traction was reduced, you tried to change speed too quickly, or you tried to change direction too quickly.

Reduced Traction

A loss of traction or a reduction in traction can be frightening and dangerous even for experienced drivers. When traction is reduced because of a change in conditions, your tires can lose their grip on the road's surface and the vehicle can begin to slide. Drivers should always be aware of conditions that could result in reduced traction. See Chapter 12 for more information on driving in conditions of reduced traction.

Changing Speed Too Quickly

You are on a slippery road, and you want to slow down. You step firmly on the brake pedal, and your vehicle starts to skid. What happened? You tried to change speed too quickly. Traction could not overcome the vehicle's kinetic energy and momentum as fast as you wanted it to.

Changing Direction Too Quickly

Turning a vehicle quickly is like a large football player trying to make a sharp turn at

---

TIPS

FOR NEW DRIVERS

Dealing with Skids

Skidding can be frightening. You can minimize trouble, however, by remembering the following points.

- The most important thing you must do is respond quickly and correctly. Concentrate. Do not panic.
- Do not brake. This will only make the skid worse.
- Look and steer in the direction in which you want the front of the vehicle to go.
- Make steering corrections quickly but smoothly.
- Do not give up. Keep steering.

---

a full gallop. Sometimes it works, but sometimes it doesn't. If you're driving at a high speed, your vehicle has a tremendous amount of momentum and kinetic energy. Inertia is also at work, trying to force your vehicle to move in a straight path. Tire traction may not be great enough to compensate for momentum, kinetic energy, and inertia when you turn or enter a sharp curve.

How fast is a high speed? It depends on the road. Look at the speed limit signs posted just below the warning signs as you near a curve. They tell you the maximum safe speed you should use to enter the curve. Then you need to adjust speed downward according to conditions.

What Are the Kinds of Skids?

Knowing the kind of skid you are experiencing will help you manage the risk involved, and it may even help you prevent skidding.

KINDS OF SKIDS

Type	Braking skid	Power skid	Cornering skid	Blowout skid
Reason	The brakes are applied so hard that one or more wheels lock.	The gas pedal is pressed suddenly and too hard.	The tires lose traction in a turn.	A tire suddenly loses air pressure.
Conditions	A sudden stop A wet, slippery, or uneven road	A sudden, hard acceleration A slippery road surface	A turn made too fast Poor tires or a slippery road surface	A punctured, worn, or overinflated tire An overloaded vehicle
What can happen	Steering control is lost. If the front wheels lock, the vehicle skids straight ahead. If only the rear wheels lock, the rear of the vehicle slides sideways. The vehicle may spin around.	A vehicle with front-wheel drive plows straight ahead. In a vehicle with rear-wheel drive, the back end can skid to the side. The vehicle may spin around.	Steering control is lost. The rear wheels skid away from the turn. The vehicle keeps going straight ahead.	There is a strong pull toward the side on which a front tire has blown out. A rear-tire blowout may cause a pull toward the blowout, side-to-side swaying, or fishtailing.
What to do	Take your foot off the brake pedal. Steer. When the wheels start turning again and moving forward, steering control will return.	Ease up on the gas pedal until the wheels stop spinning. Steer to straighten the vehicle. Countersteer if the vehicle starts to spin.	Take your foot all the way off the accelerator. Steer to straighten the vehicle.	Do not brake. Make firm, steady steering corrections. Do not change speed suddenly. Slow down gradually, and drive off the road.

There are four basic kinds of skids: braking, power, cornering, and blowout. If you know the causes and results of these kinds of skids and the conditions under which they occur, you can deal with them safely.

- A **braking skid** occurs when you apply the brakes so hard that one or more of the wheels lock.
- A **power skid** occurs when you suddenly press on the accelerator too hard.
- A **cornering skid** occurs when you lose steering control in a turn, curve, or lane change.
- A **blowout skid** occurs when a tire suddenly loses air pressure.

◆ *Accelerate and brake gradually to reduce the risk of skidding on snowy roadways.*

How Do You Respond to a Skid?

Suppose you are driving carefully on an ice-covered roadway. Vehicles are parked alongside the traffic lane, and traffic is heavy in both directions. Suddenly your vehicle begins to skid. How can you manage the risk of a skid and safely drive out of it?

1. Ease off the gas pedal and shift into Neutral. Stay off the brake.
2. With your foot off the pedals, look well ahead and steer in the direction in which you want the front of the vehicle to go.
3. As the skid starts to change direction, turn the wheel smoothly and quickly in the direction in which you want the front of the vehicle to go.
4. Keep steering until you are out of the skid.

WHAT WOULD YOU DO?

You have a blowout. What is likely to happen? What should you do? Why?

Lesson 3 Review

1. What conditions can make your vehicle skid?
2. Describe four kinds of skids.
3. Describe how to safely steer out of a skid.

Natural Laws, Risk Management, and Collisions

OBJECTIVES

1. Explain how speed control can help you avoid a collision.
2. Describe how knowledge of natural laws can help you avoid a collision.
3. Tell how to minimize the risks of a collision.

KEY TERMS

antilock brake system (ABS)
force of impact

The goal of any driver is to avoid collisions and injuries. Good drivers understand how to use accelerating, braking, and steering to help them achieve this goal.

How Can You Use Speed Control to Avoid a Collision?

Braking is a natural reaction to avoid a collision. However, it is not always the correct evasive action.

Accelerating

Accelerating may sometimes be your only means of reducing risk. Such situations occur most often at intersections or in merging traffic. A vehicle may be coming at you from one side. Braking may leave you in the vehicle's path. Steering to the side may be impossible if there are objects on both sides of you. If the road ahead is clear, a quick burst of speed may take you to safety, or at least move the crash farther back on the vehicle.

Braking

Steering to the side or accelerating may not be possible. Under 25 mph, it takes less time and distance to stop than to steer into another lane.

When braking, you want to stop fast without making the wheels lock, or stop turning. Locking of the wheels reduces traction and will cause loss of steering control. To brake quickly, use the threshold/squeeze braking method. Use your body to sense how the brakes are working. Keep your heel on the floor and your foot on the brake. "Squeeze" the pedal down with a

◆ *The driver in the left lane accelerated to avoid the possible collision in the right lane.*

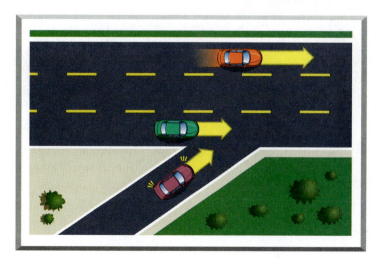

◆ *For best braking control, squeeze the brake pedal with steady, firm pressure.*

steady, firm pressure until just before the brakes lock. If they lock, ease up about 2 or 3 degrees. Immediately squeeze down again, but not as firmly. Continue until you reach your desired speed. This type of braking allows you to maintain steering control. An **antilock brake system (ABS)** eliminates the problem of locked brakes. Sensors detect when a wheel stops turning. Pressure on the wheel's brakes is reduced until the wheel starts turning again. This action is independent of the pressure the driver applies to the brake pedal. Antilock brakes permit maximum brake pressure while retaining steering control. Do *not* pump these brakes.

How Can Knowledge of Natural Laws Help You Avoid a Collision?

A knowledge of natural laws is vital to vehicle control. Knowing how natural laws work is also important when making evasive maneuvers.

Steering to Avoid a Collision

You are driving at 55 mph. At the top of a hill, you see a vehicle with a flat tire stopped in your lane about 3 seconds ahead. You are going too fast to stop in time. With normal traction, it takes about 4 to 5 seconds to stop your vehicle. You have only 3 seconds. What can you do?

You should steer to the right, if possible. Take the following steps.

1. Turn the steering wheel just enough to get onto the shoulder.
2. Once past the disabled vehicle, immediately turn the steering wheel back about twice the amount you turned it to the right.
3. Turn the wheel right to bring your vehicle back into its original path.

You use what you know about traction to steer out of trouble. If you turn the wheel more than half a turn, your speed may be too high for traction to overcome centrifugal force.

Controlled Off-Road Recovery

You see a passing vehicle coming toward you. It will not return to its lane in time. You steer to the right. The vehicle passes on the left, but now your two right wheels are on the unpaved shoulder. You want to get back on the road.

Tires rolling on different surfaces have different amounts of grip. Paved areas give more traction than unpaved areas. Braking may cause

More than 39 percent of all vehicle occupant fatalities involve a single vehicle. The driver leaves the roadway, brakes hard, or oversteers. The driver loses control. The vehicle skids, rolls over, or strikes an object.

your vehicle to skid. Turning the wheel sharply could cause your vehicle to skid, flip over, or shoot back across the roadway. Do the following.

1. Let the vehicle move right until the wheels on the shoulder are about 12 to 18 inches from the road edge.
2. Look for a spot where the road edge appears to be no more than 2 inches higher than the shoulder.
3. Signal your intention to return to the roadway.
4. Move the steering wheel ¹⁄₁₆ to ⅛ of a turn to the left. As soon as you feel the right front tire contact the road edge, steer back to the right ¼ to ½ of a turn.
5. Turn the steering wheel straight without braking or accelerating.

This maneuver is called controlled off-road recovery.

How Can You Minimize the Risk and Consequences of a Collision?

It is not always possible to avoid a collision. Knowing what to do before a collision happens will help minimize its effects. You should understand the factors that contribute to the force of impact of a collision.

Force of Impact

The force with which a moving vehicle hits another object is called the **force of impact.** Three factors affect the force of impact.

Speed of the vehicle The force of impact at 20 mph is four times that at 10 mph. And the force of impact at 30 mph is nine times that at 10 mph.

Weight of the vehicle The heavier a vehicle is, the harder it will hit any other object.

Impact distance The force of impact also depends on the distance a moving vehicle travels between first impact with an object and the point where the vehicle comes to a full stop. When a vehicle hits an unmoving solid object, the impact distance is short. The object does not "cave in" at impact, and so kinetic energy is spent immediately on impact. The shorter the impact distance, the greater the damage.

Reducing the Force of Impact

These energy-absorbing features help increase impact distance.

Sand canisters You often see canisters filled with sand in front of concrete barriers on highways. If a vehicle hits these canisters, they break apart. The sand helps reduce the vehicle's force of impact.

Vehicle features New vehicles include a number of features that help increase impact distance by absorbing energy. These features include

FYI CULTURAL CROSSROADS

In the 1400s, the Inca Empire stretched from the border between Colombia and Ecuador to central Chile in South America. From Cuzco, the empire's capital, roads that were well-constructed ran to all parts of the empire. The total length of this road system was about 9,500 miles, and it was designed for people on foot. Relay runners were stationed at posts along the road to carry messages and parcels quickly to and from the capital.

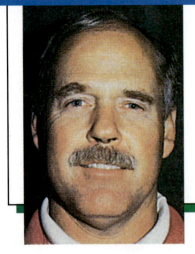

Bruce Reichel
Driving Instructor, Bill Scott Racing (BSR), Inc.

If you understand the factors involved when a vehicle is in motion, you can learn how to adjust the speed and position of the vehicle to work with the natural laws.

Controlling a vehicle is controlling its energy, and its weight and speed determine the vehicle's energy. A car weighing 2,000 pounds traveling at 30 mph has half the energy of a 4,000-pound car traveling at the same speed. A 2,000-pound car traveling at 60 mph has four times the energy of the same car traveling at 30 mph.

air bags; crumple zones; automatic safety belts; head restraints; and padded dashboards. See Chapter 7 for more information about energy-absorbing features.

If a Collision Is Unavoidable

Suppose a collision seems unavoidable. What should you do? If you can increase the impact distance, you will lessen the force of impact, which in turn will reduce the risk of serious damage or injury.

Head-on A head-on collision with a vehicle or an immovable object, such as a large tree, is the worst type of collision. If you can reduce speed, the force of impact will be less. Driving into something that is movable, such as a bush or a snowbank, will also reduce the force of the impact.

Side Suppose you are about to be broadsided in an intersection and cannot avoid it. How can you minimize the damage? You can accelerate to make impact behind the passenger compartment or with the rear end of your vehicle. This will help minimize damage or injury because impact will occur behind the passengers.

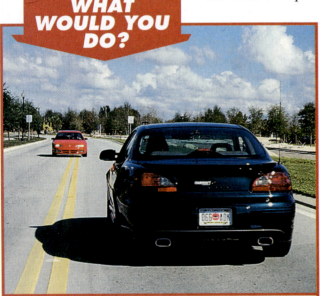

WHAT WOULD YOU DO?

A driver has lost control of a vehicle, and it is swerving into your lane. What should you do?

Lesson 4 Review

1. Under what conditions can accelerating or braking help you avoid a collision?
2. How can traction and steering help you avoid a collision?
3. How would you use knowledge of force of impact to respond to a head-on or side collision?

Using the Distance Numbers

The distance numbers shown on a map can give you a more accurate idea than the map scale of how far apart two places are. On this map, distance numbers are either black or red. The numbers indicate the distance in miles between towns, junctions, and interchanges.

Here's an example of how the numbers work. Find Lake Butler and Starke on the road map. Along the highway running between the two cities, you'll see a red number 15. This means that Lake Butler and Starke are 15 miles apart.

Along Route 301 between Starke and Waldo, you'll see the red number 11. It tells you that it is about 11 miles from Starke to Waldo.

If you add the numbers—15 + 11—the sum is 26. The distance by road from Lake Butler to Waldo, going through Starke, is about 26 miles.

In general, you can estimate driving time more accurately by using distance numbers rather than the map scale, especially if the road to be driven has many curves and loops. Keep in mind, though, that distance numbers indicate only the mileage, not the condition of the road. Six miles of travel along a twisting back road can take twice as long as 10 miles of highway driving!

Try It Yourself

1. How many miles is it from Otter Creek to Trenton along Routes 98 and 129?
2. You're going from Jasper to Branford along Route 129. How far is it?
3. What is the shortest route between Greenville and Branford?

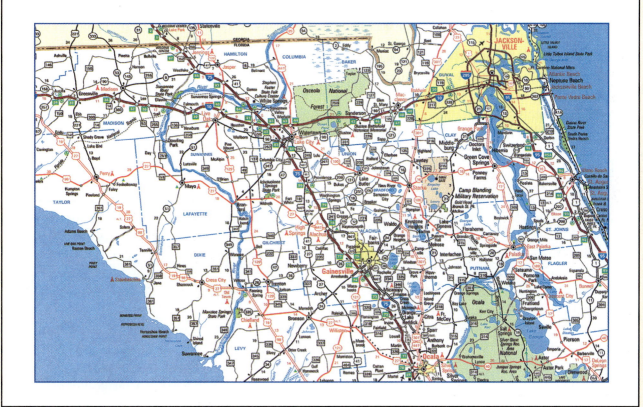

KEY POINTS

Lesson One

1. Natural laws include the laws of inertia, friction, momentum, kinetic energy, and gravity.
2. Inertia causes passengers to keep moving forward when a vehicle is stopped abruptly. Friction between the road and tires holds a vehicle on the road. Momentum determines the extent of damage in a collision. Kinetic energy affects braking and acceleration. Gravity can slow your vehicle when you are driving uphill or increase its speed when going downhill.

Lesson Two

1. Braking is a result of friction between the brake linings and the wheel drums or wheel discs and pads.
2. Friction and inertia affect steering, as do road conditions and a vehicle's tires, steering mechanism, suspension, and wheel alignment.
3. As you enter a curve, inertia and centrifugal force can be overcome by the friction between the tires and roadway, allowing you to change direction.
4. Gravity pulls a vehicle into the curve on an inwardly banked curve, thus aiding steering

control. If the banking is toward the outer part of the curve, gravity pulls the vehicle away from the curve, making steering more difficult.

Lesson Three

1. Reduced traction and too rapid changes in either speed or direction can cause skidding.
2. Four kinds of skids are braking, power, cornering, and blowout.
3. To respond to a skid, do not brake. Look well ahead in the direction in which you want to go. Steer smoothly and quickly in that direction.

Lesson Four

1. It is possible to avoid some collisions by accelerating and steering if the roadway is clear. At speeds under 25 mph, braking can help avoid a collision.
2. You may be able to avoid a collision by understanding the relationship between steering, speed, and friction.
3. Reducing speed, choosing something that will "cave in," and protecting the passenger compartment from impact are three ways to reduce the force of impact in a collision.

PROJECTS

1. Make a photo display of potential low-traction areas in your community. Label each photo, and list the potential danger. Return to the area to check out your suspicion. Make sure to position yourself so that you are safe and will not become a danger to traffic.
2. Check the shoulders and off-road areas of some local highways. Are they well designed and maintained? Do they provide an escape path in an emergency? What dangers do they pose to drivers? How could they be improved?

*inter*NET
CONNECTION

Pick two of the natural laws studied in the chapter. Use Glencoe's driver education Web site to gather more information on these natural laws. Learn more about how each law will help you maintain control of your vehicle and reduce driving risk.
www.glencoe.com/sec/driver.ed

CHAPTER TEST

Write the letter of the answer that best completes each sentence.

1. A vehicle's momentum depends on its
   a. kinetic energy.
   b. speed and weight.
   c. center of gravity.

2. If only the outer edges of a tire grip the road,
   a. the tire is properly inflated.
   b. the tire is overinflated.
   c. the tire is underinflated.

3. Three factors that affect braking distance are
   a. car and roadway conditions and speed.
   b. steering ability, centrifugal force, and ocular tracking.
   c. tread depth, controlled recovery, and the motion of energy.

4. If you are trying to get out of a skid,
   a. look for wet leaves to slow you down.
   b. keep your foot off the pedals and steer in the direction that you want the vehicle to go.
   c. slam on the brakes.

5. If your vehicle has good directional control,
   a. you can decrease total stopping distance by 3 seconds.
   b. you will be able to keep the vehicle moving in the direction in which you steer it.
   c. you can make sharp turns at high speed.

6. After driving through a deep puddle,
   a. only use engine braking for a while.
   b. apply light pressure to the brake pedal.
   c. stop at the nearest service station for brake fluid.

7. A power skid occurs when you
   a. apply the brakes too hard.
   b. press the accelerator too hard.
   c. downshift too quickly.

8. A driver can turn successfully as long as there is enough
   a. friction to overcome centrifugal force.
   b. centrifugal force to overcome friction.
   c. adhesion to overcome friction.

9. Because of inertia,
   a. objects at rest move in a straight line.
   b. moving objects continue to move in a straight line.
   c. moving objects continue to move along a curved path.

10. A vehicle's speed and weight both affect
    a. the center of gravity.
    b. friction.
    c. force of impact.

Write the word or phrase that best completes each sentence.

| skidding | kinetic energy | inertia |
| centripedal | center of gravity | |

11. Any object in motion has _____.
12. Safety belts work against _____ to keep you from being thrown forward.
13. A higher _____ makes a vehicle less stable and harder to control on turns and curves.
14. _____ is loss of control over the direction in which your vehicle is moving because of reduced traction.

DRIVER'S LOG

In this chapter, you have learned about the effect that natural laws have on a variety of driving situations. Summarize, in a few sentences for each, the meaning of inertia, gravity, and momentum. Explain how these laws help you anticipate and manage risk.

CHAPTER 15

Responding to an Emergency

Emergencies happen even to the most experienced and careful drivers. It is important to learn how to assess and respond to emergencies safely, efficiently, and calmly. When you can do this, an emergency need not turn into a disaster.

OBJECTIVES

1. Describe what to do in case of brake failure.
2. Explain what to do in case of engine stalling or other engine failure.
3. Describe what to do in case of steering failure.

Brake, Engine, and Steering Failures

You see the stop sign at the intersection ahead and step on the brake. The pedal goes all the way to the floor, but your vehicle doesn't slow down. Two teenagers start across the street. Your mind races: "What should I do?"

Emergencies can occur suddenly and without warning. Brakes can fail, engines can stall, steering systems can malfunction. If you are prepared to deal with such emergencies, however, you can keep a dangerous situation from becoming a tragedy.

◆ *Learn how to deal with emergency vehicle failures to manage risk.*

What Actions Can You Take When Your Brakes Fail?

All new vehicles have a dual-service brake system. Some vehicles have separate systems for the front and back wheels. Other vehicles use an "X" brake system, which links each front wheel with its diagonal rear wheel. Total failure of both systems at once is very unlikely, although partial or temporary brake failure does happen occasionally.

In Case of Brake Failure

When brake failure occurs, the foot brake may have no resistance. The brake pedal may sink to the floor and the brake warning light may come on. Here is what to do.

1. Rapidly pump the brake pedal. Doing so may build up pressure in the brake-fluid lines, providing some braking force. After a few pumps you'll know whether or not you've restored braking power. If power is restored, stop pumping.
2. Shift down to a lower gear to slow the movement of the vehicle.
3. If pumping the brakes does not work, use the parking brake. Either keep your thumb on the release button or hold the brake handle so that you can alternately apply and release brake pressure. Applying

the parking brake too abruptly may lock the rear wheels—usually the only ones the parking brake affects—and send the vehicle into a spin. Use an apply-release-apply-release pattern with the parking brake to slow down the vehicle.

4. If you still have little or no brake control, look for a place to steer against the curb if there is one. Scraping the tires against a curb can help reduce speed.

5. Other ways to slow the vehicle after you've applied the parking brake and downshifted include steering into an open area, such as a parking lot and shifting into lower gears as quickly as possible; steering onto an uphill road; and turning the ignition to the off position, *not* the lock position, which would lock the steering wheel. After you have brought the vehicle to a stop, put the gear selection in Park to keep the vehicle where it is.

6. If you cannot avoid a collision, steer so that you sideswipe an object rather than hit it head-on. If possible, steer your vehicle into bushes or scrape along a guardrail or even parked vehicles rather than move toward pedestrians or occupied vehicles.

Note: If your vehicle has power brakes, engine failure may cause brake malfunction. If that is the case, your brakes will still work, but you'll have to press harder on the pedal.

Other Brake Problems

If you apply your brakes hard for a long time, such as when traveling down a long mountain slope, you could over-heat them and cause "brake fade," a kind of temporary brake failure. To help prevent this, shift to a lower gear before starting down the slope. You can also pull off the road to let your brakes cool.

Drive more slowly through puddles. Driving at normal speeds through deep puddles or on flooded roadways can make your brakes wet and lead to temporary brake failure as well as cause hydroplaning. To dry your brakes, drive slowly with your left foot gently on the brake pedal. The friction will produce heat that will dry the brakes.

TIPS FOR NEW DRIVERS

Emergency Items

It is wise to keep emergency items in the trunk of your vehicle. Include such items as these:

- flashlight with extra batteries
- jumper cables (for starting a dead battery)
- flares, warning triangles, or reflectors
- coolant
- windshield-washer fluid
- wiping cloth
- ice scraper, snow brush, and snow shovel
- jack with flat board for soft surfaces
- lug wrench (for changing a flat tire)
- screwdriver, pliers, duct tape, and adjustable wrench (for making simple repairs)
- extra fan/alternator belt
- extra fuses (if needed for your car)
- fire extinguisher
- heavy gloves
- blanket
- drinking water
- first aid kit
- pencil and notebook (for recording emergency information)
- spare headlamp and bulb

◆ *Your car's engine may stall and your brakes may get wet in rainy weather.*

How Can You Respond to Engine Failure?

Engine failure occurs more often than any other kind of vehicle failure. Engines fail for many different reasons, such as a broken timing gear, a fuel system problem, lack of fuel, an electrical system malfunction, or problems caused by extreme heat or cold.

If Your Vehicle's Engine Stalls

If your vehicle's engine stalls (stops suddenly) while you are driving, check traffic around you and determine the best point at which to leave the roadway. Signal, then steer off the road or to the curb as quickly as possible while you still have momentum. Keep in mind that if your engine stalls and you have power brakes and power steering, the brakes and steering will still work, but they will be much harder to operate. If your vehicle has power brakes, do not pump the brake pedal. Use firm, steady pressure instead. When you are off the road, shift to Neutral, and try to restart the engine. If the engine starts, shift into Drive and continue driving. If you're driving a vehicle with a manual transmission, shift into First gear and continue moving forward.

If the engine won't start, make sure your flashers are on, and raise the hood. Place flares or warning triangles 100 feet in front of your vehicle and at least 100 feet behind it. Signal or wait for help.

If You Flood the Engine

If you pump the accelerator more than once when trying to start your vehicle, too much gas and not enough air may be supplied to the engine. The result is a flooded engine that won't start. When your engine is flooded, you can often smell gas. In vehicles with fuel injection, there is no need to pump the accelerator before starting; in fact, a flooded engine may result.

To start a flooded engine, press the accelerator pedal all the way to the floor and hold it there. At the same time, turn on the ignition switch, and hold it on for 5 to 10 seconds. If the vehicle starts, slowly release the accelerator. If the vehicle doesn't start, wait about 10 minutes and try again.

If the Engine Overheats

Your engine may overheat for any of various reasons: driving in slow-moving traffic during hot weather, with the air conditioner running; driving up long, steep hills; a loose or broken fan belt; a broken water pump or hose; not enough coolant or antifreeze in the cooling system; a stuck or broken thermostat; or a clogged radiator.

When engine temperature is too high, the temperature gauge or warning light on your instrument panel indicates that the engine is overheating. You may also see steam or smoke rising from under the hood.

If your engine overheats, follow these steps.

1. Turn off all accessories, especially the air conditioner.
2. If the temperature gauge continues to show hot or the warning light stays on, signal and pull off the road. Raise the hood, let the engine cool, and get professional help.

    If you can't pull off the road immediately, turn on the heater to draw heat from the engine. Doing so will not solve the problem, but it will help temporarily until you can get off the road safely.
3. If there is no steam or smoke coming from the engine, carefully open the hood (wear gloves to protect your hands). Look for such problems as a broken hose or belt. Note whether the radiator overflow tank is empty, but do not touch the radiator.
4. When the engine has cooled completely, check the fluid level in the radiator overflow tank again. If the fluid level is low, you need to add coolant. Many overflow tanks have a fill line to help you determine the proper level of fluid. Start the engine, and let it run at idle speed as you add the coolant.

If the Engine Is Wet

If you drive through water, your vehicle's engine may get wet, start to sputter, and stall. The water may short out your vehicle's electrical system or be drawn into the combustion chamber by way of the air filter and the carburetor.

If your engine gets wet and stalls, steer off the road and turn off the ignition. Wait a few minutes, keeping the hood closed to let the heat of the engine compartment dry out the moisture. Then try to restart the engine. If it doesn't start, the engine may need more time to dry. If it's a hot, sunny day, you may speed up the process by raising the hood.

◆ **Let the temperature cool before you check an overheated engine.**

SAFETY TIPS

To prevent your brakes from getting wet when driving through deep water, apply pressure to the brake pedal as you move slowly through the water.

Two kinds of steering failure are possible: power-assist failure and total steering system failure. The former is far more common than the latter.

If Power Steering Fails

Power-steering failure can occur if your engine stalls or the power-assist mechanism fails. When power steering fails, your steering wheel suddenly becomes very difficult to turn.

If your vehicle's power steering fails, grip the steering wheel firmly and turn it with more force. Check surrounding traffic, signal, and when it's safe to do so, steer off the road and stop. As soon as you possibly can, have a mechanic check your steering system.

Total Steering Failure

Sudden and total steering failure is a rare occurrence. However, if a breakdown in either the steering or suspension system does happen, your ability to control your vehicle will be drastically reduced.

In case of total steering failure, bring your vehicle to a stop as quickly and safely as possible, using the parking brake, not the foot brake. If you step on the foot brake it might cause your vehicle to pull sharply to one side. Just as when responding to brake failure, keep hold of the parking brake release button or handle to avoid locking the rear wheels and going into a spin. Downshift.

WHAT WOULD YOU DO?

As you prepare to slow your vehicle, you find that the brakes don't work and the vehicle does not slow down. What do you suppose has happened? How will you handle this situation?

Lesson 1 Review

1. What actions would you take if your vehicle's brakes failed?
2. What would you do if your engine stalled while you were driving? What if the engine overheated?
3. What would you do if your vehicle's power steering suddenly failed?

Tire Failure and Other Serious Problems

A motor vehicle is a complex machine that must endure years of stop-and-go driving, rough roads, and harsh weather. No matter how well you maintain your vehicle, there's always the possibility that a part may break or a system may malfunction.

In addition to the major vehicle failures you read about in the previous lesson, you should be prepared to deal with a number of other serious problems.

What Actions Can You Take in Case of a Blowout or Flat Tire?

A blowout and a flat tire are similar but not the same. A **blowout** is an explosion in a tire while the vehicle is in motion. The tire suddenly loses air pressure, and the vehicle may become difficult to control.

A tire can also lose pressure gradually, through a slow leak. If you don't detect the leak in time, the tire is likely to go flat. A tire can go flat either while the vehicle is parked or when it is moving.

If Your Tire Loses Pressure

When a tire fails while you are driving, you may feel a strong pull to the right or left. The rear of your vehicle may shimmy or swerve back and forth. You may even hear a thumping sound. The effect may be gradual if the tire has a slow leak or sudden if the tire blows out.

If a tire loses pressure, take these steps:

1. Keep a firm grip on the steering wheel with both hands. Look well ahead along your intended path. Maintain or slightly increase pressure on the accelerator until your steering is stable.
2. Release the accelerator slowly. Do not brake—you could make the vehicle swerve out of control.
3. Check the traffic around you. When you find a gap, signal and steer off the road. You'll have to change the tire, so move as far off the main

◆ Tire failures are fairly common. You should become familiar with emergency procedures for handling tire failure.

roadway as you can. As the vehicle slows, brake gradually and come to a stop on a flat surface.

4. Shift to Park (Reverse in a manual-shift vehicle), set the parking brake, and put on your emergency flashers.

5. Get out of the vehicle, and have passengers get out too, on the side away from traffic.

How to Change a Tire

Changing a tire requires caution and may require more strength than some people possess. Between 300 and 400 people are killed yearly while changing tires when the vehicle falls off the jack and onto them or they are struck by passing vehicles.

Position your vehicle on a flat, hard surface as far from traffic as possible. Set out flares or warning triangles at least 100 feet in front and back to alert other drivers.

Use two rocks, bricks, or pieces of wood (each at least 4 inches by 8 inches by 2 inches) to block the wheel that is diagonally across from the flat tire. Put one block in front of the wheel and another behind it. The blocks will keep the vehicle from rolling when it is jacked up.

You'll find complete instructions for changing a tire in your owner's manual or inside the trunk of your vehicle. Here are the basic steps.

1. After the wheel blocks are in place, remove the jack, lug wrench, and spare tire from your vehicle and place them near the flat tire.

2. Assemble the jack, and position it according to instructions in the owner's manual. Jack up the vehicle until the flat tire is just in contact with the ground.

◆ When you change a tire, get as far from traffic as possible. Then continue to watch for traffic approaching you.

3. Remove the hubcap or wheel cover from the wheel. Use the lug wrench to loosen the lug nuts enough so that they'll move easily, but do not remove them.

4. Jack up the vehicle until the tire clears the ground.

5. Take off the lug nuts and put them inside the hubcap or in some other safe place.

6. Pull off the wheel with the flat tire. Replace it with the spare tire. Put the lug nuts back on by hand, and tighten them slightly with the wrench.

7. Carefully let the vehicle down, and remove the jack. Tighten the lug nuts with the lug wrench.

8. Put the flat tire, jack, wrench, and other equipment back in the vehicle.

9. If the spare is an undersized tire or limited-mileage tire, drive no faster than 50 mph to the nearest service station. Have the flat tire repaired or replaced right away.

What Should You Do If Your Accelerator Pedal Sticks?

As you're driving along, you decide to decrease speed. You lift your foot from the accelerator pedal but nothing changes; the vehicle keeps moving at the same speed. The problem is a stuck accelerator: The engine does not return to idle when you take your foot off the pedal.

A stuck accelerator pedal may be caused by a sticking linkage or accelerator spring, a broken engine mount, a crumpled floor mat, or ice or snow on the floor around the pedal. Here's what to do.

1. Apply the brakes, and shift to Neutral. The engine will race, but power will be disengaged from the wheels.
2. Check traffic, and signal a lane change.
3. Choose a safe path, and steer off the road, continuing to apply the brakes.
4. When you are off the roadway, shift to Park, turn off the ignition, and apply the parking brake.
5. Do not attempt to unstick the pedal until after you've steered off the road and come to a stop. Test the pedal before reentering traffic. If the pedal problem is mechanical, have it repaired before driving again.

TIPS FOR NEW DRIVERS

15-Minute Checkup

To keep your vehicle in good working order, follow the suggestions in your owner's manual for periodic checkups and maintenance. In addition, if you drive 10,000 or more miles a year, do a 15-minute check of the following items every month:

- all lights for burned-out bulbs
- the battery fluid level or, if your vehicle has a sealed battery, the green battery-charge indicator
- the engine oil level and transmission fluid level
- the brake pedal for firmness and proper operation
- the brake fluid level
- the air pressure in all tires
- the tires for uneven wear
- the cooling system
- the hoses and belts that operate the fan, compressor, and the like
- the windshield washer and wipers
- the power-steering fluid level

What Should You Do If the Hood Flies Up?

Anything that blocks your forward view is a threat to your safety. If the hood of your vehicle suddenly flies up while you're driving, you must take action to avoid a collision and get off the road.

1. Lean forward and look through the space between the dashboard and the hood. If this view is blocked or limited, roll down your side window and look around the hood. Continue to steer in the direction in which you were moving.
2. Check your mirrors to see what traffic is behind you. Check the traffic to either side of you.
3. Signal to indicate the direction you want to move. Maintain your lane position while waiting for a gap in traffic. Then steer off the road.

What Actions Can You Take If Your Vehicle Catches Fire?

Vehicle fires don't occur often, but when they do, prompt action minimizes risk to people and property.

If the Engine Catches Fire

Engine fires are usually fuel-fed or electrical. You'll see and smell smoke coming from under your hood. Follow these steps.

1. Steer off the road to an open space. Turn off the ignition.
2. Get out of the vehicle, and have all passengers get out too. Move far away from the vehicle. Call for help.
3. Decide how serious the fire is. If it is serious—high heat and flames around the hood—do not attempt to put the fire out yourself. Wait for the fire department.
4. If the fire is not serious and you have a fire extinguisher, you can try to put it out yourself. *Do not use water;* it is not effective against fuel, electrical, and oil fires. Wear gloves, or wrap your hands in cloth. Face away from the vehicle, and crouch down so that your head is at the level of the hood. Do not open the hood. Just pull the hood release to create a small space into which you can spray the extinguishing agent.

◆ *Get out of the vehicle as soon as you safely can if your car catches fire.*

If There Is a Fire in the Passenger Compartment

A fire in the passenger compartment is usually caused by carelessness of a passenger or the driver. A common cause of such fires is a burning cigarette or match that drops to the floor or gets blown into the backseat.

If there's a fire in the passenger compartment, steer off the road and stop clear of traffic. Turn off the ignition. Get out of the vehicle, and have all passengers get out. Use a fire extinguisher or water to put out the fire.

What Should You Do If Your Vehicle's Battery Is Dead?

It's a freezing-cold winter night. You turn the ignition switch to start. Nothing happens—no sound, no engine turnover, nothing. Your vehicle's battery is dead.

A battery may go dead if you keep your headlights on or play the radio for a long time while the engine is not running. An old battery may no longer have enough power to start a vehicle in very cold weather.

If the battery is dead, you can't start the engine. However, you may be able to restore power to your battery by using jumper cables.

Jump-Starting Your Vehicle

The most common way to recharge your battery is to **jump-start** it. To do this, you need another vehicle with a working battery that is the same voltage as yours and a pair of jumper cables.

Before you decide to jump-start your battery, make sure the battery fluid is not frozen or the level of fluid low. If it is, do *not* attempt to jump-start your battery because it might explode.

To jump-start your vehicle, follow these steps.

1. Position the vehicle so that the cables can reach between the two batteries. Do not let the vehicles touch.
2. Turn off ignition and electrical equipment in both vehicles. Shift both vehicles into Park or Neutral. Put on their parking brakes.
3. Double-check to make sure both vehicle batteries have the same voltage (usually 12 volts).
4. If either battery has cell or vent caps, remove them. Check again to make sure your dead battery is not frozen.
5. Cover each battery with a heavy cloth to protect against splashing of boiling battery fluid.
6. Attach the positive jumper cable (red, or marked P or +) to the positive terminal of the good battery. Clamp the other end of the same cable to the positive terminal of the dead battery.
7. Attach the negative jumper cable (black, or marked N or –) to the engine or frame of the vehicle with the good battery. Be sure the cable does not touch the fan or drive belts.
8. Attach the other end of the negative cable to the engine or frame of the vehicle with the dead battery. Connect as far as possible from the battery or moving parts, such as the fan.
9. Start the engine of the vehicle that has the good battery. Hold down the accelerator so that the engine runs at a high idle.
10. Start the engine of the vehicle with the dead battery, and with the cables still attached, run it for several minutes.
11. With both engines still running, remove the cables in reverse order from the order in which you attached them.
12. Replace battery caps if they've been removed, and dispose of the cloth covers in case they contain acid.

◆ *It's a good idea to keep jumper cables in the trunk of your car.*

What Should You Do If Your Headlights Fail?

Headlight failure at night is dangerous because without lights, your ability to see is reduced, as is the ability of other drivers to see your vehicle.

Rarely do both headlights fail at the same time. However, if one headlight goes out, you may not notice it until the other also goes out. Headlight failure is usually the result of a burned-out low-beam headlamp.

If you're driving at night and suddenly your lights flicker or die, you have to get off the road, but without making any sudden, possibly dangerous moves. Here's what to do.

1. Slow down and continue in the same direction you were going. Be aware of the traffic around you.
2. Try switching to high beams. Headlights seldom burn out on both high and low beams at the same time. If switching to high beams gives no light, try turning on parking lights, turn indicators, and the emergency flashers. These can give you enough light to help you get off the road.
3. When you see a gap in traffic, steer off the roadway. If you have no lights at all, look for the side-lane markers on the pavement. You can also use available light from other vehicles on the roadway.
4. If possible, stop your vehicle off the roadway near a lighted place, such as a lighted sign, building, or streetlight. Call for help.

WHAT WOULD YOU DO?

Suddenly your front hood flies up, obstructing your vision. What steps will you take to avoid a collision?

Lesson 2 Review

1. What would you do if one of your vehicle's tires suddenly lost pressure while you were driving?
2. How would you deal with a stuck accelerator pedal while driving?
3. What would you do if your vehicle's hood flew up while you were driving?
4. How would you respond to an engine fire? To a fire in the passenger compartment?
5. List the steps for jump-starting a dead battery.
6. What would you do if your headlights failed while you were driving at night?

Waiting for Help and Protecting the Scene

OBJECTIVES

1. Describe how you would get help if your vehicle broke down.
2. Explain how you would protect yourself at the scene.

In an emergency, you may need assistance even though you may be miles from a phone. You may be able to correct a minor mechanical problem yourself. You might also choose to call on passing vehicles and pedestrians to get the help you need.

What Should You Do at the Scene of a Vehicle Breakdown or Other Emergency?

If your vehicle breaks down, you may be able to remedy the problem yourself—by changing a flat tire, for example. If you can't fix the problem, you'll need to get help.

After pulling completely out of traffic, you'll have to communicate your situation to passing drivers or pedestrians in a way that keeps you and other roadway users safe.

◆ *Raising the hood of your car is one action you can take to let others know you need help.*

Make Others Aware of Your Problem

If you have a cellular phone, you'll be able to call for help immediately from your vehicle.

If you have no cell phone and must pull off the road at a place where there's no telephone within safe walking distance, you'll need to get the attention of other drivers. To do this safely—in a way that protects you as well as other drivers—raise the hood of your vehicle, and tie a handkerchief or scarf to the antenna or left door handle. You can also hold the handkerchief or scarf in place by closing a window on it. Set out flares or warning triangles to alert other drivers. Stay in the vehicle if you have pulled well off the roadway. Otherwise, get as far away from the road as you can. Switch on your emergency flashers to alert passing drivers to your situation.

Protect Yourself

You can wait inside your vehicle if the weather is bad and you're far enough off the road. Keep the windows almost closed and the doors locked. Do not sit in a stopped car with windows closed, engine running, and heater on. You could be putting yourself and your passengers at risk of carbon monoxide poisoning.

It is very dangerous to lower your window or open your vehicle door to strangers. If a stranger does stop to offer help, just ask the person to call for emergency road service.

If your vehicle is not far enough from roadway traffic or if you think it might be struck from behind by another vehicle, leave your vehicle and walk to a safe place. Proceed carefully—especially at night or in bad weather, when visibility is limited.

Never stand behind or directly in front of your vehicle. Other roadway users will have trouble seeing you, and you could be struck by an oncoming vehicle.

Make Decisions When Help Comes

Emergency road service operators can usually change a flat tire or do minor repairs on the spot. They may also have gasoline and a booster battery in case you've run out of gas or have a dead battery.

If you need to be towed to a service garage, you should know whether or not your insurance covers all or part of the towing charge. You should also find out how many miles away the service garage is and what the charge is for towing.

If your vehicle is towed, you'll have to arrange transportation for yourself and your passengers. Passengers are not allowed to ride in a vehicle when it's being towed.

WHAT WOULD YOU DO?

Your vehicle has broken down and you have moved it to the side of the road. What actions will you take to find assistance?

Lesson 3 Review

1. What steps would you take to get help if your vehicle broke down?
2. How would you protect yourself at the scene?

First Aid Guidelines and Procedures

OBJECTIVES

1. List several basic first aid guidelines.
2. Describe procedures for controlling bleeding, treating shock, and restoring breathing.
3. List the items that should be in a first aid kit.

KEY TERMS

first aid
mouth-to-mouth resuscitation
hemorrhaging
shock

First aid is emergency treatment given to a person who is injured or ill, before professional medical care arrives. Learning about first aid procedures may help you prevent further injury or even save someone's life in an emergency.

What Are Some Basic First Aid Guidelines?

Because it is usually another motorist and not a medical professional who is first on the scene, all drivers should have some knowledge of first aid. You can learn first aid by taking a course given by the American National Red Cross. You can also read about first aid procedures in a manual or book. However, to really know what you're doing, you need both training and practice in first aid.

Here are some basic first aid guidelines for emergency situations.

- Quickly search the scene and decide if you can help. If you feel confused and uncertain, do not try to give first aid. Call for help.
- The person with the most experience should give first aid. If there are other uninjured people nearby, quickly find out who among you has the most experience with first aid.
- If more than one person is injured, care for the most seriously injured person first.
- Keep calm and act quickly and quietly. Speak in a normal tone of voice. Try not to worry the injured.
- Check that the injured person is breathing. If not, start mouth-to-mouth resuscitation. (See page 286.)
- Find out if the injured person is bleeding. Try to stop any serious bleeding as quickly as possible.
- *Never* move an injured person unless you must do so for his or her safety. Moving an injured person can worsen the injury. Try to keep injured people from moving.
- Get trained medical help as soon as possible. However, if you are the only uninjured person at the scene, do not leave the victim in order to get help unless you have no other choice.

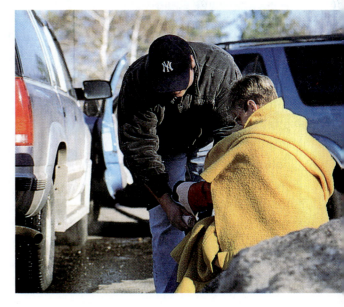

◆ **First aid can be given to injured persons before an ambulance arrives on the scene.**

Professional medical personnel are the only ones who should move an injured person.

- A person who looks uninjured but is unable to move may have an injury to the spine. Do *not* try to move the person. Cover him or her with a blanket if available, and go for help.
- Take precautions to protect yourself against exposure to an injured person's blood or body fluids.

What Are Some Specific First Aid Procedures?

You should learn procedures for restoring breathing, controlling bleeding, and treating shock. They could help you save a life.

Restoring Breathing

Two or three minutes without breathing can cause permanent brain damage. Six minutes without breathing can cause death. To try to restore breathing, apply **mouth-to-mouth resuscitation.**

1. Place the person faceup. Then kneel down and clear the victim's mouth with your fingers.
2. Put one hand under the victim's neck. Gently tilt the head backward, pushing the chin up. Using your thumb and index finger, pinch the victim's nostrils closed.
3. Put your mouth right over the victim's mouth. Blow air into the victim's mouth until you see his or her chest rise. Remove your mouth. Let air escape from the victim's lungs while you take another breath.
4. Repeat the procedure. You should blow air into an adult's mouth at a rate of about 12 times per minute. For children, the rate should be about 20 times per minute. Continue until you are sure the victim is breathing independently or until medical help arrives.

Controlling Bleeding

Someone who is bleeding heavily, or **hemorrhaging,** can die within minutes, so it is very important to try to stop heavy bleeding as quickly as possible.

You can control heavy bleeding by applying direct pressure. Remember to wear protective equipment, such as disposable gloves. Put a clean cloth—such as a folded handkerchief or piece of a shirt—directly over the wound and press down firmly. If you don't have a clean cloth, press directly on the wound with your gloved hand. Keep pressing, without lifting your hand, until medical help arrives.

SAFETY TIPS

Wear protective equipment when giving first aid to a seriously injured person. For example, disposable gloves will decrease the risk of contracting an infectious disease. Keep one or two pairs of disposable gloves in your vehicle's first aid kit. Consult a first aid manual for additional information.

Other means of stopping heavy bleeding are to apply arterial pressure or to use a tourniquet. Do not use either of these methods unless you are fully trained to do so.

Treating Shock

Serious injury, bleeding, or burns can cause shock. When a person is in a state of **shock,** the blood does not circulate properly. As a result, the brain and other tissues fail to get enough oxygen. Shock can cause death if it is not treated.

A shock victim usually feels faint, weak, cold, and often nauseated. The person's skin will feel cold and clammy and may look pale—even blue. Breathing is irregular, and the pulse is weak and fast.

It is wise to treat seriously injured people for shock even if they do not show signs of it. Keep the victim warm with a blanket or coat. Try to keep the body temperature near normal. Control any bleeding, and loosen tight clothing. Do not give the injured person anything to eat or drink. This could induce vomiting and aggravate any internal injuries.

What Items Should You Include in a First Aid Kit for Your Vehicle?

Always keep a first aid kit in your vehicle. The contents of the kit may enable you to save a life—or enable someone else to save your life.

CONNECTIONS

History

In 1881 Clara Barton founded the American Red Cross in Washington, D.C. It is a nonprofit humanitarian organization with the express purpose of preventing and easing human suffering. In 1905 the organization was renamed the American National Red Cross. It made a commitment to provide a worldwide network of emergency relief.

Throughout the 20th century, the American National Red Cross has been a pioneer in the field of emergency relief and medical assistance. The organization provided assistance during World Wars I and II, contributing medical supplies, blood plasma, and able-bodied volunteers. Following World War II, the organization launched a program to provide blood to people of all races, colors, and creeds who need it.

During the past 40 years, the American National Red Cross has become deeply involved in the field of public health. The organization offers many instructional programs in first aid, lifesaving, nurse's aide training, baby care, and home nursing. Many people serve in first aid stations and mobile units along highways.

There are now more than 2 million Red Cross volunteers nationwide. In addition, more than 20 million Junior Red Cross members participate in activities geared toward helping people in their communities as well as underprivileged children in other countries.

Loretta J. Martin
Coordinator, Safety and Driver Education, Chicago Public Schools

Roadside emergencies can happen anytime. You can minimize their consequences if you mentally prepare for them, know how to handle common vehicle failure, and know what to do at the scene of an emergency.

- *Don't drive unless you are fit.*
- *Wear your safety belt.*
- *Carry an emergency car kit.*
- *Carry a good first-aid kit and know how to use it.*
- *Protect the scene.*
- *Know how to get help quickly.*

The American National Red Cross suggests that the following items be included in a first aid kit:

- bottle of syrup of ipecac; bottle of activated charcoal (both for use only on advice of a medical professional)
- change for phone calls
- pencil and notebook
- disposable gloves
- plastic adhesive bandages (25, in various sizes)
- gauze dressings (12, 4 inches square)
- roller gauze bandages (2 rolls, 3 inches wide)
- safety pins (10, in various sizes)
- adhesive tape (1 roll, 1 inch wide)
- scissors
- triangular bandages (5)
- moist towelettes (6)
- combine dressings (3)
- tweezers

Check the contents of your first aid kit regularly, and replace any items as needed. Be sure to keep the kit out of children's reach.

WHAT WOULD YOU DO?

You have been involved in a collision with another vehicle. You are uninjured, but the other driver is bleeding. How can you help?

Lesson 4 Review

1. What first aid guidelines should you follow in an emergency?
2. What are the first aid procedures for restoring breathing, controlling bleeding, and treating shock?
3. What items should you include in a first aid kit for your vehicle?

Benjamin Banneker

To drivers traveling through the United States, it seems as though many major cities just grew, without any plan at all. In many cases, this is true. However, our capital city, Washington, D.C., is one of the few cities in this country that was designed before it was built. This is particularly evident in the area surrounding the United States Capitol, which is located near the center of Washington. Like the spokes of a wheel, broad streets extend out from the Capitol in all directions. This roadway pattern can also be seen near Union Station, the Lincoln Memorial, and Mt. Vernon Square.

President George Washington chose Pierre L'Enfant, a French engineer, to draw up the plans for the new capital. Benjamin Banneker helped L'Enfant to work out the city's plan and to survey, or measure, the size, shape, and area of the land. Banneker was the first African American ever to be appointed to work for the government.

L'Enfant left the United States before the building of Washington, D.C., was completed, taking the plans with him. However, Benjamin Banneker stepped in and finished laying out the city from memory.

Benjamin Banneker was the son of a free woman and a slave father. He was born free in 1731 on a farm in Maryland. Banneker was educated in a Quaker school, where he became interested in mathematics and science. He later taught himself astronomy.

Banneker used his knowledge to make astronomical and tidal calculations in order to write a yearly almanac predicting weather conditions. He sent a copy of his almanac to Thomas Jefferson along with a letter urging the abolition of slavery. Those against slavery held Banneker up as an example of the talents and abilities of African Americans.

What Do You Think Now?

What do you think was Benjamin Banneker's most important accomplishment? Why?

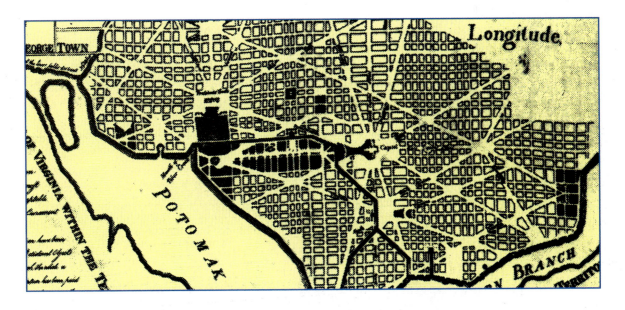

KEY POINTS

Lesson One

1. In case of brake failure, rapidly pump the brake pedal. If that doesn't work, use the parking brake. Downshift.
2. If your engine stalls while you're driving, signal and steer off the road. If your vehicle is in motion, shift to Neutral and try to restart the engine. If the engine won't start, steer near the curb or onto the shoulder and stop.
3. If your vehicle's power steering fails, grip the steering wheel firmly and turn it with more force than usual. Steer off the road and stop. In case of total steering failure, use the parking brake to stop.

Lesson Two

1. If your vehicle has a blowout or flat tire, keep a firm grip on the steering wheel. When steering is stablized, release the accelerator slowly but do not brake. Steer off the road.
2. If the accelerator pedal sticks, brake and shift to Neutral. Carefully steer off the road.
3. If the hood flies up, look through the space between the dashboard and the hood or out of the driver's side window. Continue to steer in the direction in which you were moving until you can leave the road.

4. In case of a vehicle fire, steer off the road to an open space. Turn off the ignition. Get out and move away from the vehicle. Call for help.
5. To jump-start a dead battery, turn off the ignition in both vehicles, and shift both into Park. Attach the jumper cables properly. Start the engine of the vehicle with the good battery, then the engine of the other vehicle.
6. If your headlights fail, slow down and switch to high beams. If that doesn't work, turn on the parking lights, turn indicators, and flashers to see how to get off the road.

Lesson Three

1. If your vehicle breaks down, get off the road. Let other drivers know you need help.
2. Protect yourself at the scene. Wait inside your vehicle. Don't open your vehicle to strangers.

Lesson Four

1. If you encounter an injured motorist, see if you can help. Give first aid if necessary. Never move an injured person.
2. To restore breathing, give mouth-to-mouth resuscitation. To control bleeding, apply direct pressure to the wound. To treat shock, keep the victim warm.

PROJECTS

1. Look over a vehicle owner's manual. What special directions does the manual contain for avoiding and responding to vehicle failures and emergencies? What preventive maintenance tips does the manual offer?
2. Interview a member of a first aid squad. Ask what collision-related injuries occur most frequently. Also find out what kinds of first aid treatments are given most frequently.

*inter*NET CONNECTION Use the Internet to gather more information on AAA and the educational and other services they provide in addition to emergency road service.
www.glencoe.com/sec/driver.ed

CHAPTER TEST

Write the letter of the answer that best completes each sentence.

1. If your vehicle breaks down, you should
   a. phone for help or get the attention of passing drivers.
   b. stand directly in front of your vehicle until help arrives.
   c. stand in the road and wave your arms.

2. If your steering wheel suddenly becomes very hard to turn, the problem probably is
   a. power-steering failure.
   b. engine overheating.
   c. wet brakes.

3. If one of your tires suddenly loses pressure,
   a. release the accelerator slowly.
   b. brake hard.
   c. immediately shift into Park.

4. A collision victim who looks uninjured but cannot move
   a. should try to get up and walk around.
   b. may have a spinal injury.
   c. should be moved as quickly as possible.

5. If the fluid in your battery is frozen and the engine won't start,
   a. use jumper cables.
   b. do not use jumper cables.
   c. turn on the heater and use jumper cables.

6. If the hood flies up while you're driving,
   a. stop immediately.
   b. honk your horn and move right.
   c. look through the space between the hood and the dashboard.

7. If your foot brake suddenly loses power,
   a. turn the ignition to the lock position.
   b. shift into Reverse.
   c. rapidly pump the brake pedal.

8. A victim who feels faint, weak, and cold
   a. needs artificial respiration.
   b. should be kept as cool as possible.
   c. may be suffering from shock.

9. To dry wet brakes,
   a. drive slowly with your left foot pressing gently on the brake pedal.
   b. stamp down on the pedal several times.
   c. drive in low gear.

10. To put out a minor engine fire, use
    a. a fire extinguisher.
    b. water.
    c. a heavy cloth.

Write the word or phrase that best completes each sentence.

engine flooding	first aid	hemorrhaging
cooling system	brake fade	resuscitation

11. A person who is _____ can die in minutes.

12. Applying your brakes hard for a long time may cause _____.

13. Your engine may overheat if there is not enough coolant in the _____.

14. _____ is emergency treatment given to a person who has been injured.

15. Pumping the accelerator repeatedly when trying to start your vehicle can result in _____.

DRIVER'S LOG

In this chapter, you have learned about how to deal with emergency situations caused by vehicle failures and those in which personal injury is involved. Write two paragraphs giving your ideas on the most important factors to keep in mind when confronted with both types of emergency.

UNIT 3 CUMULATIVE REVIEW

This review tests your knowledge of the material in Chapters 1–15. Use the review to help you study for your state driving test. Choose the answer that best completes each statement.

1. The penalties for DWI and DUI
   a. are the same in all states.
   b. differ from state to state.
   c. are set by the National Highway Safety Act.
   d. are not very severe.

2. When driving at 55 mph, your following distance should be at least
   a. 10 seconds.
   b. 6 seconds.
   c. 4 seconds.
   d. 1 minute.

3. When turning left from a two-way street,
   a. yield the right-of-way to traffic behind you.
   b. yield the right-of-way to oncoming traffic.
   c. use hand signals.
   d. shift into Reverse gear.

4. While driving, you should
   a. aim low and look down.
   b. keep your head moving.
   c. keep your windows open.
   d. keep your eyes moving.

5. Lane-use lights are mounted
   a. on slow-moving vehicles.
   b. below warning signs.
   c. above reversible lanes.
   d. on telephone poles.

6. The best way to avoid becoming a problem drinker is to
   a. drink only on weekends.
   b. drink beer only.
   c. avoid drinking in the first place.
   d. drink at home.

7. A problem common to rural roads in spring and fall is the presence of
   a. busy intersections.
   b. slow-moving vehicles.
   c. HOV lanes.
   d. smog.

8. A driver can avoid skidding in the rain by
   a. changing speed gradually instead of abruptly.
   b. driving between 45 and 60 mph.
   c. frequently changing gears.
   d. riding the clutch.

9. Inertia, friction, and kinetic energy are
   a. difficult to manage.
   b. natural laws.
   c. different terms for visibility, time, and space.
   d. culprits.

10. Vehicles made since 1986 are required to have
    a. air bags and safety belts at all seats.
    b. a third, centered, high-mounted brake light.
    c. power windows.
    d. antilock brakes.

11. To make a turnabout safely, you need
    a. 100 yards of visibility.
    b. 1,000 feet of visibility in each direction.
    c. 500 feet of visibility in each direction.
    d. at least 1 minute.

12. Friction between the road and tires is
    a. latex.
    b. adhesion.
    c. centrifugal force.
    d. gravity.

13. If your accelerator sticks, you should
    a. reach down and grab it.
    b. shift to Neutral and steer off the road.
    c. jump out of the vehicle.
    d. pump the brakes.

14. Crosswalks are most frequently located at
   a. bridges.
   b. steep grades.
   c. campsites.
   d. intersections.

15. A good driver is one who has learned
   a. to eliminate risk completely.
   b. how to manage risk.
   c. to drive very fast.
   d. to read a map while driving.

16. Parking at an angle of 90 degrees to the curb is called
   a. parallel parking.
   b. illegal parking.
   c. double parking.
   d. perpendicular parking.

17. *Jaywalking* refers to the act of
   a. walking across a street without regard for traffic rules.
   b. smoking marijuana in public.
   c. obeying traffic rules.
   d. yielding the right of way to others.

18. Gravity pulls objects
   a. toward a collision.
   b. across a banked road.
   c. toward the Earth's center.
   d. into kinetic energy.

19. When making a right turn, you should wait until there is a
   a. 2-second gap to your left.
   b. 6- to 8-second gap to your left.
   c. 7- to 9-second gap to your right.
   d. 12-second gap to your right.

20. You can reduce glare in snowy weather by wearing
   a. sun visors.
   b. sunglasses.
   c. a defroster.
   d. a hat.

21. Points at which you can safely enter or exit a limited-access highway are called
   a. intersections.
   b. HOV lanes.
   c. crosswalks.
   d. interchanges.

22. As you enter a turn or a curve, you should
   a. decrease speed.
   b. increase speed.
   c. maintain an even speed.
   d. apply centrifugal force.

23. A way to restore breathing is using
   a. direct pressure.
   b. mouth-to-mouth resuscitation.
   c. a tourniquet.
   d. an air bag.

24. A vehicle with a manual shift has
   a. an automatic transmission.
   b. two brake pedals.
   c. a selector lever.
   d. a clutch and a gearshift.

25. A vehicle's rate of acceleration is
   a. lower at high speeds.
   b. lower at low speeds.
   c. perception distance.
   d. set by the Uniform Vehicle Code.

26. Truck drivers have poor visibility
   a. behind a car.
   b. in daylight.
   c. at speeds of 55 mph.
   d. to the sides.

27. Engine fires are often
   a. caused by cigarette smoking.
   b. electrical in nature.
   c. best ignored.
   d. easily extinguished by water.

UNIT 4

Planning for Your Future

As a driver, you will make many important decisions. This unit will help you develop guidelines so that your decisions will be based on understanding your needs, intelligent planning, and informed judgment.

CHAPTER 16

Buying a Vehicle

Purchasing a vehicle requires mature judgment, evaluation of needs, and ability to manage expense. It is important to learn how to assess safety features, fuel efficiency, comfort, and insurance needs to make a wise choice.

LESSON ONE

Determining Personal Need When Considering Buying a Vehicle

LESSON TWO

Factors That Are Involved in Selecting a Vehicle

LESSON THREE

How to Obtain Financing for a New or Used Vehicle

LESSON FOUR

Choosing and Purchasing Insurance for a Vehicle

OBJECTIVES

1. List factors to consider that may determine your need to buy a vehicle.
2. Describe what you should consider in determining the kind of vehicle you need.

Determining Personal Need When Considering Buying a Vehicle

If you are considering buying a vehicle, the first question you should ask yourself is not about the vehicle—it's about you. The question is "Am I responsible enough to own and drive a vehicle?" Examine the reasons you are considering the purchase—including both your wants and your needs.

There are many reasons to *want* your own vehicle.

- A vehicle makes you more independent.
- A vehicle saves you time in getting from one place to another.
- Owning a vehicle makes you feel more mature.
- Going places in your own vehicle is fun.

Make your own *want list*. Why do you really want a vehicle? Then think about another question: "Do I really *need* to own a vehicle?"

How Can You Tell Whether You Need Your Own Vehicle?

The following questions may help you focus on your needs.

- How close to your home are the places that you go to most often?
- How do you get to these places now?
- How available is public transportation?
- Is there a family vehicle, and if so, how available is it to you?

Think about your answers. If you live close to the places you normally go to, if public transportation is convenient, or if the family vehicle is available to you, you may not need to own a vehicle at all.

You still have other questions to consider.

Can you afford a vehicle? You will need to examine all of the costs involved in buying and owning a vehicle. In addition to the purchase price, you'll have to pay for fuel, oil, maintenance, repairs, insurance, licensing, registration, tolls, and often, parking.

How will a vehicle affect your schedule? For students who have to earn the money to pay for buying and operating a vehicle, the cost can be measured in hours as well as dollars. Working to pay vehicle expenses takes away time needed for studies, and a balanced social life.

Are you mature enough to manage the responsibilities of owning a vehicle? Often, increased responsibility means increased stress. Can you cope with that stress? Are you mature enough to distinguish your wants from your needs? Are you able to evaluate honestly all of the costs (both in time and in money) involved in vehicle ownership?

Can you deal in a mature way with the social pressures of driving and owning a vehicle? Driving a vehicle always involves risk to yourself and to others. If you're not mature enough to manage that risk responsibly, you shouldn't buy—or drive—a vehicle, regardless of your age.

What Personal Factors Influence the Kind of Vehicle You Need?

Be prepared when you shop for a vehicle. Think about how your vehicle will be used and what your needs are. The following questions will help you sort out what *you* should be looking for in a vehicle.

How many passengers will you usually have? The answer may help you decide what size vehicle you should buy.

What age are your passengers? Considering your passengers' comfort and space needs can help you decide what size vehicle you need and whether it should be a two- or four-door model. For example, if your regular passengers include elderly people, you need to think about the ease with which they can enter or leave the vehicle.

How many miles do you expect to drive each day, month, or year? Consider your expected mileage to help you determine how fuel efficient your vehicle needs to be.

What is the cost of the vehicle plus the cost of insurance? Expensive vehicles cost more to insure than less expensive ones. Insurance rates are also higher for sports vehicles than for family-type sedans.

How much will you have to spend to maintain the vehicle? A new vehicle usually costs much less to maintain than a used vehicle. You need to make sure that you can afford repairs and maintenance.

Lesson *1* Review

1. How can you tell if you really need a vehicle?
2. How should passenger comfort and maintenance costs influence the kind of vehicle you buy?

WHAT WOULD YOU DO?

How would you explain to the drivers what factors they should think about before buying a vehicle?

Factors That Are Involved in Selecting a Vehicle

You have decided that you really need to own a vehicle. You've thought carefully about how your vehicle will be used and what your needs are. Now you need to know what to look for in a vehicle in order to choose one that is safe, comfortable, and fuel efficient.

There's a great deal to think about when you really get down to choosing a vehicle. However, the very first thing you should check out is the vehicle's safety. In fact, if safety is *not* your first concern, you shouldn't be buying a vehicle.

How Can You Select a Vehicle That Is Safe?

You should ask a number of questions about safety before purchasing a vehicle. To find the answers, you may have to do a little research.

Does the vehicle have air bags? In head-on crashes, most fatalities occur when the driver hits the steering wheel and suffers head or chest injuries. Air bags help prevent such injuries. Passenger-side air bags help protect front-seat occupants.

◆ *The presence of air bags is a safety factor you should consider when buying a car.*

How does the vehicle hold up in a crash test? Crash test data are available from the U.S. Department of Transportation's National Highway Traffic Safety Administration.

Does the vehicle have an antilock brake system (ABS)? Vehicles with antilock brakes can stop in a shorter distance on slick surfaces than can vehicles without such brakes. However, the main advantage of antilock brakes is that they let you steer around an obstacle even if you panic and slam on the brakes.

What is the size of the vehicle? Most recent studies show death rates in the smallest vehicles to be more than twice as high as those in the largest vehicles.

What is the death rate per 10,000 registered models of the vehicle? Getting all of the information you can about your potential vehicle's safety record could save your life. Vehicle models differ by as much as 800 percent in their safety records. The Insurance Institute for Highway Safety analyzes the safety records of most vehicles sold in the United States.

The institute examines the death rate by manufacturer and model. Vehicle death rates range from 0.5 to 4 deaths per 10,000 registered vehicles. Generally, the higher the death rate, the less safe the vehicle. If the death rate of a particular model is more than 2 per 10,000 registered vehicles, think twice before buying.

The institute also examines the death rate in single-vehicle crashes compared to multivehicle crashes. If more than 50 percent of the deaths occurred in single-vehicle crashes, the particular vehicle model may encourage unsafe driving.

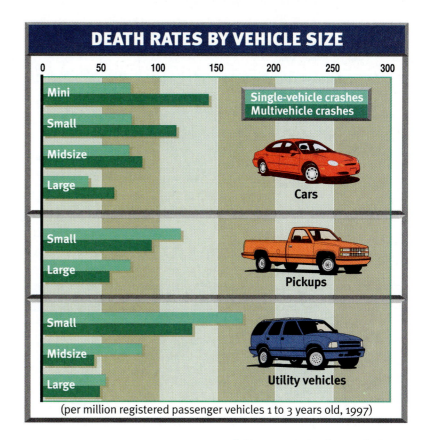

DEATH RATES BY VEHICLE SIZE

(per million registered passenger vehicles 1 to 3 years old, 1997)

◆ *You can see by the graph that small two-door cars are the least safe.*

How Can You Check a Vehicle's Comfort Features?

You will spend a lot of time in your vehicle, so check to be sure that it's comfortable for you. Get into the vehicle. Does it fit you? Are the seats adjustable? Can you adjust the steering wheel height so that the top of the wheel is at or below the top of your shoulders? Do the seat and steering wheel positions give you maximum control of the vehicle?

Ask to take the vehicle for a test drive. Be sure that you can reach all accessory switches and dials easily. Be sure the seat is comfortable enough so that a long drive won't leave you with an aching back.

How Can You Determine Whether a Vehicle Is Fuel Efficient?

Fuel consumption is an important consideration when choosing a vehicle. An energy-efficient vehicle can save you money, reduce pollution, and help conserve this planet's energy resources.

Energy Tips

If you are buying a new vehicle, look carefully at the dealer's sticker. It contains information about miles per gallon of gasoline. The greater the number of miles per gallon, the more fuel efficient the vehicle.

The Insurance Institute for Highway Safety provides free information on death rates and crash test data. You can write to the institute at 10005 N. Glebe Road, Arlington, Virginia 22201.

Fuel consumption depends on a vehicle's weight, type of engine, design, and type of transmission, among other factors.

The Weight of the Vehicle

The less weight an engine pulls, the more efficiently it works. This saves fuel. In general, however, the heavier the vehicle, the more protection it provides you in a crash.

The Type of Engine

The more cylinders in the engine the more fuel it uses. A 4- or 6-cylinder engine probably will meet the needs of most intermediate-size vehicles. This size engine is also fuel efficient.

The Design of the Vehicle

One key to fuel economy is how well the vehicle overcomes air resistance. A streamlined vehicle has less air resistance than a vehicle with a boxy design.

The Type of Transmission

A manual transmission consumes less fuel than an automatic one. A vehicle with a manual transmission also is less expensive to buy. However, again there are trade-offs. An automatic is easier to use and to learn to drive than a manual one, and more models are available.

In addition, most drivers have more control driving vehicles with automatic transmissions.

The Power Train

The power train powers the wheels that move the vehicle. The number of times that the driveshaft revolves to make the wheels turn once is known as the axle-gear ratio. The higher the axle-gear ratio, the greater the fuel consumption.

TIPS

FOR NEW DRIVERS

Used-Vehicle Checks

When purchasing a used vehicle, check the following.

The condition of the paint New paint can indicate collision damage.

For rust Don't buy a vehicle with rusted-out areas unless you can afford repairs.

For worn tires, including the spare Uneven wear on any tire may indicate front-end problems.

The tailpipe A light gray color indicates proper combustion.

The radiator Remove the radiator cap. Is the coolant clean? Is there caked-on rust on the cap? Are there signs of leaks on the back of the radiator?

The transmission Pull out the transmission dipstick and sniff it. A burned smell may indicate an overheated transmission. Feel the oil on the crankcase dipstick. If it is gritty, there may be dirt in the engine.

The service stickers Service stickers tell you how often a vehicle has been tuned and had the oil changed.

All windows and door locks Check for ease of operation.

The engine Listen for loud or unusual noises when you start the vehicle. Check all gauges and warning lights.

The headlights, taillights, brake lights, and turn indicators

For slamming sounds or lurching as the vehicle starts An automatic transmission should take hold promptly when in gear.

Safety belts, air bags, and head restraints

Power Equipment

Power equipment and accessories add extra weight and energy requirements to a vehicle, which leads to higher fuel use. When choosing a vehicle, evaluate whether ease of operation is worth extra fuel cost to you.

What Should You Know About Buying a Used Vehicle?

Many consumers decide to buy a used vehicle, usually for economic reasons. You should consider many of the same factors when buying a used vehicle that you would when buying a new one. However, there are other considerations as well.

You can buy a used vehicle from a private owner or a used vehicle dealer. Buying from the owner can cost less, but you will not get a **warranty,** a written guarantee that the seller will repair the vehicle if something goes wrong within a given period of time. Dealers, on the other hand, often offer warranties.

The **Blue Book** is a guide to the average price paid to dealers for different makes and models of used vehicles. Actual price may differ from the "book" price depending on the condition of the vehicle and its mileage.

Before buying a used vehicle, test-drive it. Shaky steering and a wobbly ride may mean front wheels are misaligned or need balancing. Make several sharp turns at a low speed. Steering should not stiffen up. If the vehicle has power steering, there shouldn't be any squeaks or other noises.

Slow down from 50 mph to 15 mph without braking. Step hard on the accelerator. If there is blue exhaust smoke, the vehicle may need an engine overhaul. Having diagnostic tests performed on the vehicle you choose *before* you buy it may save you money in the long run.

Lesson **2** Review

1. How can information from the Insurance Institute for Highway Safety help you evaluate a vehicle's safety?
2. Describe how test-driving a vehicle can help you evaluate how comfortable it is.
3. How does the type of engine a vehicle has affect its fuel efficiency?
4. What should you check when you select a used vehicle?

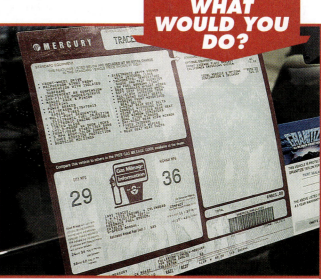

WHAT WOULD YOU DO?

You want some of these features, but you also want fuel economy. What will you do?

How to Obtain Financing for a New or Used Vehicle

Once you have chosen the vehicle you want to buy, you have to decide how to pay for it. Very few people can afford to pay cash for a new vehicle or for a late-model used vehicle. Most people have to take out a loan to pay for the vehicle. How do you get a loan?

What Should You Know About Financing a Vehicle?

To finance the purchase of a vehicle, you need to know where to get a loan and the amount of the monthly payments.

Where to Get Financing

If you are a full-time high school student, you will not be able to obtain financing on your own. The lending institution will require that an adult be responsible for loan repayment. You may be able to get a loan if you are 18 years old and work full-time. In most cases, however, a responsible adult will need to co-sign the loan.

Drivers finance their vehicles through banks, credit unions, finance companies, and if buying a new vehicle, often through the dealer. You

CONNECTIONS

Math

Calculate the interest on a vehicle loan to estimate the monthly payments. Suppose that you want to buy a used vehicle for $6,000. You've saved $2,000 and want to borrow the rest. Further suppose that a bank will lend you $4,000 for 24 months (2 years) at 12 percent interest. Follow these steps to estimate the amount you'll pay in interest and what your monthly payments will be.

1. Multiply the amount of the loan by the interest: $4,000 × 0.12 = $480.
2. Multiply the interest by the number of years: $480 × 2 = $960.
3. Add the interest to the amount of the loan: $4,000 + $960 = $4,960.
4. Divide the total by the number of months to find out how much you'll pay per month: $4,960 ÷ 24 = $206.66.

Amount of loan	$4,000
Interest on loan	12%
Total amount of loan	$4,960
Loan period	24 mos.
Monthly payments	$206.66

should check out each possible source of financing as carefully as you've checked out the vehicle you want to buy.

The Amount of Monthly Payments

Loan agencies lend money to make money. They make money by charging interest on the money they lend. Different sources of financing often charge different interest rates. Compare rates to get the best deal.

The amount of the loan is based on the cost of the vehicle. The amount of time you have to pay back the loan is based on whether the vehicle is new or used. Used vehicle loans have to be repaid more quickly than new vehicle loans.

You should try to pay as much as you can toward the purchase of the vehicle—the down payment—and then borrow the rest. The lender will give you a schedule of monthly payments. The amount of these payments will depend on how much money you borrow, the interest rate on your loan, and whether or not your vehicle's insurance is included in the loan.

◆ *In order to finance a vehicle, you can ask about a loan at the bank where you have a checking or savings account. Dealerships may also offer financing at low interest rates as part of their sales promotions.*

WHAT WOULD YOU DO?

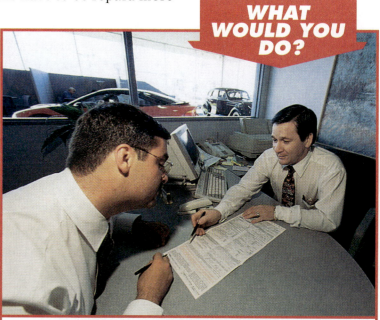

The buyer can make a down payment of either $1,000 or $1,500 on a used vehicle. Which should he choose to do? Why?

Lesson 3 Review

1. Where would you go to get financing for a vehicle?
2. What advice would you give someone about financing a vehicle?

Choosing and Purchasing Insurance for a Vehicle

In most states, when you buy a vehicle, you must purchase insurance. Many different kinds of vehicle insurance policies are available, and you should investigate each kind carefully before deciding what you will need. It should be noted that insurance laws sometimes vary from state to state.

What Kinds of Insurance Might You Need?

Suppose you are involved in a collision that results in property damage and serious injury. How will you pay the costs involved? Unless you're very rich, you'll need automobile insurance. That's why many states require anyone who owns a vehicle to have one or more kinds of motor vehicle insurance.

Liability Insurance

The word *liable* means "responsible." **Liability insurance** is proof that you will be financially responsible if you cause damage to property or injure other people. Many states require drivers to prove that they have a certain amount of liability insurance before their vehicles can be registered.

Liability insurance is the most important motor vehicle insurance protection you can have. It protects you against claims if you are at fault in a collision. It helps you pay for any injury or property damage caused by your actions. Liability insurance not only protects you, it also protects anyone else who has your permission to drive your vehicle. (Check your policy first to see if there are restrictions on who can and who cannot drive your vehicle.)

Most drivers have two kinds of liability insurance: bodily injury liability insurance and property damage liability insurance. Both are usually sold in amounts of $10,000 to $500,000.

◆ *Liability insurance provides coverage if you cause injury or property damage.*

Bodily injury liability insurance covers you if your driving causes injury to or the death of another person or persons. It also covers legal fees, court costs, and lost wages.

Property damage liability insurance covers you if your driving causes damage to the property of other people. It covers damage to their vehicles and property in their vehicles and damage to buildings, telephone poles, and traffic lights.

Of course, you are covered only for the amount of insurance you have purchased. If a court determines that you have caused more damage than your insurance will pay, you are held personally liable.

Uninsured Motorist Insurance

Although many states require that vehicle owners have liability insurance and show proof of it before their vehicles can be registered, some drivers allow their policies to lapse or cancel their policies after registration. If you are involved in a collision with such a driver, or if you are involved with a hit-and-run driver, **uninsured motorist insurance** protects you. Uninsured motorist insurance also protects you in states where no liability insurance is required. It pays for any bodily injury that you may suffer. Generally, it does not pay for damage to your vehicle.

Collision Insurance

Collision insurance pays for damage to your vehicle even if you are to blame in a crash or are involved with an uninsured driver. Collision insurance also covers repairs if your vehicle is damaged in a parking lot or in a parking space on the street.

Because of the increasing cost of repairing collision damage, very few insurance companies offer full-coverage collision insurance that pays the entire amount of any damages. Most drivers have a deductible policy. With this kind of policy, you agree to pay a fixed amount, such as the first $50, $100, $250, or $500 worth of damages. The insurance company pays the rest. The greater the fixed amount, or **deductible,** you pay, the less this insurance costs.

Banks and companies that finance motor vehicle loans usually require a vehicle's owner to have collision insurance with a deductible of no more than $250. However, once the vehicle loan is repaid, it is a good idea to raise the deductible to $500 in order to lower the cost of the insurance.

◆ *Collision insurance covers the cost of damage to a vehicle no matter who is at fault.*

♦ *You are responsible for the cost of repairs up to and including the deductible amount.*

Comprehensive Insurance

If your vehicle is damaged by anything other than a collision, **comprehensive insurance** pays the bills. For example, comprehensive insurance covers theft or damage caused by fire, explosions, natural disasters, falling objects, or vandalism.

Medical Payment Insurance

Medical payment insurance covers medical, hospital, or funeral costs regardless of who is at fault. It pays a fixed amount if you or passengers in your vehicle are injured or killed in a collision. It also pays if you or a member of your family is injured or killed while riding in someone else's vehicle. Very often, medical payment insurance pays if you or a member of your family is struck as a pedestrian or the rider of a bicycle, bus, or taxicab. The amount paid is determined by the policy.

No-Fault Insurance

An increasing number of states have no-fault insurance laws. In this system, your insurance company pays your medical bills and any other costs resulting from a collision-related injury. The system is called **no-fault insurance** because blame is not considered before the insurance company pays your bills. In very serious crashes, the injured parties can still go to court and sue the person responsible for damages.

Towing Insurance

Towing insurance covers the costs of on-road repairs and the cost of having your vehicle towed.

What Factors Determine the Cost of Insurance?

You purchase vehicle insurance by paying a premium, or a set amount of money, to an insurance company, usually every six months. How is this premium determined?

Insurance companies rely on statistics to determine their rates. The statistics indicate the likelihood that people of a certain age, gender, or marital status will be involved in a crash. They also indicate the likelihood of certain types of vehicles being involved in a crash. Insurance companies use the following factors to determine rates.

Your age Drivers under the age of 25 pay the highest premiums.

Your driving record Traffic-violation convictions, collisions, and insurance claims can increase your insurance costs. Some companies offer discounts to those who drive a specified number of years without a collision or traffic ticket.

Mileage per year The farther you drive, the more your vehicle insurance will cost.

If you drive to work Carpooling reduces the cost of insurance.

Where you live If you live in a city, your insurance costs will be greater than those of a person who lives in the country.

Your gender Women pay lower insurance rates than men. Statistics show that men drive more often and farther and are involved in more collisions.

FYI

Insurance companies usually pay damages only up to a vehicle's "book" value. This amount can be less than an owner thinks the vehicle is worth. Any special or custom equipment may not be covered either unless specifically noted in your policy.

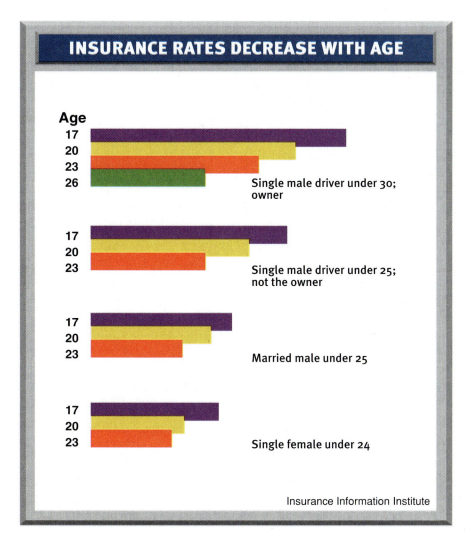

INSURANCE RATES DECREASE WITH AGE

Age

17
20
23
26
Single male driver under 30; owner

17
20
23
Single male driver under 25; not the owner

17
20
23
Married male under 25

17
20
23
Single female under 24

Insurance Information Institute

◆ *Many drivers receive minimum coverage at a base rate. You can see that single males pay the highest insurance premiums.*

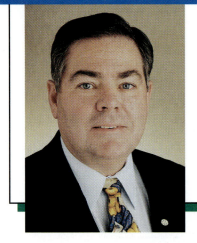

David Van Sickle
Director, Auto and Consumer Information, AAA International

Shopping for a car? Consider safety features first. Safety belt systems, air bags, antilock brakes, and traction control should top your list.

Stick to basics with your first car. Features like a 4-cylinder engine and a manual transmission can make a vehicle more affordable to buy, operate, and maintain.

Try to stay away from high-performance vehicles. Even though they can be affordable to buy, high insurance rates for young drivers can make them unaffordable to operate.

Your marital status Young married men pay less than men of the same age who are single. Young married men are involved in fewer collisions than young single men.

The value of your vehicle The more expensive the vehicle, the greater the cost of insurance.

The type of vehicle A sports car or sport utility vehicle costs more to insure than a larger sedan.

Other factors Many insurance companies offer discounts to students who have completed a driver education program and to students whose grade average is B or higher. Companies may also offer discounts to drivers whose vehicles have air bags or antilock brakes. Discounts may be given as well to drivers who garage their vehicles. Those who buy cars with antitheft devices, or who have antitheft devices installed in their vehicles, may also qualify for a discount.

WHAT WOULD YOU DO?

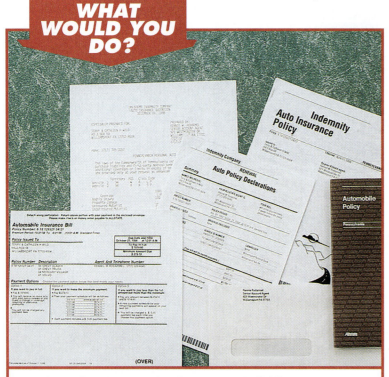

You plan to drive in a state that does not require liability insurance. What will you do to be sure you are adequately covered?

Lesson 4 Review

1. How is liability insurance different from other kinds of motor vehicle insurance?
2. How does being male or female play a role in the amount you pay for motor vehicle insurance?

Understanding Map Symbols

Look at the symbols and the legend on a map to learn about the area you are traveling through.

You can see that there is an airport near Great Falls, Montana, at D, 7, and a campground near Choteau at C, 6.

Try It Yourself

1. At what coordinates can ski areas be found?
2. How many campgrounds can you find in the Blackfeet Indian Reservation?
3. What does 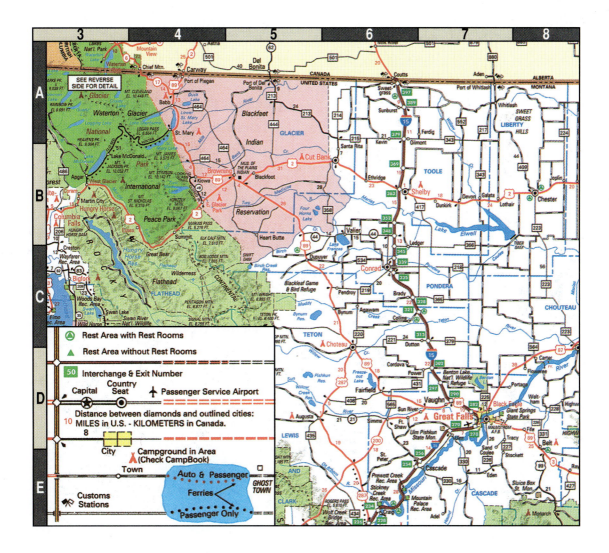 stand for at A, 4?

KEY POINTS

Lesson One

1. To determine your need for a vehicle, think about how close you are to places that you go to most often, how available public transportation is for you, how available the family vehicle is, and whether you are mature enough to take on the responsibilities of owning a vehicle.

2. Before buying a vehicle, think about the number of passengers you will have and their age; the number of miles you expect to drive; and the cost of the vehicle plus the cost of maintenance and insurance.

Lesson Two

1. To select a safe vehicle, consider its equipment; what its death rate per 10,000 models is, how it holds up in crash tests, and its size.

2. To select a comfortable vehicle, sit in the driver's seat and adjust the seat and steering wheel (where possible), making sure you can reach accessory switches and dials easily.

3. Factors that affect fuel efficiency are a vehicle's weight, engine and transmission type, design, power train, and whether it has power equipment and other fuel-consuming accessories.

4. If you're thinking of buying a used vehicle, find out if a warranty is available, know the *Blue Book* value, test-drive the vehicle, and have it checked by an independent professional.

Lesson Three

1. You can get financing through banks, credit unions, finance companies, or the vehicle dealer.

2. Shop around to get the best interest rates, and know what your monthly payments will be.

Lesson Four

1. The basic types of insurance are liability (bodily injury and property damage), uninsured motorist, collision, comprehensive, medical payment, no-fault, and towing insurance.

2. Factors that determine insurance cost include age, driving record, mileage per year, where you live, gender, marital status, and the vehicle's value. Insurers may offer discounts to students who have completed a driver education course and to drivers who have safety devices, keep their vehicle in a garage, and have antitheft devices.

PROJECTS

1. Visit several vehicle dealerships in your area. Talk to salespeople and compare prices, safety features, and service facilities. Select a vehicle that you might want to own. Interview a mechanic certified by the National Institute for Automotive Service Excellence (NIASE) about the vehicle you have selected.

2. Interview a local insurance agent to find out if there are differences in rates for new drivers under the age of 25. Use what you learn to propose ways a new driver can reduce insurance costs. Share your information and ideas with your class.

*inter*NET CONNECTION

Cruise Glencoe's Web site to investigate how vehicles for sale are advertised over the Internet.
www.glencoe.com/sec/driver.ed

CHAPTER TEST

Write the letter of the answer that best completes each sentence.

1. A driver interested in fuel efficiency would
   a. buy a vehicle with 4 cylinders.
   b. buy a vehicle with 8 cylinders.
   c. buy a vehicle with 16 cylinders.

2. When buying a vehicle, most people
   a. pay with a credit card.
   b. pay cash.
   c. take out a loan.

3. Before buying a vehicle, consider
   a. how clean it is.
   b. how many passengers you will have.
   c. whether it is a convertible.

4. A driving record and marital status can affect
   a. the cost of your insurance.
   b. the purchase price of a vehicle.
   c. your concentration at the wheel.

5. Expensive vehicles
   a. cost more to insure than inexpensive vehicles.
   b. cost less to insure than inexpensive vehicles.
   c. use less fuel than inexpensive vehicles.

6. The death rate in the smallest vehicles is
   a. lower than that in the largest vehicles.
   b. the same as that in the largest vehicles.
   c. twice as high as that in the largest vehicles.

7. The *Blue Book* is a guide to
   a. vehicle dealerships in the United States.
   b. the average price paid to dealers for various used vehicles.
   c. different types of vehicle engines.

8. Liability insurance
   a. protects you against claims if you are at fault in a collision.
   b. is available to drivers over 21 years of age.
   c. protects you if you are accused of lying.

9. The purchase price of a vehicle is
   a. one of the many expenses associated with owning a vehicle.
   b. the only expense in owning a vehicle.
   c. generally lower than it was ten years ago.

10. Bodily injury insurance covers
    a. any damages to the body of your vehicle.
    b. the death or injury of other people while you are driving.
    c. only the driver of a vehicle.

Write the word or phrase that best completes each sentence.

fuel consumption	warranty
comprehensive insurance	financing
uninsured motorist insurance	deductible

11. A(n) _____ is a written guarantee that the seller will repair your vehicle.

12. If your vehicle is damaged by anything other than a collision, _____ will pay the bills.

13. There can be large differences in _____ among different vehicle models.

14. Vehicle dealers can offer you a(n) _____ arrangement when you buy a new vehicle.

15. If you are involved in a collision with a hit-and-run driver, _____ can protect you.

DRIVER'S LOG

In this chapter, you have learned some considerations to keep in mind when you are ready to buy a vehicle. Write a paragraph in response to each of the following questions.
- Describe the guideposts you use to measure maturity. Which do you need to work on?
- What will you look for when you buy a vehicle? What do you think your choice will say about your maturity? Why?

CHAPTER 17

Vehicle Systems and Maintenance

Good drivers make sure that their vehicles are safe to drive. Good drivers understand their vehicles' different systems and make sure that those systems are properly maintained.

OBJECTIVES

1. List several things on your vehicle that you can inspect before entering it.
2. List what to check after starting the engine.
3. Explain when to have your vehicle serviced.

Checking Your Vehicle Before and After You Start the Engine

You've probably heard the old saying that an ounce of prevention is worth a pound of cure. That maxim is especially important for drivers.

Inspecting and caring for your vehicle before something goes wrong can save you both money and aggravation. More important, maintaining your vehicle can save your life.

Different makes and models are alike in some ways, different in others. To be able to check your particular model properly, you should refer to the owner's manual. If you don't have the manual for your vehicle, obtain a copy from a dealer or order one from the manufacturer. Manuals are also available in many bookstores. Keep the manual in your glove compartment so you'll have it handy when you need it.

◆ *Before you enter your vehicle, check under the hood for items such as the coolant level.*

What Can You Inspect Before Entering Your Vehicle?

You don't need to be a mechanic to inspect your vehicle. You can check many items quickly and easily before driving. Make these checks at least once a month and before long drives.

In addition to the guidelines below, refer to Chapter 7 for other important predriving checks and procedures.

Fluid Levels

You can inspect the different fluid levels. Check:

- the engine oil (when the engine is cool and not running).
- the level of coolant in the radiator overflow tank or radiator.
- the transmission fluid and the fluid level in the power-steering and master-brake-cylinder reservoirs.
- the battery fluid (if necessary for your battery).
- the windshield-washer fluid.

Belts, Hoses, and Wires

Before you enter your vehicle, inspect belts, hoses, and wires.

- Check the fan belt and the belts that run the power-steering and air-conditioning units. Many new vehicles have only one belt that drives these units. Belts may need tightening or adjustment. Replace frayed or cracked belts as soon as possible.
- Check all hoses and hose connections for leaks.
- Look for loose, broken, or disconnected wires. Also check for cracked insulation on wires.
- Make sure the battery cables are tightly connected and the terminals are free of corrosion.

◆ *Learning how to do your own maintenance can save you the cost and inconvenience of repairs.*

What Can You Check After Starting the Engine?

Once your engine is running, you should make several routine checks to ensure that your vehicle is operating properly and safely.

Gauges and Warning Lights

You have already read about the various gauges and warning lights that provide information about your vehicle. Check these gauges and lights regularly as you drive. They will warn you of a wide range of problems, such as low oil pressure or fuel level, engine overheating, and alternator malfunction.

Brakes

Your vehicle's brake-warning light will make you aware of some—but not all—problems with your brake system.

For this reason, always test your brakes as soon as you begin driving. When you step on the brake pedal, you should feel firm resistance, and your vehicle should come to a smooth, straight stop. The pedal should stay well above the floor.

Specific warning signs of a brake system malfunction are discussed later in this chapter.

TIPS | **FOR NEW DRIVERS**

Having Your Vehicle Serviced or Repaired

- To find a reliable mechanic or garage, ask friends and relatives for their recommendations. You can also call your local American Automobile Association.
- Ask the mechanic for a cost estimate of the work to be done.
- Find out for how long the mechanic will guarantee any work done. Save your bill or receipt.
- Know what you're paying for. If there's something you don't understand, ask for an explanation.
- If the mechanic replaces a part, ask to see the old part.
- Warranties may cover many repairs. Know what your warranty does and does not cover.

Always check radiator coolant level by looking at the radiator overflow tank. If additional coolant is needed, add it to the overflow tank, not to the radiator. Rarely should it be necessary to remove the radiator cap. If you do have to remove the radia-tor cap, do so *only when the radiator is cool.* If you remove the cap when the radiator is hot, boiling water could spurt out and scald you.

Horn

Periodically check to make sure your horn works. If you're driving an unfamiliar vehicle, always locate and try the horn *before* you begin driv-ing. Horn position on the steering wheel varies from vehicle to vehicle.

Lights and Turn Signals

Vehicle safety checks find that nearly one out of four vehicles has at least one lightbulb or headlight burned out. Check all exterior lights and turn signals before you drive. Periodically have a friend or family member stand outside the vehicle and tell you if your brake lights work when you press the brake pedal.

How Do You Know When Your Vehicle Should Be Serviced?

Your owner's manual contains guidelines for servicing and main-taining your vehicle. The guidelines vary, depending on the kind and amount of driving you do and on the manufacturer's recommendations.

Some systems and parts require more frequent attention than others. Recommended intervals for servicing may be based either on time or on miles driven. For example, your manual might recommend checking tire pressure once a month, changing the oil every few months, and having the suspen-sion checked every 20,000 miles.

Keeping complete records will help you maintain a schedule of care. An easy way to keep track of repairs and maintenance is to keep a small notebook in your vehicle. Each time you or a mechanic services or repairs the vehicle, jot down exactly what was done and the date. Save your receipts in an envelope in the glove compartment.

WHAT WOULD YOU DO?

A friend has agreed to let you use her car while she's on vacation. What checks will you make before getting into her car? What checks will you make after starting the engine?

Lesson *1* Review

1. What kinds of problems might you spot as you check your vehicle before entering it?
2. What can you check after you start the engine?
3. What can help you determine when to have your vehicle serviced?

Becoming Familiar with the Engine and Power Train

OBJECTIVES
1. Explain how a typical vehicle engine works.
2. Tell what the power train is and what it does.
3. Describe four guidelines for maintaining the engine and power train.

KEY TERMS
internal combustion engine
cylinder
spark plug
piston
crankshaft
power train
drive wheel
differential

Many parts work together to produce a vehicle's power and motion. By keeping these parts operating smoothly, you help your vehicle run safely and fuel efficiently.

How Does the Engine Work?

Your vehicle's engine is known as an **internal combustion engine.** It is called that because the power it produces comes from burning a mixture of fuel and air inside, rather than outside, the engine.

When you start your vehicle's engine, you're setting off a chain of events.

1. Turning the key in the ignition causes power to be drawn from the battery to a small electric starter motor, commonly called the starter.
2. The starter turns the flywheel of the engine. When the flywheel turns, it turns the crankshaft.
3. A piston in each **cylinder** of the vehicle is attached to the crankshaft. Most vehicles have 4, 6, or 8 cylinders. The more cylinders in a vehicle, the more power the engine has, but also the more gasoline the engine uses.

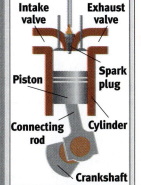    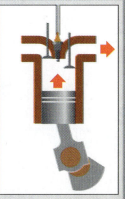

The parts of a cylinder. Most cars have four, six or eight cylinders. The piston in each cylinder is attached to a part of the crankshaft.

Step 1. As the piston moves down, the air-fuel mixture is drawn into the cylinder through the intake valve or valves.

Step 2. The piston moves up and compresses the air-fuel mixture. (The intake and exhaust valves are both closed.)

Step 3. A spark explodes the compressed air-fuel mixture. This pushes down the piston, which turns the crankshaft.

Step 4. The piston moves up and forces the burned gas out the exhaust valve or valves. The cycle begins again.

4. In each cylinder, a **spark plug** produces a spark. This spark causes the fuel-air mixture inside the cylinder to explode. The explosion pushes down the **piston,** which turns the **crankshaft.**

5. The continuous up-and-down motion of the pistons keeps the crankshaft turning. Power sent from the crankshaft is transmitted to the wheels, making the vehicle move.

What Is the Power Train and What Does It Do?

Several parts of your vehicle work together to transmit power from the engine to the wheels. These parts make up the **power train.**

In most vehicles, the power train sends power from the engine to only two of the four wheels. The wheels that receive the power are called the **drive wheels.** If the two front wheels are the drive wheels, the vehicle has front-wheel drive. If the two rear wheels receive the power, the vehicle has rear-wheel drive. A vehicle has four-wheel drive if all four wheels receive power.

The transmission is part of the power train. Gears in the transmission allow it to transfer power to the drive wheels. With a manual transmission, the driver uses the clutch pedal and the gearshift lever to shift gears and change the amount of power that goes to the drive wheels. With an automatic transmission, the clutch works automatically, so the gears are shifted automatically too.

In a vehicle with rear-wheel drive, the transmission is connected by a driveshaft to the differential, rear axle, and rear wheels. The **differential** allows the rear wheels to turn at different speeds when the vehicle turns.

◆ *Power is transmitted differently to vehicles with rear-wheel drive, front-wheel drive, and four-wheel drive.*

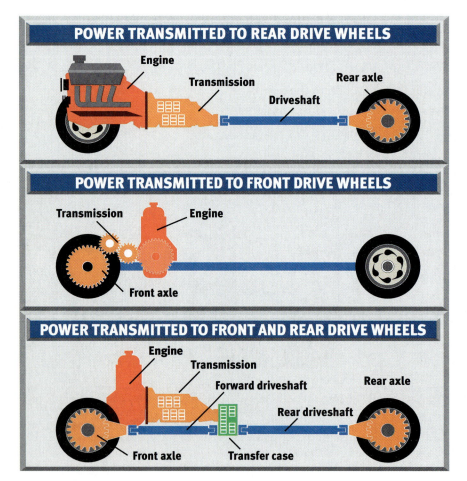

POWER TRANSMITTED TO REAR DRIVE WHEELS

Engine
Transmission
Rear axle
Driveshaft

POWER TRANSMITTED TO FRONT DRIVE WHEELS

Transmission
Engine
Front axle

POWER TRANSMITTED TO FRONT AND REAR DRIVE WHEELS

Engine
Transmission
Forward driveshaft
Rear axle
Rear driveshaft
Front axle
Transfer case

In a vehicle with front-wheel drive, engine power is sent to a combination transmission and differential and then directly to the front wheels.

How Can You Maintain the Engine and Power Train?

Vehicles that are well maintained perform better, are more fuel efficient, and last longer than vehicles that are neglected.

Here are some basic guidelines for keeping your vehicle's engine and power train in top condition. Your owner's manual will give you additional specific recommendations.

Check and Change the Oil Regularly

Check your vehicle's oil every second time you fill the fuel tank. Change the oil according to the recommendations in your owner's manual. Most manufacturers give two schedules for oil changes: one for normal use and one for severe use. Severe use is often described as plenty of short trips, stop-and-go driving, or regular travel in dusty conditions. Failure to follow the recommended schedule can void your warranty.

Have Regular Tune-Ups

Some older vehicles require regular tune-ups, but most new ones do not have any need for such attention beyond regular checks and replacement of fluids and filters. Emission regulations require a vehicle's computer to make the necessary "tune-ups" as the vehicle ages to ensure the most complete combustion of fuel and to prevent pouring unburned hydrocarbons into the atmosphere. Consult your vehicle manual to determine your recommended tune-up intervals. Do a visual check of belts, hoses, and wires under the hood for any obvious signs of wear or problems as you check the oil—every second time you fill the vehicle's fuel tank.

WHAT WOULD YOU DO?

The used car you've just bought is running beautifully. You'd like to keep it that way. Describe the actions you will take to maintain your car in top shape.

Lesson 2 Review

1. What is an internal combustion engine, and how does it work?
2. What parts make up the power train, and how do they supply power to the wheels?
3. What are some of the tasks a mechanic might do when giving your vehicle a tune-up?

OBJECTIVES

1. Explain how the fuel and exhaust systems work and how to maintain them.
2. Explain how the electrical and light systems work and how to maintain them.
3. Describe how the lubricating and cooling systems work and how to maintain them.

KEY TERMS

electronic fuel-injection (EFI) system
exhaust manifold
muffler
catalytic converter
battery
alternator
engine control module (ECM)
coolant
antifreeze
radiator

Understanding and Maintaining Vehicle Systems

Today it's easy to take motor vehicles for granted. But they are still among the most complicated machines ever invented. Every time you get behind the wheel, you take control of a network of many different systems that work together to make your vehicle work the way it does.

How Do the Fuel and Exhaust Systems Work?

The fuel and exhaust systems in a vehicle must operate properly to maximize engine efficiency and minimize pollution.

The Fuel System

Your vehicle's fuel system includes the fuel tank, fuel lines, fuel pump, fuel filter, **electronic fuel-injection (EFI) system,** and air filter. Fuel is stored in the tank, where in some cases the fuel pump resides. The pump forces fuel through the fuel lines and filter. The air-fuel mixture forms a vapor that is injected at a specific time into each cylinder, where it is ignited by a spark plug.

Most vehicles now have electronic multipoint fuel-injection systems. Multipoint means that there is a separate nozzle or injector fed by a separate fuel line for each cylinder.

◆ *The fuel system both stores fuel and delivers the correct air-fuel mixture to the engine.*

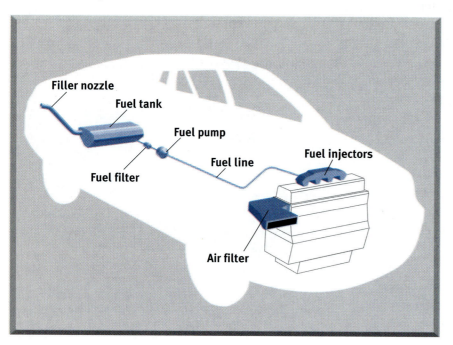

Filler nozzle
Fuel tank
Fuel pump
Fuel filter
Fuel line
Fuel injectors
Air filter

The Exhaust System

The exhaust system serves two main purposes. First, it carries off carbon monoxide and other harmful gas by-products of combustion. Second, it muffles engine noise.

The pipes that make up the **exhaust manifold** collect unburned gases from the engine and carry them to the muffler. The **muffler** absorbs noise created from the explosions in the cylinders. Exhaust gases exit through the tailpipe. Pollution-control devices, such as the **catalytic converter,** reduce the amount of harmful gases coming from the tailpipe.

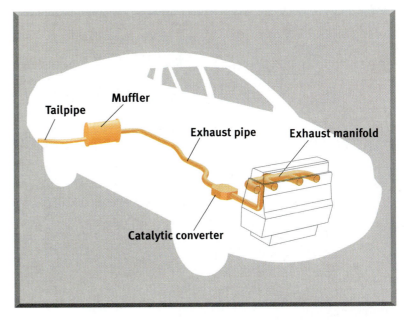

◆ *The exhaust system carries off poisonous gases and muffles engine noise.*

How Can You Maintain the Fuel and Exhaust Systems?

To maintain your vehicle's fuel system, replace the air and fuel filters as needed.

Most vehicles today operate on lead-free gasoline. Using leaded gasoline will destroy the catalytic converter.

How much maintenance or repair the exhaust system requires varies with the conditions under which you drive. Short trips, for example, are harder on a vehicle than long highway drives. Be on the lookout for loose, rusting, or damaged parts. Always have your exhaust system thoroughly inspected as part of a tune-up.

◆ *The electrical system supplies energy to start the vehicle and sends electrical current to the spark plugs.*

How Do the Electrical and Light Systems Work?

The electrical and light systems help keep your vehicle running smoothly and safely.

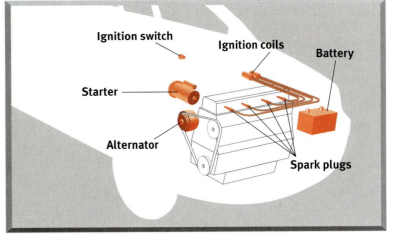

◆ *In order to keep your battery in top working condition, keep terminals free of corrosion.*

The Electrical System

The heart of your vehicle's electrical system is the battery. The **battery** provides the power to start the engine. It also enables you to operate, for a short time, such equipment as your radio and lights when the engine is not running.

After you turn the ignition key and start the vehicle, the battery supplies the electricity to fire the spark plugs, operate the stereo, air-conditioning, and other systems. The **alternator,** or generator, provides a constant charge for the battery. The **engine control module (ECM)** controls the electrical and other engine systems.

To prevent electrical overloads and damage to delicate electronic components, the electrical system is equipped with fuses, usually located in a clearly labeled pod beneath the instrument panel or under the hood.

The Light System

Your vehicle's light system enables you to see and be seen.

Exterior lights include headlights, taillights, side-marker lights, brake lights, signal lights, parking lights, and emergency flashers. Interior lights include the dome light on the inside roof of the vehicle and the various dashboard lights that provide you with information about the vehicle or warn you of malfunctions.

How Can You Maintain the Electrical and Light Systems?

The first step in maintaining the electrical and light systems is to keep your battery in top working condition. Keep the battery terminals free of corrosion and the battery cables firmly connected. Most current batteries are maintenance-free, but if you have an older one, check the fluid level at least once a month, and add water when needed.

The electrical system is constantly monitored by the engine control module or computer. If it detects a problem, the "check engine" light on the instrument panel may come on.

Keep headlights clean and properly aligned. Even a thin layer of dirt can cut light output by as much as 90 percent. Misaligned lights

FYI

If the "check engine" light comes on, make sure the gas cap or lid is fully tightened to the point of at least one click or notch. The emission control equipment is so sensitive that it can detect if the cap is not correctly tightened and will cause the warning light to come on. You may or may not need to computer reset it.

can reduce your ability to see the roadway and can momentarily blind oncoming drivers.

Check exterior lights at least once a week, and promptly replace any burned-out bulbs.

How Do the Lubricating and Cooling Systems Work?

As the parts of your vehicle's engine move rapidly and rub against each other, they produce friction and heat. At the same time, the fuel-air explosions in the cylinders create more heat. Small wonder then that the engine temperature may exceed 4,000°F.

Too much heat can destroy your vehicle's engine. The lubricating and cooling systems are designed to keep that from happening.

The Lubricating System

Oil is the key element in your vehicle's lubricating system. Coating engine parts with oil reduces friction, heat, and wear. Oil also helps clean internal engine surfaces and prevent rust and corrosion.

An oil pump moves oil from the oil pan, where it is stored, to all moving engine parts. The oil filter cleans the oil as it circulates.

In addition to oil, grease is used to lubricate parts of the vehicle, such as the steering system. Like oil, grease reduces friction and helps parts move smoothly.

Energy Tips

The engine control module or computer in a modern vehicle automatically adjusts the engine's systems for whatever grade of fuel you use. Some engines will perform better with higher, more expensive grades of fuel, but most will not. See your owner's manual for the manufacturer's recommendations.

FYI

Each year, electrical system failures disable more vehicles than the combined next two causes of vehicle breakdowns.

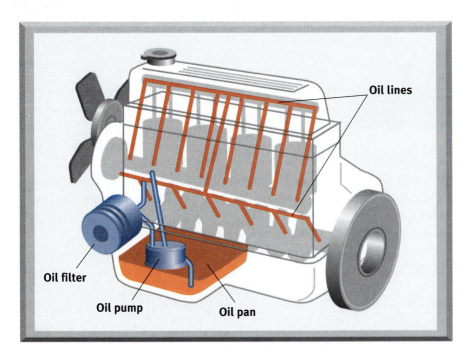

Oil lines

Oil filter

Oil pump

Oil pan

◆ *The lubricating system reduces heat by coating the parts of the engine with oil.*

The Cooling System

The purpose of the cooling system is to keep your vehicle's engine from overheating. To do this, the cooling system circulates **coolant**— a mixture of water and antifreeze— through the engine by means of a network of pipes, channels, and connecting hoses.

Antifreeze has a lower freezing point and higher boiling point than pure water. Without it, the liquid in the cooling system would freeze in very cold weather and could boil over in hot weather, especially in traffic jams and on long trips. Frozen or boiling coolant does not circulate, and this can cause the engine to overheat.

Your vehicle's coolant is stored in the radiator and in the radiator overflow tank. A water pump pumps the coolant through the radiator and the circulating network. A fan forces the air through the **radiator** to cool the liquid. A thermostat in the system works to control the flow of the coolant in order to maintain the best operating temperature.

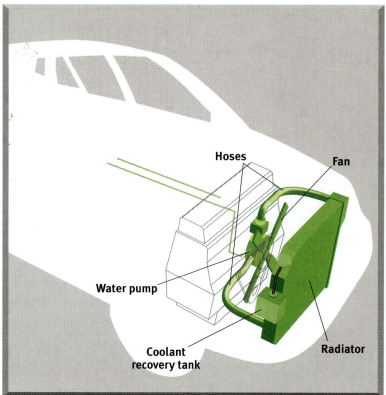

Hoses

Fan

Water pump

Coolant recovery tank

Radiator

◆ *The so-called water-cooled engine actually uses a coolant in its cooling system.*

CONNECTIONS

Science

Carbon monoxide is an odorless, colorless, and tasteless gas. Small amounts of carbon monoxide can make you sleepy or nauseated or give you a headache by interfering with the ability of your red blood cells to carry oxygen. Large amounts of carbon monoxide can kill you.

Avoid driving a vehicle that has an exhaust leak or a broken tailpipe. Such defects allow carbon monoxide and other harmful exhaust gases to be trapped beneath the vehicle, even when it is moving. These gases may leak up into the vehicle's interior.

To guard against carbon monoxide poisoning, also avoid:
- running a vehicle's engine in a closed garage.
- sitting in a parked vehicle with the windows closed, the engine running, and the heater on.
- driving with the trunk lid up.
- driving with the rear window of a station wagon open.
- stopping so close to the vehicle ahead that your heater or air conditioner draws in exhaust gases from that vehicle's tailpipe.

How Can You Maintain the Lubricating and Cooling Systems?

Checking and changing the oil and oil filter regularly is the key to maintaining your vehicle's lubricating system. Low oil pressure allows the engine to become too hot, which may cause excessive wear of moving parts.

Keep in mind that the oil-pressure gauge or warning light does not indicate how much oil is in the engine, but it will signal a drop in oil pressure. To check the actual level of oil, use the oil dipstick. *Never* drive your vehicle with insufficient oil: you could destroy the engine. The engine oil level can only be checked after the engine has been turned off for some period of time, preferably an hour or more. This is necessary to give the oil time to drain back into the oil pan from throughout the engine. Checking it before that has happened will give you a false low reading.

Driving with an overheated engine can also damage your vehicle. If the temperature gauge or warning light indicates overheating, stop driving as soon as possible. Let the engine cool before you look for the cause of the problem.

To maintain the cooling system, use the proper coolant, and check the fluid level whenever the vehicle is serviced. Also check the fan belt and connecting hoses. Have the cooling system completely drained, flushed, and refilled every two years.

◆ You can learn to use a dipstick to check whether or not your vehicle needs more oil.

WHAT WOULD YOU DO?

You've been stuck in bumper-to-bumper traffic for nearly an hour on a hot summer day. The temperature warning light has just come on. How will you handle this situation? What safety precautions will you take?

Lesson **3** Review

1. Why is it important to keep the fuel and exhaust systems of your vehicle in good condition?
2. Explain how your vehicle uses electricity, and name the source of electrical power in your vehicle.
3. How do the lubricating and cooling systems work?

Suspension, Steering, Brakes, and Tires

Your comfort and safety in a vehicle depend not only on how well you drive but also on how your vehicle handles. To protect yourself and others, make sure your vehicle's suspension, steering, and brake systems as well as all four tires are in good operating condition.

What Vehicle Systems Are Important for Comfort and Safety?

The suspension, steering, and brake systems, and tires, work together to give you control over your vehicle and to provide a comfortable ride.

The Suspension System

The suspension system supports your vehicle's weight, cushions the ride, and helps keep the vehicle stable when you drive over bumps or uneven roadway surfaces.

Most vehicles today use suspensions—especially in the front of the vehicle—where the spring and shock absorber are contained in one unit called a **strut.**

The springs soften the impact of bumps in the roadway. If your vehicle had only springs, however, it would continue bouncing after hitting a bump. This bouncing would reduce the contact between the tires and the road and make it harder for you to control the vehicle.

The **shock absorbers**—or shocks, as they're commonly called—work to control bouncing. By absorbing the shocks of driving, they make the ride smoother and help you maintain steering and braking control.

◆ *The suspension system cushions the vehicle's frame against bumps in the road.*

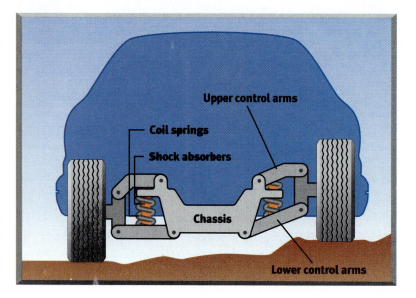

Upper control arms

Coil springs

Shock absorbers

Chassis

Lower control arms

The Steering System

The steering system enables you to turn the front wheels. The steering wheel is connected to the front wheels by a steering shaft and movable rods.

The front wheels are designed to remain in an upright position and move up and down over bumps, even when they are turned.

The Brake System

Brakes slow or stop a vehicle by applying **hydraulic pressure**—pressure created by the force of a liquid—against the four wheels. Stepping on the brake pedal forces brake fluid from the master brake cylinder through the brake-fluid lines to the wheel cylinders. There are two types of brakes: disc brakes and drum brakes.

Disc brakes In a **disc brake,** pressure squeezes the brake pads against a flat metal wheel disc, producing the friction needed to stop the wheel from turning.

All new vehicles now have disc brakes on the front wheels. Many have them on the rear wheels as well. All new vehicles now also have power brakes, which require less pressure on the brake pedal than older non-power systems. Power brakes do *not,* however, shorten a vehicle's stopping distance.

Drum brakes In a **drum brake,** the fluid pressure causes the brake shoes to push against the brake lining. The lining then presses against the round hollow metal drum inside the wheel. Friction slows and stops the wheel's turning motion.

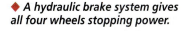

◆ *A hydraulic brake system gives all four wheels stopping power.*

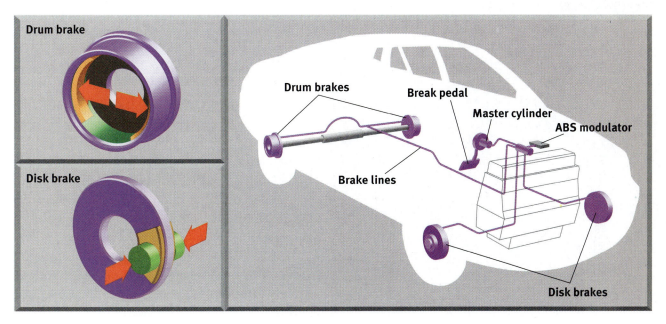

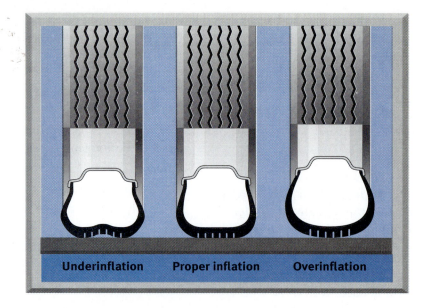

Underinflation   Proper inflation   Overinflation

◆ *It is important for fuel efficiency and traction that a vehicle's tires be properly inflated.*

To minimize the risk of brake failure, brake systems are designed so that front and rear brakes are controlled independently. If one pair of brakes fails, the other pair will still work to stop the vehicle.

Antilock brakes Many newer vehicles have an antilock brake system (ABS), which is designed to keep the wheels from locking when the driver presses too hard on the brake pedal in an emergency. Since the wheels do not lock, the driver can continue to steer the vehicle. Antilock brakes do not shorten the stopping distance of a vehicle.

Parking brake A parking brake is a mechanically operated brake that is separate from the hydraulic brake system. Attached by cable to the rear wheels, it is used to prevent a parked vehicle from rolling.

The Tires

A driver's control of a vehicle depends largely on the condition of the tires. Nevertheless, more than 40 percent of nearly 250,000 vehicles inspected between 1982 and 1993 had defective tires.

Tire inflation Tires must be inflated properly to provide maximum traction and control. Too little tire pressure (underinflation) or too much tire pressure (overinflation) reduces traction, makes a vehicle harder to handle, and lowers fuel efficiency.

Most vehicles require different pressures for the front and rear tires. To find the recommended maximum air pressures for your vehicle, check your owner's manual or look for a sticker that may be affixed to a doorpost or inside the fuel filler door. Usually two tire pressures are listed—one for normal and a higher number for long trips or when carrying heavy loads. The lower number may result in a softer ride but will likely mean lower tread life. The higher number will improve both handling and wear at the cost of some ride quality.

◆ *The vehicle manufacturer often places maximum tire air pressure on the inside of the door.*

WEIGHT

TIRE PRESSURE COLD   32 PSI   220 kPa

MINIMUM TIRE SIZE

P165/80R13

STANDARD LOAD

SEE OWNERS MANUAL FOR OPTIONAL TIRES, HIGH SPEED OPERATION & ADDITIONAL DATA

PRINTED IN USA   F 4472 984

Tire tread The grooved outer surface of a tire is its **tread.** On wet or slippery surfaces, the amount of tread on your tires determines how much traction your vehicle will have. Compared with tires that have good tread, overly worn tires have double the risk of skidding and are also more likely to go flat or blow out.

Tires should be replaced when the depth of the tread is $\frac{1}{16}$ inch. To help you judge tread depth, all tires have tread wear bars that run across the tire.

Tire rotation Front tires generally wear faster than rear tires. To equalize tire wear, have your vehicle's tires rotated about every 5,000 to 6,000 miles. Rotating tires means switching their position from front to rear and sometimes from one side to the other. Check your owner's manual for the recommended tire-rotation pattern.

When tires are rotated, they often need to be balanced. This helps ensure that weight is evenly distributed as the wheel turns. Balanced tires provide better steering control, a smoother ride, and longer tire life.

What Are Some Warning Signs of Vehicle Problems?

Sometimes vehicle problems appear unexpectedly. More often, though, advance warnings signal that a part or system needs attention.

◆ *Have a mechanic check the vehicle if any warning signs of suspension or brake problems appear.*

Suspension and Steering Problems

Most problems affecting the suspension and steering system develop gradually as a result of wear. Watch for the following warning signs.

- There is too much play (free movement) in the steering wheel. With rack and pinion power steering, there should be virtually no play in the wheel. In a manual system, there should be no more than 2 inches of play.
- The steering wheel vibrates or is difficult to turn.
- The front end of the vehicle wobbles or shimmies.
- The vehicle bumps as you turn the wheel while driving on a smooth road.
- The vehicle pulls to one side as you drive.
- The vehicle bounces too much after hitting a bump.
- Tread wear on the front tires is uneven.

Have a mechanic check your vehicle if any of these warning signs appear. The front end of your vehicle may need aligning, the tires may need to be balanced, or some other problem may need correction.

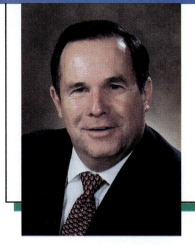

Richard Russell

Member, Society of Automotive Engineers, nationally certified Master Driving Instructor, and consultant to AAA

Tires are arguably the most important safety feature on your vehicle. The four small patches of rubber in contact with the road determine how you stop, steer, and go. Don't think of buying new tires as a "grudge buy." Tires are the one area where a purchase decision can directly affect the safety of your vehicle. This is not an area to try to save money. Generally speaking, the more you spend on a tire, the better the grip it will provide and the safer you will be.

Brake Problems

See Chapter 14 for a description of brake failure. Neglecting a problem with the brake system can have fatal consequences. Check with a mechanic if any warning signs appear.

Tire Problems

Inspecting your tires regularly *before* you drive will help avoid problems on the road. Watch for the following warning signs of tire troubles:

- tread wear bars appear, indicating less than 1/16 inch tread
- areas of little or no tread— "bald" spots
- uneven wear
- bulges
- embedded nails, glass, or metal
- frequent pressure loss in one particular tire, suggesting a slow leak

WHAT WOULD YOU DO?

You just test-drove this car. As you stepped on the brake, the car pulled to the right. What could cause this problem? Would you buy the car?

Lesson 4 Review

1. How are the steering, suspension, brakes, and tires important to your safety?
2. What are some warning signs that indicate tire problems?

Graphing Braking Distances

After you apply the brakes, the distance it takes to come to a stop depends in part on the speed at which your vehicle is moving.

The formula for figuring out braking distance is

$$D = S \times \tfrac{1}{10}S \div 2.4$$

where S = speed and D = distance in feet.

Here is how you would figure braking distance at 35 mph.

$$D = 35 \times (\tfrac{1}{10} \times 35) \div 2.4$$
$$D = 35 \times 3.5 \div 2.4$$
$$D = 51.04$$

Thus, braking distance at 35 mph is 51.04 feet, or a little more than 17 yards.

Make a graph to show how braking distance changes in relation to speed.

Try It Yourself

1. First, use the formula to figure the stopping distance for these speeds:
   20 mph 30 mph 40 mph 50 mph 60 mph
2. On a sheet of graph paper, write the speeds along the bottom of the graph at regular intervals, as shown below.
3. On the left side of the graph, write distances in regular intervals, as shown below.
4. For each distance you figure, put a dot at the appropriate place on your graph.
5. Finally, draw a line from the first dot to the second, from the second to the third, and so on, beginning with the dot at the shortest braking distance.

What conclusion can you draw from your graph?

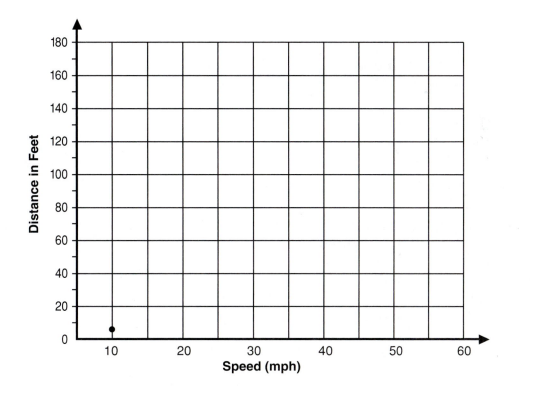

KEY POINTS

Lesson One

1. At least once a month, before entering your vehicle, check fluid levels, belts and hoses, and connections.
2. After starting the engine, check gauges and warning lights, and test your brakes and horn.
3. Service your vehicle according to the kind and amount of driving and manufacturer recommendations.

Lesson Two

1. An internal combustion engine burns a mixture of fuel and air. In each cylinder, a spark causes the mixture to explode, pushing down the piston, turning the crankshaft.
2. The power train sends engine power to the wheels through the transmission.
3. Regularly check and change the oil, check the transmission fluid, and change filters.

Lesson Three

1. The fuel pump forces fuel from the tank to the fuel-injection system to mix with air. The vapor is ignited in the cylinders. Unburned gases from the engine exit through the tailpipe. Replace filters as needed. Have your exhaust system inspected at least twice a year.
2. The battery is the source of electrical power. Keep headlights clean and aligned, and replace any burned-out bulbs.
3. Lubricating and cooling systems keep heat from destroying the engine by sending oil to moving engine parts. A mixture of fluid and antifreeze cools the engine.
   Change oil and oil filters regularly. Use coolant, and check the fluid level when the vehicle is serviced.

Lesson Four

1. The suspension supports a vehicle's weight, cushions the ride, and stabilizes the vehicle; the steering system enables the front wheels to turn; brakes stop the vehicle; tires help it grip the road.
2. Warnings of possible suspension problems include too much play in the wheel; front-end wobble; and pulling to one side.

PROJECTS

1. In an owner's manual, find the sections that deal with the vehicle systems discussed in this chapter. What information does the manual provide that applies specifically to the particular make and model vehicle? In what other ways does the manual help the owner maintain the vehicle?
2. Research and report on the various types of tires, including summer, all-season, and winter or snow tires. What are the advantages and limitations of each? Where should you put two new tires or snow tires on a vehicle with front-wheel drive?

*inter*NET
CONNECTION

To learn how car systems have changed with the use of computers, visit Glencoe's Web site.
www.glencoe.com/sec/driver.ed

CHAPTER TEST

Write the letter of the answer that best completes each sentence.

1. A catalytic converter is part of a vehicle's
   a. transmission.
   b. exhaust system.
   c. fuel system.

2. You should check your engine oil
   a. while your engine is running.
   b. before starting your engine.
   c. every 12,000 miles.

3. Springs and shock absorbers are parts of a vehicle's
   a. transmission.
   b. front-end alignment.
   c. suspension system.

4. Most vehicles' engines are
   a. turbine engines.
   b. external combustion engines.
   c. internal combustion engines.

5. When you step on your brake pedal, you should feel
   a. firm resistance.
   b. no resistance.
   c. the floor.

6. The temperature of a vehicle's engine may exceed
   a. 212°F.
   b. 500°F.
   c. 4,000°F.

7. You should rotate your vehicle's tires to
   a. equalize tire wear.
   b. increase fuel efficiency.
   c. improve suspension.

8. Most vehicles today operate on
   a. lead-free gasoline.
   b. leaded gasoline.
   c. diesel fuel.

9. Many vehicles are equipped with
   a. a power clutch.
   b. drum brakes on the front wheels and disc brakes on the back wheels.
   c. disc brakes on the front wheels and drum brakes on the back wheels.

10. Your vehicle's alternator
    a. controls suspension.
    b. mixes oxygen with gasoline.
    c. supplies electricity to run the engine.

Write the word or phrase that best completes each sentence.

| pistons | hydraulic pressure | power train |
| muffler | electrical system | owner's manual |

11. The parts of a vehicle that transmit the engine's power to the wheels make up the _____.

12. The heart of a vehicle's _____ is called the battery.

13. Brakes slow or stop a vehicle by applying _____ against the four wheels.

14. A(n) _____ contains specific guidelines for servicing and maintaining a vehicle.

15. The pipes that make up the exhaust manifold collect unburned gases from the engine and carry them to the _____.

DRIVER'S LOG

In this chapter, you have learned how the systems that operate a vehicle function and what the maintenance requirements of these systems are. Based on your observations, do most drivers pay attention to these maintenance requirements? Write a paragraph about what you would tell those who do not.

CHAPTER *18*

Planning a Trip

Planning is essential to travel, whether it is to a local supermarket or across the country. Vehicle preparation, wise route decisions, and time management are key ingredients to responsible planning.

LESSON ONE

Preparing Yourself and Your Vehicle for a Short Trip

LESSON TWO

Getting Ready for a Long Trip

LESSON THREE

Loading and Driving with a Trailer

LESSON FOUR

Traveling Safely in a Light Truck: A Pickup, Sport Utility Vehicle, or Van

OBJECTIVES

1. Describe how you would prepare yourself for a short trip.
2. Discuss how you would prepare your vehicle for a short trip and the reasons for doing so.

Preparing Yourself and Your Vehicle for a Short Trip

Most traffic fatalities happen within 25 miles, or a short trip's distance, of the driver's home. Have you thought about ways to reduce your chances of being in a collision when you take a short trip away from home?

What Steps Should You Take When Planning a Short Trip?

A short trip can be a 5-mile drive to a neighborhood shopping center, a 2-mile drive to work or school, or a 45-mile trip to visit a relative who lives in another town. Even if you make the same trip every day, being prepared can help you reduce the risk of being in a collision.

Prepare Yourself

You need to make advance preparations for a trip even if you'll only be driving a short distance. Ask yourself these questions before you get into the car.

Do I know how to get where I'm going? If you are going someplace you have never been before, work out your route in advance. Make sure that you have specific directions to follow, and use a map to check them out. Know the names of the streets and roads that you have to follow. Make sure that you are able to drive on them in the direction you want to go.

Do I know another way to get there? Sometimes even the best plans just don't work out. Your planned route may be

TIPS

FOR NEW DRIVERS

Working a Self-Service Gas Pump

To operate a self-service gas pump, pull up to the pump that dispenses the kind of fuel your vehicle uses. If a sign says "Pay Cashier Before Pumping," the pumps will not operate until you pay. Otherwise, pump the amount you need, and pay when you are done.

1. Open the fuel filler door, and take off the gas cap.
2. Take the pump nozzle off its cradle, and place the nozzle in the fuel tank opening.
3. Turn on the pump switch. It is usually located near the pump nozzle cradle.
4. Squeeze the lever on the pump nozzle to begin pumping the fuel.
5. If you have prepaid or when the tank is full, the pump will shut off automatically. Otherwise, release the lever, and put the nozzle back on its cradle. Turn off the pump switch. Then put the gas cap back on, and shut the fuel filler door.

blocked for many reasons, so it's smart to have alternative plans to get where you're going by another route.

Do I have everything I need? Even though you will probably not take any luggage on a short trip, you may need some or all of the following items: identification, money, addresses, directions or a map, and a list of things to do, see, or buy.

Have I given myself enough time? Hurrying can make you nervous and careless. First figure out how long the trip should take, then add some time for the unexpected. You can anticipate some delays by listening to the radio for weather conditions and traffic reports.

Am I going at a good time? Try to avoid rush-hour traffic. There's no reason to get involved in a traffic jam if you don't absolutely have to. As you plan your route, remember that roads leading into urban areas will be busiest during the morning rush hours and roads leading out will be busiest in the evening rush hours.

◆ *Use a map to make sure you know how to get where you're going.*

Prepare Your Vehicle

Every time you use your vehicle, you should check to be sure that it is in proper condition to be driven. (See Chapter 7 for predriving checks.) You should check to see that:

- tires are properly inflated.
- signal lights are working.
- front and back lights are working.
- you have enough fuel and oil.

Preparing yourself and your vehicle for a trip does not take much time. However, the time you spend in preparation will save you time and trouble in the long run.

WHAT WOULD YOU DO?

You had last-minute errands and are going to be late for an appointment. What will you do next time to avoid this situation?

Lesson *1* Review

1. What are some helpful questions to ask yourself as you prepare for a short trip?
2. What items should you check as you prepare to drive your vehicle?

OBJECTIVES

1. Explain how you would prepare yourself for a long trip.
2. Describe how you would prepare your vehicle for a long trip.

Getting Ready for a Long Trip

You face risk when you take a long trip, just as you do when you take a short trip. Fatigue, unfamiliarity with the area, and uncertain weather conditions are some factors that can increase driving risk on a long trip. Long trips also present you and your vehicle with some different needs.

What Should You Do to Prepare for a Long Trip?

If you plan to take a long trip, some of the preparations you should make are similar to those you make for a short trip. Others, however, are important only when you are traveling long distances.

Prepare Yourself

Here are some questions that you should ask yourself to prepare for a long trip.

How will I get to where I want to go? You may choose the most direct route to your destination, or you may choose to drive on a more leisurely route through scenic country. Whichever you choose, plan your route carefully. Use a map, and keep in mind the risks that each route may pose. The most direct route may involve expressway driving, where high speeds and large trucks present special problems. On the other hand, a scenic route may lead through congested towns or wilderness areas with no gas stations or places to stay.

Plan your route before you start the trip. Don't try to read a map while you're moving on the roadway. If you need to check the map, pull into a rest area or onto the shoulder when it is safe to do so.

You may want to write to or visit an auto club or travel agency to obtain maps, route suggestions, and recommendations on places to stay.

◆ *Call ahead to make reservations at hotels or motels along your route and at your destination.*

Where will I spend the night while I am on the road? Plan where you will spend each night, and make your reservations in advance. Ask about rates and parking facilities, and figure this information into your budget and schedule.

Will I have had enough sleep the night before driving? Be sure that you get enough rest before getting behind the wheel. If you become tired while driving, pull over at a rest stop.

A good plan is to drive in 2-hour stretches with 15-minute breaks in between. Don't try to drive more than a total of 8 hours in a day. If you're traveling with another person who also drives, share the driving task.

Budgeting Your Money and Planning Your Time

A long trip can be expensive. To figure out how much money you'll need, make a budget. Use the categories above, adding others if you need to. Figure your budget by the day or by the week. Your emergency supplies should include an extra set of vehicle keys as well as replacements for or additions to supplies you normally carry in your trunk or other vehicle storage area. (See Chapter 15 for a list of emergency supplies.)

Energy Tips

Although a scenic route may be more enjoyable, a limited-access highway tends to be much safer and more energy efficient. You'll have fewer stops, starts, curves, and hills, and you'll be able to maintain a steady speed for longer periods of time.

BUDGET

	Food	Lodging	Gas	Tolls	Parking	Recreation
Day 1	$75	$95	$18	$5	—	$20
Day 2	$120	$70	$15	—	$5	—
Day 3	$70	$80	$15	$3	—	$15

SCHEDULE

	Depart		Average	Arrive	
	Place	Time	Speed	Place	Time
Day 1	Holyoke	7 A.M.	40 mph	Boston	9 A.M.
Day 2	Boston	2 P.M.	45 mph	NYC	6 P.M.
Day 3	NYC	6 A.M.	45 mph	Washington, D.C.	11 A.M.

BEFORE-THE-TRIP CHECKLIST

Emergency supplies	Professional vehicle checkup	Maps and travel books
Extra fuses	Brakes	City maps
Gloves	Transmission	State maps
Duct tape	Shocks	Places of interest
Flashlight		
First aid kit		
Keys		

FYI

To find the recommended air pressures for your tires, check your vehicle owner's manual or look for a sticker that may be affixed to a doorpost or to the inside of the fuel filler door. *Never* exceed the maximum tire pressure recommended for your vehicle.

Planning your travel time by making a schedule is also helpful. In making up your schedule, consider such factors as rush-hour traffic, speed limits, the kind of route you want to take, how far you want to drive at a time, and occasional stops for stretching, eating, and relaxing. Plan your driving time so that you avoid morning and early-evening rush-hour traffic.

Prepare Your Vehicle

Your vehicle should always be in good condition. However, before a long trip, you should have a mechanic check the following:

- brake shoes and pads
- exhaust system for leaks
- front-end alignment
- tire condition
- fluid levels in the engine, transmission, and battery
- shock absorbers
- belts and hoses

Pack the vehicle carefully. Overloading can have an adverse effect on your vehicle's handling, acceleration, and fuel efficiency.

Before you load your vehicle, consult your owner's manual for the maximum weight load recommended per tire. Then be sure that your tires are inflated to the tire pressure recommended to carry any extra weight.

When you pack the vehicle, follow these additional guidelines.

- Pack the heaviest objects at the bottom of the trunk or storage area.
- If you use a vehicle-top carrier, be sure to place only lighter objects in it.
- Do not put anything on the rear-window shelf that will obstruct your view of the roadway behind you or that can be thrown forward in a sudden stop. Do not obstruct the back seat windows by hanging clothes over them.

You and your family are about to take a three-week driving trip. What will you do to make this vehicle trip-worthy?

Lesson 2 Review

1. How can you prepare yourself and your vehicle for a long trip?
2. How can making a budget and a schedule help you with your plans for a long trip?

Loading and Driving with a Trailer

LESSON THREE

OBJECTIVES
1. Describe factors you should be aware of when planning to use a trailer.
2. Explain the procedures for driving a vehicle with a trailer attached.

KEY TERM

hitch

Many drivers tow boats, campers, or other kinds of trailers behind their vehicles. Towing a trailer, however, can make driving more difficult.

What Do You Need to Know About Trailers?

Knowing some of the special features and needs of trailers can help you minimize the risk when driving with one attached to your vehicle.

Weight of the Trailer and Its Load

Many vehicles are limited in the amount of weight they can pull in a trailer. Consider the weight of your vehicle, the weight of the trailer you're planning to haul, and the weight of the load. Check your owner's manual for recommended factory load limits.

Necessary Equipment

If you tow a trailer frequently, your vehicle may need additional equipment, such as a heavy-duty suspension, anti-sway bars, a large-capacity radiator, transmission cooler, and heavy-duty shock absorbers. You will need to add mirrors on your vehicle to increase visibility. You also need extra emergency equipment for heavier trailers, including a hydraulic jack, blocks for holding on grades, and tow ropes.

To tow a trailer, you need a **hitch,** a device that attaches to the back of the vehicle, and safety chains. For ordinary loads, use a hitch that is welded or bolted to the frame of the vehicle. For heavier loads, there are special hitches for load equalizing. When your hitch is installed, also install an electrical outlet for the trailer's taillights, stoplights, and turn signals.

Preparing to Tow a Trailer

The increased load that a trailer puts on your vehicle means that you will need to check your oil and transmission fluid more often than

FYI

The poorest trailer hitch is a bumper attachment unit. Do not use this kind of hitch for anything except the very lightest loads.

◆ *Pack a trailer so that 60 percent of the load is in the front half.*

usual. You will also need to replace air, oil, and fuel filters sooner than you ordinarily would. You may need to increase the air pressure in your tires.

Packing a Trailer

The rear end of your vehicle will have to support 10 to 15 percent of the trailer load. Therefore, the vehicle itself should carry 10 to 15 percent less than the maximum weight recommended by the owner's manual. Too much weight in the back of the vehicle will cause its front to rise and will affect steering, braking, and the aim of the headlights.

When you pack the trailer, follow manufacturer's guidelines. Load the heaviest items at the bottom, over the trailer wheels. About 60 percent of the weight should be packed in the front half of the trailer, and the total weight should be about equal from side to side. Be sure to pack all items tightly or tie them down so that they cannot shift during driving maneuvers.

Check what you have done. The bottoms of both the vehicle and the trailer should be nearly parallel to the ground.

How Do You Drive a Vehicle with a Trailer Attached?

Towing a trailer requires new driving skills and plenty of practice.

Starting

Maneuverability and acceleration are limited when you tow a trailer. Check traffic carefully. Signal before moving. Allow a large gap before entering traffic. Start slowly, and check traffic in the mirrors frequently.

Backing

Backing is a difficult maneuver. Use these guidelines to back with a trailer: back slowly; to go left, turn the steering wheel to the right and then straighten it; to go right, turn the steering wheel to the *left* and then straighten it. Do not turn the steering wheel too much or hold it in the turned position too long. Doing so can cause the trailer to jackknife.

◆ *Practice backing with a trailer before you actually need to do it.*

Turn wheel this way to make trailer go right.

Turn wheel this way to make trailer go left.

Making a Right Turn

To turn right, follow these steps.

1. Check traffic and signal for the right turn in advance of the intersection.

2. Position farther from the curb than if you didn't have a trailer attached.

3. Steer the vehicle straight ahead until the front wheels are well beyond the curb line.
4. Turn the steering wheel sharply right.
5. Complete the turn by straightening the steering wheel.

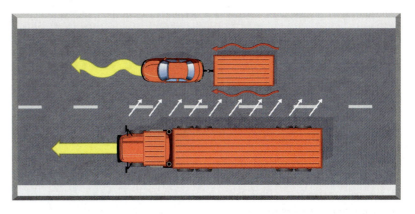

Making a Left Turn

To turn left, follow these steps.

1. Check traffic and signal early.
2. Proceed farther into the intersection than usual to allow for the trailer.
3. Swing wide enough so that the trailer will not cut the corner.
4. Complete the turn and move into traffic.

◆ *A draft from large vehicles can make a trailer move from side to side. Be ready to adjust steering.*

Overtaking, Passing, and Being Overtaken

When you plan to overtake and pass another vehicle, allow much more time and space because of the length and weight of the trailer.

When you are being passed by a light vehicle, observe the same rules that you do in a car. (See Chapter 9.) However, if a heavy vehicle is passing you, the air that it displaces will tend to push the trailer to the side. Be ready to adjust your steering.

Slowing and Stopping

If your trailer does not have brakes, the brakes on your vehicle control all slowing and stopping. If the trailer does have brakes, then your vehicle's brakes control the trailer's brakes.

The additional weight and length of the trailer mean that you will need more time and space to stop. When you do enter traffic, allow a greater following distance than you ordinarily would.

Before driving with a trailer, check your insurance to be sure that you are covered for towing a trailer. Also check the laws about trailers in states that you will be traveling through.

SAFETY TIPS

If you are pulling a trailer, you will need twice the usual distance to merge into traffic, to pass another vehicle, or to stop.

Lesson **3** Review

1. Why is it important to pack a trailer carefully?
2. In what ways is driving with a trailer different from driving without one?

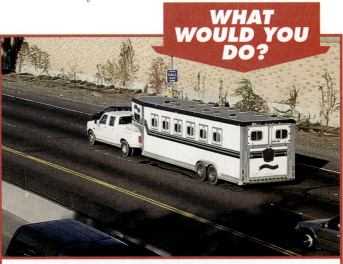

WHAT WOULD YOU DO?

You want to make a left turn. What will you do?

OBJECTIVES

1. Explain the importance of visibility and vehicle size when traveling in a pickup truck, sport utility vehicle, or van.
2. Describe how you can protect yourself and other motorists when driving a large vehicle.

KEY TERM

sport utility vehicle (SUV)

Traveling Safely in a Light Truck: A Pickup, Sport Utility Vehicle, or Van

The most popular vehicles on American roads today are light trucks. This category includes pickups, vans, and **sport utility vehicles (SUVs).** An SUV is designed for a variety of uses and usually incorporates four- or all-wheel drive. It features increased ground clearance and a cargo area included within the interior of the vehicle. Driving a light truck or sharing the road with light trucks requires consideration for their size and limitations.

How Do You Drive a Pickup, Sport Utility Vehicle, or Van?

A number of factors make light trucks more difficult than cars to drive and more difficult to share the road with.

Visibility

A taller vehicle allows the driver to see over surrounding traffic and take advantage of that height to search farther down the road for pending problems. This gives the driver an advantage in planning driving strategy.

◆ *Because you sit higher in a van or sport utility vehicle, you can see farther ahead than you do in a car.*

Vehicle Size

Most pickups, SUVs, and vans are wider and higher than cars. This greater width and height, along with a greater weight, pose special problems that you must learn to deal with in order to manage risk.

Know the height of your vehicle. The extra height of most light trucks means that vehicles sharing the road with them often cannot see through, around, or past them to determine what lies ahead. While you can see through the glass area of a car, the same cannot always be said for these taller vehicles. When following one, stay farther behind to increase your ability to see around it.

Because these vehicles are taller than cars, the headlights and bumpers are above the rest of the traffic. In case of a collision, the bumpers will not match up with those of surrounding cars but will more likely strike the cars' bodies above their bumpers, resulting not only in more damage to the vehicles but also an increased possibility of injury to the cars' occupants.

Because headlights are higher they cause more glare when approaching or following other traffic. As the driver of the taller vehicle, you should be aware of this and stay farther back from vehicles you are following and pay strict attention to keeping your lights on low beam when approaching other vehicles.

Additional height also causes problems when you are trying to turn or stop suddenly. The center of gravity is higher, and the vehicle will roll to the side or pitch forward more easily than a car. The additional size and weight makes pickups, SUVs, and vans handle much less securely than cars in emergency situations.

Don't forget to check the height of your vehicle, especially a van, which might not fit into some garages or enclosed parking spaces.

Know the weight of your vehicle. Pickups, vans, and sport utility vehicles, because of their construction and additional components, weigh more than cars. Weight is the enemy of fuel mileage, handling, and braking. Being larger, these vehicles take longer to stop, turn, or accelerate than does a lighter vehicle.

Be alert for wind. The square shape and taller height mean that light trucks present a greater surface to the wind and are more susceptible to it.

Know about your vehicle's tires. Tires determine how well any vehicle can stop, turn, or accelerate. Tires used on pickups, SUVs, and vans have a more open and rugged tread design to allow them to deal with off-road use. However, this makes them less efficient on wet or dry pavement because they place less rubber on the road, limiting the ability of these larger, heavier vehicles to stop or turn. On average, a pickup or sport utility vehicle will take between 10 percent and 20 percent more distance to stop from highway speeds than a passenger car.

Protecting Other Motorists

Adjust your driving to take into account that you are driving a larger and wider vehicle than

◆ *Look for signs on underpasses that tell you what the maximum clearance is.*

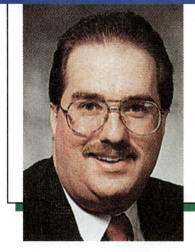

Bill Hughes
Director, National Travel, AAA

Allow sufficient time to get to your destination to avoid feeling rushed and making last-minute decisions. Keep a sufficient amount of fuel in your vehicle—you may not know how long it is to the next service station. Plan your stops so that you don't find yourself in an area where suitable accommodations cannot be found. Select a map that offers the proper level of detail to ensure that you can find your way safely. Check the map for toll roads to make certain you have enough cash to get to your destination.

many others on the road. Maintain a greater margin of space around the vehicle. Keep in mind that you may be blocking the visibility of other drivers. Take this into consideration when you spot potentially threatening conditions ahead that cars behind you may not see.

Increase your following distance to give yourself more time to maneuver and stop. Manage the risk to yourself and to others by staying alert and allowing extra time and space to accomplish driving maneuvers.

Protecting Yourself

Driving long distances is always strenuous and requires frequent rest stops and careful planning. Because of size and the increased difficulty in maneuvering a pickup, sport utility vehicle, or van, you may get tired more quickly than when you are driving a car. Manage risk to yourself and to your passengers by planning to drive shorter distances and resting more often than you would if you were driving a car. If possible, share driving duties.

WHAT WOULD YOU DO?

Since you're driving a vehicle larger and wider than many others, how should you adjust your driving to protect other motorists?

Lesson 4 Review

1. How would the size, weight, and height of a pickup, sport utility vehicle, or van make driving more difficult than driving a car?
2. How do you protect yourself and other motorists when driving a light truck?

Reading City Maps

Driving in a new city is often very confusing. Most maps have insets that show major cities in larger scale. Below is an inset map of Wichita, Kansas.

Suppose you are coming into Wichita from the north, on Interstate 135. To get to Wichita State University, you would leave Route 15 at the interchange for 13th Street. Then you would head east to Hillside Avenue. To get from Washington Road to the Historical Museum, you would drive about 1 mile east on Douglas Avenue.

Try It Yourself

1. How would you get from Wichita State University to Friend University?
2. Suppose you are at the airport. How would you drive to Planeview Park?
3. How would you get from the corner of 25th Street and Amidon Avenue to the Wichita Center for the Arts?

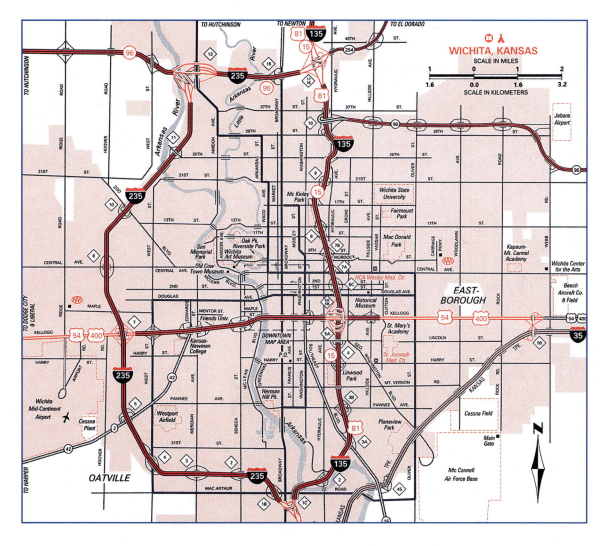

CHAPTER 18 REVIEW

KEY POINTS

Lesson One

1. To prepare yourself for a short trip, have good directions or a map, know an alternate route, take all the items you need, allow extra time, and avoid rush-hour traffic.
2. To prepare your vehicle, be sure that tires are properly inflated, signal lights are working, front and back lights are in order, and that you have enough gas and oil.

Lesson Two

1. Prepare yourself for a long trip by planning your route, making a budget and schedule, making reservations, and getting enough rest.
2. Prepare your vehicle by having it checked by a mechanic and making sure you have adequate emergency equipment.

Lesson Three

1. When planning to use a trailer, consider the weight of the trailer and its load, the weight of your vehicle, and whether your vehicle can tow and control the loaded trailer. Be sure you have any necessary additional equipment to help you tow the trailer safely. Pack the trailer so that 60 percent of the load is in the front half and the heaviest items are on the bottom, making sure the load is secure.
2. To start out in a vehicle with a trailer attached, check traffic, signal, allow a very large gap when entering traffic, and begin slowly. To back with a trailer, move slowly and turn the wheel left when going right and right when going left. To turn, signal early, position the vehicle beyond the curb line, and turn the steering wheel so that the trailer does not cut the corner. Allow extra time and space to pass, to be passed, and to slow and stop.

Lesson Four

1. Although drivers of pickups, sport utility vehicles, and vans sit higher and can see farther ahead and around them than other drivers, this additional height means that people following them will not see as much as they would otherwise.
2. When you are driving a light truck, allow extra stopping distances by following farther behind vehicles. Allow an extra margin of space in all directions at all times.

PROJECTS

1. Choose four neighboring states through which you might take a long trip. Find out what their laws are regarding driver licensing for pickups, SUVs, vans. Compare other state laws with the laws in your own state. Prepare a report on their differences and similarities.
2. Find out where your ancestors lived or where they entered this country. Plan a trip to that place. Plot out your route, and make a budget and schedule. Mark your route on a map for display, and report on your travel plans.

*inter*NET CONNECTION

Explore the Glencoe Web site to find more information on the advantages and disadvantages of driving an SUV. Find out which SUVs are the safest. **www.glencoe.com/sec/driver.ed**

CHAPTER TEST

Choose the letter of the answer that best completes each sentence.

1. When packing a trailer, 60 percent of the load should be
   a. over the wheels.
   b. in the front half of the trailer.
   c. at the bottom of the trailer.

2. You should not drive more than a total of
   a. 8 hours a day.
   b. 5 hours a day.
   c. 12 hours a day.

3. Most traffic fatalities occur
   a. within 50 miles of the driver's home.
   b. within 25 miles of the driver's home.
   c. when a vehicle is changing lanes.

4. If you are going someplace you have never gone before, you should
   a. use a road map while you are driving.
   b. stop periodically to ask directions.
   c. plan your route ahead of time.

5. If you tow a trailer frequently, you may need a
   a. hydraulic jack.
   b. vehicle-top carrier.
   c. boat.

6. You can anticipate some delays by
   a. using a map.
   b. having an alternate route.
   c. listening to the radio for traffic and weather reports.

7. Before starting on a long trip, you should
   a. choose the quickest route.
   b. choose the most leisurely route.
   c. keep in mind the risks that each route may have.

8. You can make a schedule to
   a. know when to exceed the speed limit.
   b. plan your travel time.

   c. keep track of how much money you spend on a trip.

9. When backing a trailer,
   a. turn right to go left.
   b. turn left to go left.
   c. look over your right shoulder.

10. Drivers of taller vehicles can see farther ahead because they
    a. have better eyesight.
    b. have bigger mirrors.
    c. can see over smaller vehicles.

Write the word or phrase that best completes each sentence.

overloading	shock absorbers
restrictions	following distance
trailer hitch	urban areas

11. Roads leading into _____ are busiest during the morning rush hour.

12. _____ can have an adverse effect on your vehicle's acceleration.

13. Have a mechanic check for worn _____ before a long trip.

14. Use a(n) _____ that is welded or bolted to the frame of your vehicle.

15. When you drive a vehicle heavier or taller than a car, you should increase your _____.

DRIVER'S LOG

In this chapter, you have learned how to plan long and short trips, how to tow trailers safely, and how to drive pickups, sport utility vehicles, and vans. Make a personal checklist to remind you of considerations that you would take into account when planning a cross-country trip in such vehicles.

UNIT 4 CUMULATIVE REVIEW

This review tests your knowledge of the material in Chapters 1–18. Use the review to help you study for your state driving test. Choose the answer that best completes each statement.

1. To stop heavy bleeding, use
   a. an air bag.
   b. shock.
   c. adhesion.
   d. direct pressure.

2. At a flashing red traffic signal, you must
   a. slow down.
   b. yield to an emergency vehicle.
   c. come to a full stop.
   d. reverse direction.

3. A vehicle's weight, body design, and engine type all contribute to
   a. the driver's popularity.
   b. oil consumption.
   c. fuel efficiency.
   d. night vision.

4. Plan your time on a trip by
   a. making a budget.
   b. making a schedule.
   c. taking a scenic route.
   d. wearing a watch.

5. At least once a month, check your vehicle's
   a. brake linings.
   b. fluid levels.
   c. shock absorbers.
   d. front-end alignment.

6. At a four-way stop, yield to the
   a. vehicle at your right.
   b. vehicle behind you.
   c. truck at your left.
   d. oncoming car.

7. To prove your identity at the department of motor vehicles, you can take
   a. a phone bill.
   b. your parent's tax return.
   c. a birth certificate.
   d. a report card.

8. Coolant is stored in the
   a. glove compartment.
   b. power train.
   c. radiator.
   d. steering column.

9. Vehicle financing can be obtained through
   a. a bank.
   b. your school.
   c. an insurance company.
   d. the federal government.

10. Tires should be rotated every
    a. 50 miles.
    b. 500 to 600 miles.
    c. 5,000 to 6,000 miles.
    d. two years.

11. You should pack a trailer so that
    a. 25 percent of the load is in the front half.
    b. 60 percent of the load is in the front half.
    c. the load is evenly distributed.
    d. your vehicle's rear bumper touches the ground.

12. Narcotics
    a. stimulate the central nervous system.
    b. are safe and easy to use.
    c. are often used by truck drivers.
    d. can cause death.

13. One problem common to urban driving is
    a. busy intersections.
    b. large animals on the road.
    c. high altitudes.
    d. interchanges.

14. Driving through deep puddles can lead to
    a. brake failure.
    b. front-end alignment.
    c. engine lock.
    d. clutch fade.

15. You are responsible for providing a vehicle for the
    a. in-vehicle test.
    b. knowledge test.
    c. Smith System.
    d. visual acuity test.

16. A factor in the cost of motor vehicle insurance is
    a. ethnic background.
    b. age.
    c. parents' driving records.
    d. number of school years completed.

17. The night before your knowledge test,
    a. stay awake and study.
    b. get plenty of rest.
    c. take a stimulant.
    d. go out with your friends and relax.

18. Driving faster than the posted speed limit is
    a. sometimes necessary.
    b. legal on country roads.
    c. always illegal.
    d. legal but irresponsible.

19. You can increase visibility in dense fog by using
    a. your dome light.
    b. brake lights.
    c. low-beam headlights.
    d. high-beam headlights.

20. The catalytic converter
    a. is a pollution-control device.
    b. is an optional feature.
    c. is attached to the battery.
    d. converts miles to kilometers.

21. Think twice about buying a vehicle if its passenger death rate is
    a. less than 1 per 10,000 registered vehicles.
    b. more than 2 per 10,000 registered vehicles.
    c. less than 2 per 10,000 registered vehicles.
    d. more than 1 per 100,000 registered vehicles.

22. To relax during the in-vehicle test,
    a. chat with the examiner.
    b. admit that you are nervous.
    c. hold your breath.
    d. wear loose clothing.

23. The odometer tells you
    a. the speed of the vehicle.
    b. how far you have driven.
    c. the engine temperature.
    d. how much fuel is in the tank.

24. One step of the Smith System is
    a. the SIPDE process.
    b. risk.
    c. angle parking.
    d. keep your eyes moving.

25. To start a vehicle, insert a key in the
    a. steering wheel.
    b. dashboard.
    c. ignition switch.
    d. carburetor.

26. Traction is poorest at about
    a. 32°F.
    b. 112°F.
    c. 40°F.
    d. the equator.

27. The air filter is part of the
    a. cooling system.
    b. exhaust system.
    c. protection system.
    d. fuel system.

acceleration An increase in speed.

accelerator The gas pedal; controls speed by adjusting the flow of gasoline to the engine.

adhesion Sticking together; in automotive terms, traction or friction.

administrative laws Laws that regulate driver licensing, vehicle registration, financial responsibility of drivers and vehicle owners, or minimum equipment and vehicle standards.

advisory speed limit A speed limit that interrupts normal driving speed for a limited time and provides guidelines for adjusting speed.

air bag A safety bag that automatically inflates upon impact in a collision.

alternator A generator that produces the electricity needed to run a vehicle and its electrical devices.

angle parking Parking so that a vehicle is positioned at a 30- to 90-degree angle with a curb or other boundary.

antifreeze A substance with a low freezing point, usually added to the liquid in a vehicle's radiator to prevent freezing.

antilock brake system (ABS) A braking system that is designed to keep a vehicle's wheels from locking when the driver brakes abruptly.

antitheft device Any device used to protect a vehicle from being stolen or entered.

area of central vision The area of vision directly ahead of a person.

automatic transmission A system that transmits power to the drive wheels. Gears are changed automatically in a vehicle with this type of transmission.

axle The shaft or rod connecting two opposite wheels on which the wheels revolve.

banked curve A curve that slopes up from the inside edge.

battery A unit that stores an electrical charge and furnishes current.

beltway A highway that passes around an urban area.

blind spot An area outside a vehicle that is not visible to the driver in the rearview or side-view mirrors.

blood-alcohol concentration (BAC) The percentage of alcohol in a person's blood.

blowout A sudden loss of air pressure in a tire.

blowout skid A skid occurring when a tire suddenly loses air pressure.

Blue Book A guide to the average price paid to dealers for different makes and models of used vehicles.

brake pedal A pedal that enables a driver to slow or stop a vehicle.

brake system The system that enables a vehicle to slow down and stop by means of hydraulic pressure.

braking distance The distance a vehicle covers from the time the driver applies the brakes until the vehicle stops.

braking skid A skid caused when the brakes are applied so hard that one or more wheels lock.

carbon monoxide A colorless, odorless, highly poisonous gas; a by-product of burning fuel.

catalytic converter An antipollution device, part of the exhaust system, that reduces harmful emissions.

center of gravity The point around which all the weight of an object is evenly distributed.

centrifugal force The force that tends to push a moving object out of a curve and into a straight path.

clutch In a vehicle with a manual transmission, a device that engages and disengages the engine and is connected to the drive shaft; the pedal by which the device is operated.

collision A crash; the result of one object hitting another with sudden force.

collision insurance Insurance that covers the cost of repairs to your vehicle even if you are to blame in a crash or are involved with an uninsured driver. It also covers repairs to your vehicle if it is damaged in a parking lot or in a parking space on the street.

color blindness The inability to distinguish between certain colors.

comprehensive insurance Insurance that covers the cost of repairs for vehicle damage caused by anything other than a collision, such as theft, fire, explosions, natural disasters, falling objects, or vandalism.

contrast sensitivity A person's ability to see details in the driving environment in situations such as facing the glare of headlights or driving when it is dark.

controlled-access highway See **limited-access highway.**

coolant A liquid added to a motor vehicle's radiator to reduce heat.

cooling system The system that keeps the engine cool by forcing air over metal cooling vanes that surround the cylinders. It includes the radiator, overflow tank, water pump, and thermostat.

cornering skid A skid on a turn or curve.

crankshaft The shaft that is turned as the pistons move up and down in the cylinders of the engine.

crowned road A road that is higher in the center than at either edge.

cruise control A vehicle feature that allows a driver to maintain a desired speed without manually pressing the accelerator; intended for highway driving.

cylinder A part of the engine that houses a piston; most vehicles have four, six, or eight cylinders.

deceleration A decrease in speed.

deceleration lane An expressway lane used for slowing down before an exit.

deductible A fixed amount of money that an insured person must pay for damages before the insurance company pays the rest, usually the first $100, $250, or $500 worth of damage.

defogger See **defroster.**

defroster A heating unit that clears moisture from the inside of the front and/or rear windows and ice from the outside surfaces.

depth perception Vision that gives objects their three-dimensional appearance and that enables a person to judge the relative distance between two objects.

differential An arrangement of gears that allows each drive wheel to turn at a different speed when a vehicle goes around a curve.

directional control The ability of a motor vehicle to hold to a straight line.

directional signal A device that allows drivers to communicate their intentions to move right or left by means of a blinking light; an arm or a hand signal.

disc brake A brake in which pressure squeezes the brake pads against a flat metal wheel disc, producing the friction needed to stop the wheel from turning.

downshift To shift to a lower gear from a higher one.

Drive The most frequently used forward gear in a vehicle with an automatic transmission.

drive train See **power train.**

drive wheel A wheel that moves a vehicle.

driver evaluation facility A special center where individuals with physical disabilities undergo a comprehensive medical assessment to determine their potential to drive.

driving under the influence (DUI) See **driving while intoxicated.**

driving while intoxicated (DWI) An offense with which drivers may be charged if their blood-alcohol concentration at the time of arrest is above a certain percent.

drum brake A brake in which fluid pressure causes the brake shoes to push against the brake lining, which then presses against the round hollow metal drum inside the wheel. This creates friction, which slows and stops the wheel's turning motion.

electrical system The system that carries electricity throughout the vehicle and consists of the battery, the alternator or generator, the voltage regulator, and wires.

electronic fuel-injection (EFI) system A system that times and measures fuel flow and injects gasoline into the engine.

emergency brake See **parking brake.**

emergency flashers A signaling device that makes all four turn signals flash at once; used to warn other drivers that a vehicle has stopped or is moving slowly.

engine See **internal combustion engine.**

engine control module (ECM) A computerized system that controls the electrical and other engine systems in a vehicle.

exhaust manifold A collecting system for unburned gases as they exit from the cylinders.

exhaust system The system that gets rid of waste gases and vapors from the engine and reduces the noise of the explosions within the engine cylinders.

expressway A divided highway with limited access that has more than one lane for traffic moving in the same direction; designed for high-speed travel.

field of vision The area ahead and to the left and right that can be seen when one looks straight ahead.

first aid Emergency treatment given to an injured or ill person before professional medical personnel arrive.

fixed speed limit A posted speed limit that cannot legally be exceeded.

flywheel The part of the engine that is turned by the starter and, as a result, turns the crankshaft.

following distance The time-and-space gap between vehicles traveling in the same lane of traffic.

force of impact The force with which a moving vehicle hits another object.

freeway An expressway; a highway that is not a toll road.

friction Resistance to motion between two objects when they touch.

friction point The point at which the clutch pedal and other parts of the power train begin to work together as the driver releases the clutch pedal.

fuel system A system that consists of the fuel tank, fuel pump, fuel filter, fuel-injection system, and air filter.

fuses Safety devices, usually located beneath the dashboard, that protect a car's electrical circuits from overloading.

gas pedal See **accelerator.**

gear Toothed wheels that mesh with each other to transmit motion or change a vehicle's speed or direction.

gear selector lever The lever in a vehicle with an automatic transmission that allows the driver to choose a gear.

gearshift The lever in a vehicle with a manual transmission that permits gears to be changed.

graduated driver licensing (GDL) A driver training program based on the idea that a teen with a new driver's license needs time and guidance to gain the necessary driving experience and skills in reduced-risk settings.

gravity The invisible force that pulls all objects on Earth toward its center.

ground viewing Searching beneath parked vehicles and other objects for signs of movement.

guide sign A sign, including a route marker or destination, mileage, recreational area, or roadside service sign, used to guide and direct drivers.

hand brake See **parking brake.**

hand-over-hand steering A steering method in which the driver's hands cross when turning.

hazard flashers See **emergency flashers.**

head restraint A safety device attached to the back of the seat that is designed to prevent injury to the head and neck.

hemorrhaging Bleeding heavily.

high-occupancy vehicle (HOV) lane A lane reserved for use by vehicles having two or more occupants.

highway A main public roadway, especially one that runs between cities.

highway hypnosis A drowsy state that may occur during long hours of highway driving.

highway transportation system (HTS) A system made up of roadways, motor vehicles, and people.

hitch A device attached to the back of a vehicle to haul a trailer.

hydraulic pressure The pressure created by a liquid being forced through an opening or tube.

hydroplaning Skimming on top of a film of water.

idle To operate the engine without engaging the gears or applying pressure on the accelerator.

implied consent A law stating that any licensed driver charged with driving under the influence or while intoxicated cannot legally refuse to be tested for blood-alcohol concentration.

inertia The tendency of an object in motion to stay in motion and for an object at rest to stay at rest.

inhibitions Personality elements that stop a person from behaving without regard to possible consequences.

interchange A point at which a driver can enter or exit an expressway or connect with a highway going in another direction.

internal combustion engine The part of a vehicle that produces its power by exploding an air-fuel mixture within its cylinders.

international sign A road sign that conveys meaning through symbols, not words.

intersection The place where two or more roadways cross.

jaywalking The pedestrian practice of crossing a roadway without regard for traffic rules or signals.

jump-start To attach a vehicle's dead battery by cables to a charged battery to start the vehicle.

kinetic energy The energy of motion.

lane-use light An electronic signal mounted above a reversible lane that indicates whether the lane can or cannot be used at a particular time.

liability insurance Insurance that protects you against claims if you are at fault in a collision and helps pay for any injury or property damage you cause.

limited-access highway A highway that has fixed points of entry and exit.

lubricating system A system that reduces heat by coating the engine parts with oil; consists of the oil pump, oil pan, and oil filter.

manual shift A system in which the driver changes gears by moving the gearshift and depressing the clutch.

margin of space The amount of space that should be allowed in front of, behind, and to both sides of a vehicle, giving it room to maneuver in threatening situations.

momentum The energy of motion; the product of weight and speed.

moped A low-powered, two-wheeled vehicle most commonly driven on city streets.

mouth-to-mouth resuscitation A method of restoring breathing to a victim.

muffler A device in the exhaust system that reduces engine noise.

multiple-lane highway A highway that has more than one lane for traffic moving in each direction.

Neutral A gear position in which the gears are not engaged and cannot transmit power.

night blindness The inability to see well at night.

no-fault insurance A system in which one's insurance company pays one's medical bills and any other costs resulting from a collision-related injury regardless of who is at fault.

odometer A device that measures distance traveled by a vehicle; its gauge.

overdrive The highest forward gear in many newer vehicles with automatic transmissions; it allows a vehicle to travel more efficiently at higher speeds. In a vehicle with a manual transmission, the fourth and fifth gears are sometimes identified as overdrive gears.

overdriving one's headlights Driving so fast at night that the driver is unable to stop within the range of the headlights.

parallel parking Parking parallel and close to the edge of the road.

Park Gear setting on a vehicle that locks the transmission.

parking brake The brake that holds the rear wheels. It is used to keep a parked vehicle from moving.

parkway A broad highway that may be limited to noncommercial vehicles.

passive safety device A device, such as an air bag or head restraint, that functions without the user having to operate it.

pedestrian A person traveling on foot.

peer pressure The influence of friends who are in your age group.

perception distance The distance a vehicle covers during the time in which its driver identifies a need to stop.

peripheral vision The area of vision to the left and right of the area of central vision.

perpendicular parking Parking so that a vehicle forms a 90-degree angle with a curb or line.

piston A cylinder enclosed in another cylinder within the engine. Its up-and-down movement turns the crankshaft.

point system A system used to keep track of traffic violations by individual drivers.

power brakes Brakes that make it easier to slow or stop without intense foot pressure on the brake pedal.

power skid A skid caused when the accelerator is pressed too hard and suddenly.

power steering A vehicle steering system designed so that it takes little effort to turn the steering wheel.

power train The parts of a motor vehicle that transmit power from the engine to the wheels; the engine, transmission, and clutch.

push-pull-feed steering A steering method in which the driver's hands do not cross even when changing lanes or turning.

radiator A cooling device that air-cools liquid pumped from the engine.

rate of acceleration The time it takes to speed up from a stop or from one speed to a higher one.

rate of deceleration The time it takes to slow down from one speed to a lower one or to a stop.

reaction distance The distance a vehicle covers between the time a driver identifies a situation that requires braking and the moment that the brakes are applied.

regulatory sign A sign that controls the flow of traffic.

Reverse The gear used to back a vehicle.

reversible lane A lane on which the direction of traffic changes at certain times of day.

revoke To cancel a person's license to drive a vehicle, usually for the period of a year or more, after which time the driver can apply for another license.

right-of-way The right of one roadway user to go first or to cross in front of another; right-of-way must be yielded to others in many situations.

risk The chance of injury to oneself or others and of damage to vehicles and property.

safety belt A restraining belt designed to protect the driver and riders in a motor vehicle; a seat belt.

shared left-turn lane A lane that drivers moving in either direction use to make a left turn.

shift To change gears by means of a mechanism; the mechanism itself.

shock A physical disorder often accompanying serious injury; characterized by faintness, weakness, feeling cold, and nausea.

shock absorber A device that cushions a vehicle's frame against the impact of bumps in the road.

shoulder The strip of land along the edge of a roadway, sometimes referred to as a berm.

SIPDE process A five-step driving strategy (search, identify, predict, decide, execute) that enables drivers to process information in an organized way.

skid A driver's loss of control over the direction in which the vehicle is moving.

Smith System A set of five principles that help drivers operate safely and defensively.

space margin See **margin of space.**

spark plug A device in an engine's cylinder that ignites the fuel-air mixture by means of an electric spark.

speedometer A device that measures the speed of a vehicle in miles per hour or kilometers per hour; its gauge.

sport utility vehicle (SUV) A vehicle designed for a variety of uses, usually incorporating four- or all-wheel drive, and featuring increased ground clearance and a cargo area included within the interior.

steering system The system that enables a driver to turn a vehicle's front wheels.

strut A suspension unit that contains both a spring and a shock absorber.

suspend To take away a person's driver's license for a specified period of time, usually 30 to 90 days.

suspension system The system, including shock absorbers, that protects the body of a vehicle from road shocks.

tailgate To drive too closely behind another vehicle.

three-point turn A turnabout made by turning left, backing to the right, then moving forward.

threshold braking A braking technique in which the driver firmly presses the brake pedal to a point just before the wheels lock.

total stopping distance The distance covered by a vehicle from the perception distance to the moment that the vehicle comes to a stop.

tracking Steering; keeping a vehicle steadily and smoothly on a desired course.

traction The friction between a vehicle's tires and the road surface.

traffic control signal An electronic signal, such as a colored light, used to keep traffic moving in an orderly manner.

transmission The gears and related parts that carry power from the engine to the driving axle.

tread The outer surface of a tire, with its pattern of grooves and ridges.

turnabout Any turning maneuver by which a driver moves a vehicle to face in the opposite direction.

turnpike A road, usually an expressway, that requires a driver to pay a toll.

turn signal See **directional signal.**

two-point turn A turnabout made by first backing or heading into a driveway or alley and then heading or backing into the street.

uninsured motorist insurance Protection from financial losses resulting from a collision involving a driver who does not have insurance protection or from a hit-and-run driver; also protects you in states where no liability insurance is required.

U-turn A turnabout carried out by making a U-shaped left turn.

vertical field of vision The area extending upward and downward that allows you when driving to see traffic lights overhead and pavement markings below.

visibility The distance and area a driver can see and the ability of a vehicle or pedestrian to be seen.

visual acuity The ability to see clearly.

warning lights and gauges Dashboard lights and gauges that provide information to the driver about the vehicle; include oil pressure, alternator, and fuel gauges and brake, safety belt, and temperature warning lights.

warning sign A sign that alerts drivers to potential dangers or conditions ahead.

warranty A written guarantee that a motor vehicle dealer will repair a vehicle, within a certain amount of time, at no charge to the customer.

yield sign A road sign at which you must slow and give the right-of-way to traffic on the crossroad or the road onto which you are merging.

i, v (t, b): The Terry Wild Studio; vi (t): Amy C. Etra/PhotoEdit; vi (b): Mary Kate Denny/PhotoEdit; vii (t): David Young-Wolff/PhotoEdit; vii (b): Tony Freeman/PhotoEdit; viii (t): The Terry Wild Studio; viii (b), ix (t): Tony Freeman/PhotoEdit; ix (b): PhotoEdit; x (t): Mason Morfit/FPG International; x (b): Dick Luria/FPG International; xi (t): The Terry Wild Studio; xi (b): Paul Conklin/PhotoEdit; xii (t): David Young-Wolff/PhotoEdit; xii (b): Michael Newman/PhotoEdit; xiii (t): Robert Brenner/PhotoEdit; xiii (b): David Young-Wolff/PhotoEdit; 2–3: Deborah Davis/PhotoEdit; 4–5: Tony Freeman/PhotoEdit; 8: David Young-Wolff/PhotoEdit; 9 (t): Tony Freeman/PhotoEdit; 9 (b): Frank Siteman/PhotoEdit; 10: Robert Ginn/PhotoEdit; 11: Bill Aron/PhotoEdit; 12: Sara Matthews/Visual Education; 13, 14: The Terry Wild Studio; 15: Sara Matthews/Visual Education; 16 (t): PhotoEdit; 16 (b): Mary Kate Denny/PhotoEdit; 17, 18 (b), 22–23: The Terry Wild Studio; 25: Sara Matthews/Visual Education; 27: Myrleen Ferguson/PhotoEdit; 28, 29: The Terry Wild Studio; 31 (t): Brian Haimer/PhotoEdit; 31 (bl): Michael Newman/PhotoEdit; 31 (br): Brian Haimer/PhotoEdit; 32, 34 (b): The Terry Wild Studio; 38–39: Tony Freeman/PhotoEdit; 40: Michael Newman/PhotoEdit; 41: David Young-Wolff/PhotoEdit; 42: Robert Ginn/PhotoEdit; 43, 45, 47, 48, 49: The Terry Wild Studio; 50 (b): Amy C. Etra/PhotoEdit; 51: Corbis; 54–55: Michael Newman/PhotoEdit; 57, 60: The Terry Wild Studio; 61: Rudi Von Briel/PhotoEdit; 62: The Terry Wild Studio; 64: Michael Newman/PhotoEdit; 65: The Terry Wild Studio; 67 (t): Bachmann/PhotoEdit; 67 (b): Mary Kate Denny/PhotoEdit; 68 (b): Sara Matthews/Visual Education; 74–75, 76–77: The Terry Wild Studio; 78: Tony Freeman/PhotoEdit; 81 (t): Michael Newman/PhotoEdit; 81 (b): Spencer Grant/PhotoEdit; 82 (t, b): Sara Matthews/Visual Education; 85: David Young-Wolff/PhotoEdit; 87 (t, bl, br): Sara Matthews/Visual Education; 89: Tony Freeman/PhotoEdit; 92 (b): The Terry Wild Studio; 96–97, 102, 104: Tony Freeman/PhotoEdit; 105 (t): Jonathan Nourok/PhotoEdit; 105 (b): The Terry Wild Studio; 106: Rudi Von Briel/PhotoEdit; 107: Michael Newman/PhotoEdit; 108 (b): The Terry Wild Studio; 112–113, 117: Sara Matthews/Visual Education; 118, 122, 125: The Terry Wild Studio; 126: Tony Freeman/PhotoEdit; 127: David Young-Wolff/PhotoEdit; 128 (b): The Terry Wild Studio; 132–133: David Doody/FPG International; 136, 137: Tony Freeman/PhotoEdit; 139: Sara Matthews/Visual Education; 142: Tony Freeman/PhotoEdit; 145 (t): John Neubauer; 145 (b): Tony Freeman/PhotoEdit; 150 (b): The Terry Wild Studio; 154–155: Tom McCarthy/PhotoEdit; 156, 157: Tony Freeman/PhotoEdit; 158: The Terry Wild Studio; 159 (l): Sara Matthews/Visual Education; 159 (r): Frank Siteman/PhotoEdit; 160: Christine Osborne/Visual Education; 161: PhotoEdit; 163 (t): Michael Newman/PhotoEdit; 163 (b): The Terry Wild Studio; 166 (b): Tony Freeman/PhotoEdit; 172–173: Michael Goodman/FPG International; 174–175: R. Way/The Terry Wild Studio; 177: Sara Matthews/Visual Education; 180: The Terry Wild Studio; 184: Sara Matthews/Visual Education; 190 (b): PhotoEdit; 194–195: The Terry Wild Studio; 197: PhotoEdit; 199: The Terry Wild Studio; 200: Robert Brenner/PhotoEdit; 201: PhotoEdit; 203: Tom McCarthy/PhotoEdit; 204: John Henley/The Stock Market; 205: Tony Freeman/PhotoEdit; 206: Stephen Simpson/FPG International; 207: Mason Morfit/FPG International; 208: Sara Matthews/Visual Education; 212 (b): The Terry Wild Studio; 213: Tony Freeman/PhotoEdit; 216–217: David Young-Wolff/PhotoEdit; 219: Dick Luria/FPG International; 220: Tony Freeman/PhotoEdit; 221 (t): The Terry Wild Studio; 221 (b): Sara Matthews/Visual Education; 224: Addison Geary/Stock Boston; 226 (b): Wolfgang Spunbarg/PhotoEdit; 230–231, 232: The Terry Wild Studio; 233: Spencer Grant/PhotoEdit; 234: The Terry Wild Studio; 236: Tony Freeman/PhotoEdit; 239: Sara Matthews/Visual Education; 243: Robert Brenner/PhotoEdit; 244 (t): Tony Freeman/PhotoEdit; 244 (b), 245, 246 (b): The Terry Wild Studio; 247: Sara Matthews/Visual Education; 250–251: The Terry Wild Studio; 254: Paul Conklin/PhotoEdit; 256 (t): Eugen Gebhardt/FPG International; 256 (b): Sara Matthews/Visual Education; 259, 262 (t): The Terry Wild Studio; 262 (b): Tony Freeman/PhotoEdit; 266 (b): The Terry Wild Studio; 270–271: Robert Brenner/PhotoEdit; 272: David Young-Wolff/PhotoEdit; 274: Tony Freeman/PhotoEdit; 275: Robert Ginn/PhotoEdit; 276: Jeff Greenberg/PhotoEdit; 277, 278: David Young-Wolff/PhotoEdit; 280: Tony Freeman/PhotoEdit; 281: Sara Matthews/Visual Education; 282: Tony Freeman/PhotoEdit; 283: Michelle Bridwell/PhotoEdit; 284: Tony Freeman/PhotoEdit; 285: The Terry Wild Studio; 286: Tony Freeman/PhotoEdit; 288 (b): Jeff Greenberg/PhotoEdit; 289: Library of Congress; 294–295: David Young-Wolff/PhotoEdit; 296–297: Michael Newman/PhotoEdit; 299: Jon Feingersh/The Stock Market; 300: Benelux Press/Photo Researchers, Inc.; 303: Tony Freeman/PhotoEdit; 305 (tl): Mary Kate Denny/PhotoEdit; 305 (tr): Michael Newman/PhotoEdit; 305 (b): PhotoEdit; 306, 307, 308: Tony Freeman/PhotoEdit; 310 (b): The Terry Wild Studio; 314–315: Sara Matthews/Visual Education; 316: David Young-Wolff/PhotoEdit; 317: Tony Freeman/PhotoEdit; 318: Robert Brenner/PhotoEdit; 321: Tony Freeman/PhotoEdit; 324: Sara Matthews/Visual Education; 327 (t, b): Tony Freeman/PhotoEdit; 330: Sara Matthews/Visual Education; 331: David Young-Wolff/PhotoEdit; 332 (b): José Carrillo/PhotoEdit; 336–337: The Terry Wild Studio; 339 (t): Tony Freeman/PhotoEdit; 339 (b): Robert Brenner/PhotoEdit; 340: David Young-Wolff/PhotoEdit; 342, 343: The Terry Wild Studio; 345, 346: Tony Freeman/PhotoEdit; 347: Robert Brenner/PhotoEdit; 348 (b): Tony Freeman/PhotoEdit.

All remaining photographs courtesy of AAA.

Illustration Credits
Anthony Cericola/Animated Graphics.

Maps courtesy of AAA.